RELIGION AND HUMAN RIGHTS: BASIC DOCUMENTS

Edited by
Tad Stahnke
and
J. Paul Martin

Center for the Study of Human Rights
Columbia University
1998

Established at Columbia University in 1978 to promote the teaching and research of human rights in their national and international contexts, the activities of the Center for the Study of Human Rights cover all disciplines and address both theoretical and policy questions. Support for the Center is provided in the form of project-specific grants and an endowment fund initiated by the Ford Foundation. This project is part of the Center's Religion, Human Rights, and Religious Freedom Program, funded by The Pew Charitable Trusts.

Copies of this book are available from:

Center for the Study of Human Rights
Columbia University
420 West 118th Street
1108 International Affairs Building
Mail Code: 3365
New York, NY 10027 USA TEL 212/854-2479 FAX 212/316-4578
Email cshr@columbia.edu
http://www.columbia.edu/cu/humanrights

ISBN 1-881482-04-9

PREFACE

The purpose of this book is to place into the hands of readers — in a portable and easy-to-use format — the most important and authoritative documents on human rights related to religion and belief. This task is not a straight-forward one, as there is no natural centerpiece document — such as an international convention — or international body devoted solely to the issue, nor has there ever been an official world conference on the subject. On the other hand, rights related to religion and belief are implicated in a wide variety of circumstances, and provisions protecting these rights are included in practically every significant human rights convention. We have therefore tried to walk a fine line: providing adequate material on the issue but not burdening the reader with documents that are repetitive or peripheral. The method we have chosen is to reproduce in full the most important documents and to provide explanatory notes with excerpts of or citations to additional documents.

The documents included in the volume come primarily from those international bodies — both governmental and religious — that have addressed the question of rights related to religion and belief most closely. There are a wide variety of views and practices concerning the appropriate scope and content of these rights, and we have attempted to include documents that represent that variety. Inevitably, some perspectives have been left out. In particular, the absence of a particular religious perspective does not imply a lack of concern by that religion or denomination with rights related to religion and belief. Of the massive body of historical documents on the topic, we have chosen those that express ideas important to the current debate.

As expressed in international human rights conventions, there are four primary rights related to religion and belief: (1) the right to freedom of thought, conscience and religion (2) the right to equal protection of the law and freedom from discrimination on the basis of religion or belief (3) the right to protection from the advocacy of national, racial, or religious hatred that constitutes incitement to discrimination, hostility or violence and (4) the right of persons belonging to religious minorities to profess and practice their religion. Of course, a number of other rights may overlap these or be implicated in connection with religion and belief, such as the right to privacy, rights pertaining to marriage and inheritance, the freedoms of expression, assembly and association and the right to education. Also, the right to religious freedom may conflict in some circumstances with the rights of non-believers, women, children and minorities. Finally, the myriad aspects of the relationship between religious entities and the state are extremely important to the protection of rights related to religion and belief.

The documents do not lend themselves to classification based on the four primary rights noted above, as provisions related to these rights run throughout most of them. We have therefore organized the book in a different fashion, one that we hope is most useful.

As a general introduction to the topic we have reprinted a report by United Nations Special Rapporteur Arcot Krishnaswami that is considered to be the most authoritative, lucid and comprehensive report on religious freedom and discrimination in matters of religion and belief. A practitioner or student of the subject will find no better place to start in order to understand the basic issues raised by these rights. Part I contains the Universal Declaration of Human Rights, the International Covenant on Economic, Social and Cultural Rights and the International Covenant on Civil and Political Rights — collectively known as the International Bill of Rights. Part II contains international and regional documents that delineate international standards associated with rights related to religion and belief such as (a) General Comments of the United Nations Human Rights Committee, (b) the United Nations Declaration on the Elimination of Intolerance and Discrimination Based on Religion or Belief, (c) selected provisions of related international human rights conventions and (d) selected provisions of regional human rights conventions. Part III contains the United Nations Declaration on the Rights of Minorities and important European documents on the rights of minorities. Part IV includes selected documents that represent a variety of secular and religious perspectives on the basis and scope of the right to religious freedom. Part V includes selected documents on the relationship between religious institutions and the state. A Topical Index to Document Provisions appears at the end of the book, allowing the reader to cross-reference provisions between the different documents on particular topics related to religion and human rights.

At the foundation of the book is the hope that it will be useful to those who care about human rights, religious freedom and the elimination of religious intolerance and discrimination throughout the world, and thus contribute in some small way to the realization of these goals.

We would like to thank the following people for all of their helpful comments, suggestions and assistance: Abdullahi An-Na'im, Roger Clark, Silvio Ferrari, Louis Henkin, Iván Ibán, Justo Lacunza-Balda, Natan Lerner, Ann Elizabeth Mayer, Kusumita Pederson, Borislav Petranov, Arati Rao, Michael Roan, Arvid Sharma, Juliet Sheen, Rik Torfs, John Witte, Jr., and Michael Young. Special thanks goes out to Joaquin Mantecón Sancho and Rosa María Martínez de Codes of the Spanish Ministry of Justice for their work coordinating the translation of the Spanish documents especially for this volume. We would also like to thank Carrie Gustafson and Sven Lindholm for their valuable research assistance. These documents were compiled and prepared for printing by Ms. Soraya Ahmad, Ms. Daica Skrobala, and Ms. Lesley Carson. The editors and the Center are most grateful for the many hours and skills they contributed to this publication.

Tad Stahnke
J. Paul Martin
Editors

RELIGION AND HUMAN RIGHTS: BASIC DOCUMENTS

TABLE OF CONTENTS

PART V
SELECTED DOCUMENTS ON THE RELATIONSHIP BETWEEN
THE STATE AND RELIGIOUS INSTITUTIONS 221

INTRODUCTION: UNITED NATIONS REPORTS

United Nations bodies have appointed several special rapporteurs over the years to prepare studies or reports on human rights related to religion and belief. The study by Arcot Krishnaswami, reprinted below, was the first comprehensive study on the issue, although an earlier study by Charles D. Ammoun, *Study of Discrimination in Education*, U.N. Doc. E/CN.4/Sub.2/181/Rev.1 (1957), Sales No. 1957.XIV.3, thoroughly addressed issues of discrimination on the basis of religion or belief in education. An update of the Krishnaswami study based on more current aspects of the problems of religious discrimination and intolerance was prepared by Elizabeth Odio Benito, *Elimination of All Forms of Intolerance and Discrimination Based on Religion or Belief*, U.N. Doc. E/CN.4/Sub.2/1987/26, Sales No. E.89.XIV.3 (1989).

In 1986, the Commission on Human Rights appointed a Special Rapporteur to seek information on incidents of religious discrimination and intolerance and report on the implementation by member states of the 1981 *United Nations Declaration on the Elimination of All Forms of Intolerance and of Discrimination Based on Religion or Belief* (reprinted below). Periodic reports have been submitted by Special Rapporteur Angelo Vidal d'Almeida Ribero and his successor, Abdelfattah Amor, appointed in 1993: U.N. Docs. E/CN.4/1987/35; E/CN.4/1988/45; E/CN.4/1989/44 and Add.1 and Corr.1; E/CN.4/1990/46; E/CN.4/1991/56; E/CN.4/1992/52; E/CN.4/1993/62; E/CN.4/1994/79; E/CN.4/1995/91/Add.1/Corr.1; E/CN.4/1996/95/Add.1.

Another important United Nations report on rights related to religion and belief is the report by Special Rapporteur Kevin Boyle on the United Nations Seminar on the Encouragement of Understanding, Tolerance and Respect in Matters Relating to Freedom of Religion or Belief, held 3-14 December, 1984 in Geneva, Switzerland, U.N. Doc. ST/HR/Ser.A/16. The working papers in preparation for the seminar are available in U.N. Doc. HR/Geneva/1984/WP.1-WP.19.

A comprehensive study has been prepared on the rights of ethnic, religious and linguistic minorities for the Sub-Commission on Prevention of Discrimination and Protection of Minorities by Special Rapporteur Francesco Capotorti, *Study on the Rights of Persons Belonging to Ethnic, Religious and Linguistic Minorities*, UN Doc. E/CN.4/Sub.2/384/Rev.1, Sales No. E.91.XIV.2 (1991)

1

ARCOT KRISHNASWAMI: STUDY OF DISCRIMINATION IN THE MATTER OF RELIGIOUS RIGHTS AND PRACTICES

U.N. Doc. E/CN.4/Sub.2/200/Rev.1, U.N. Sales No. 60. XIV.2
(1960).

INTRODUCTION:
DEVELOPMENT OF THE CONCEPT
OF THE RIGHT TO FREEDOM OF
THOUGHT, CONSCIENCE AND
RELIGION

Truly great religions and beliefs[1] are based upon ethical tenets such as the duty to widen the bounds of good-neighbourliness and the obligation to meet human need in the broadest sense. The precept that one should love one's neighbour as oneself was part of the faith of Christianity even before it had been organized as a Church. The same idea permeates Judaism and Islam, as well as the various branches of Buddhism, Confucianism and Hinduism, and it may also be found in the teachings of many non-religious beliefs.

While most religions and beliefs are imbued with a sense of the oneness of mankind, history probably records more instances of man's inhumanity to man than examples of good-neighbourliness and the desire to satisfy the needs of the less fortunately placed. Not infrequently, horrors and excesses have been committed in the name of religion or belief. In certain periods of history organized religions have displayed extreme intolerance, restricted or even denied human liberties, curtailed freedom of thought, and retarded the development of art and culture. In other periods, proponents of certain philosophical teachings have displayed similar intolerance towards all theistic religions or beliefs. However, it must be stressed that such manifestations of intolerance by organized religions or beliefs were usually the result of traditions, practices and interpretations built up around them: often the followers of a religion or belief considered it to be the sole repository of truth and felt therefore that their duty was to combat other religions or beliefs.

The movement towards a greater measure of freedom and tolerance has been temporarily arrested in certain periods of history. While it would of course be impossible to mention here all those who, through the ages, have raised their voices in favour of tolerance and religious freedom, a few examples will serve to indicate that they were drawn from many different faiths.

Twenty-three centuries ago King Asoka, patron of Buddhism, recommended to his subjects that they should act in accordance with a principle of toleration which sounds as alive today as when it was propounded:

" ... Acting thus, we contribute to the progress of our creed by serving others. Acting otherwise, we harm our own faith, bringing discredit upon the others. He who exalts his own belief, discrediting all others, does so surely to obey his religion with the intention of making a display of it. But behaving thus, he gives it the hardest blows. And for this reason concord is good only in so far as all listen to each other's creeds, and love to listen to them. It is the desire of the king, dear to the gods, that all creeds be illumined and they profess pure doctrines ... "

The Bible, in the Book of Leviticus (19:33-4), expressed the ideal of tolerance to strangers in the following words:

"And if a stranger sojourn with thee in thy land, ye shall not do him wrong. The stranger that sojourns with you shall be unto you as the homeborn among you, and thou shalt love him as thyself: for ye were strangers in the land of Egypt: I am the Lord your God."

St. Thomas of Aquinas, a leading exponent of Catholicism, taught as early as the thirteenth century that it was a duty of Governments to uphold freedom of dissident religions before the law and " ... to avoid the scandals and dissensions which suppression of these liberties and guarantees would entail".[2] He also taught that Governments had a duty:

" ... to avoid compromising the eternal salvation of the dissidents who, thus given their freedom, may be freely converted to the truth ... "

The sixteenth-century Catholic authority, Suárez, was no less emphatic when he wrote:[3]

"The temporal power of the Prince does not extend to the prohibition of the religious rites [of dissidents]: no reason for such prohibitions can be advanced, save their contrariety to the true Faith, and this reason is not sufficient with respect to those who are not subject to the spiritual power of the Church."

The Prophet Mohammed, founder of Islam, issued a code of conduct to his followers in Najran in which he said:[4]

"To the Christians of Najran and its neighbouring territories, the security of God and the pledge of Mohammed the Prophet, the Messenger of God, are extended for their lives, their religion, their land, their property — to those thereof who are absent as well as to those who are present — to their caravans, their messengers and their images. The *status quo* shall be maintained: none of their rights [religious observances] and images shall be changed. No bishop shall be removed from his bishopric, nor a monk from his monastery, nor a sexton from his church ... For what in this instrument is contained they have the security of God, and the pledge of Mohammed, the Prophet forever, until doomsday, so long as they give right counsel [to Moslems] and duly perform their obligations, provided they are not unjustly charged therewith."

The doctrine of tolerance was enunciated with particular clarity by John Locke, in his first *Letter concerning Toleration.* In this letter, published in 1689, the year after the English revolution, he wrote:

"Thus if solemn assemblies, observations of festivals, public worship be permitted to any one sort of professors, all these things ought to be permitted to the Presbyterians, Independents, Anabaptisits, Armenians, Quakers, and others, with the same liberty. Nay, if we may openly speak the truth, and as becomes one man to another, neither pagan nor Mahometan nor Jew ought to be excluded from the civil rights of the commonwealth because of his religion ... And the commonwealth which embraces indifferently all men that are honest, peaceable, and industrious, requires it not. Shall we suffer a pagan to deal with trade with us, and shall we not suffer him to pray unto and worship God? If we allow the Jews to have private houses and dwellings amongst us, why should we not allow them to have synagogues? Is their doctrine more false, their worship more abominable, or is the civil peace more endangered by their meeting in public than in their private houses? But if these things may be granted to Jews and pagans, surely the condition of any Christians ought not to be worse than theirs in a Christian commonwealth.

"... If anything passes in a religious meeting seditiously and contrary to the public peace, it is to be punished in the same manner, and no otherwise than as if it had happened in a fair or market. These meetings ought not to be sanctuaries for factious and flagitious fellows. Nor ought it to be less lawful for man to meet in churches than in halls; nor are one part of the subjects to be esteemed more blameable for their meeting together than others."

In another passage of the same letter he enunciated another idea which has a modern ring about it:

"No man by nature is bound unto any particular church or sect, but everyone joins himself voluntarily to that society in which he believes he has found that profession and worship which is truly acceptable to God. The hope of salvation, as it was the only cause of his entrance into that communion, so it can be the only reason of his stay there ... A church, then, is a society of members voluntarily united to that end."

It would appear that Locke's theory of toleration was meant to be universal in its applicability. However, it should be borne in mind that in another passage of the same letter, he specifically excludes Roman Catholics while arguing that the State should offer equal protection to members of the Established Church, to Protestant dissenters, and even to Jews, Muslims and pagans. Furthermore, he was definitely of the view that free-thinkers should be proscribed and not allowed to enjoy any rights or privileges. But whatever their limitations, Locke's writings have a considerable interest: they represent the first attempt to present a theory under which individuals and groups of individuals are entitled to claim freedom of thought, conscience and religion as a legal right. Furthermore, Locke made the distinction between freedom to maintain or to change religion or belief on the one hand and freedom to manifest religion or belief on the other, and expressed the view that whereas freedom to maintain one's religion or belief cannot be restrained, freedom to manifest religion or belief is subject to limitation by the State "in the same manner, and no otherwise", as freedom to exercise any other civil right.

RECOGNITION OF THE CONCEPT IN NATIONAL LAW

Although the concept of freedom of thought, conscience and religion emerged comparatively early in the writings of certain outstanding individuals, its recognition in national law took considerable time. The translation of the abstract concept into law and practice was a gradual process. Tolerance was accorded, in the beginning, to one or a few specified religions or beliefs; and only later was it extended to all such groups. Moreover, the measure of tolerance extended to various groups was often very narrow at first, and only by a gradual expansion was full equity achieved. Even today the stage reached is not the same in various areas of the world. A few illustrative examples may be cited.

In Switzerland, the right of the individual to profess the religion of his choice has gradually been recognized by national law. Every canton acquired, under the first peace of Kappel, of 1529, the right to decide for the entire territory subjected to its jurisdiction whether the Reformed or Catholic doctrine was to be the faith of its citizens and subjects. In the "common bailiwicks", which were ruled by Reformed and Catholic cantons in common, the decision was to be made not by the majority in the ruling cantons but by the majority of churchgoers in every individual commune; thus, the majority decision was binding on the minority also. The second peace of Kappel, of 1531, confirmed the exclusive adherence of all citizens and subjects of the free cantons to the church decided upon by the majority. In the "common bailiwicks", on the other hand, Catholic minorities could remain true to their hereditary faith while living side by side with Protestant majorities. It was not until 1712, after various intermediate settlements, that full equality of rights as between the two Christian confessions was guaranteed, by the fourth peace between the Confederates, to inhabitants of "common bailiwicks" of mixed population. In the individual sovereign cantons the old system was retained: the religion was chosen by majority decision and remained exclusively binding on all citizens and subjects. With the formation of the Helvetic Republic, the unitary constitution of 1798 introduced the principle that all forms of worship should be permitted, provided that they did not disturb public order and pretended to no seigneurial powers and privileges. But in 1803, by the Act of Mediation, Napoleon restored the former relationship between the State and the confessions, i.e., the system of politically determined exclusivity within the specified territory. The adoption of the Federal Constitution of 1848 marked a milestone in the development of freedom of Christian faith and conscience in Switzerland. However, full freedom of faith and conscience was first established by the Revised Federal Constitution of 1874.

In France, for many years, concessions granted to religious groups were revoked at will by the State. After the thirty-six-year period of civil strife known as the religious wars, from 1562 to 1598, Henry IV, by the Edict of Nantes, granted the Calvinists (the Huguenots) certain civil liberties and the right to worship in specified places. The edict was revoked in 1685 by Louis XIV, who ordered the destruction of the Calvinist temples and made any attempt by Calvinists to leave the country punishable by penal servitude. An edict of November 1787 returned to Protestants as individuals most of their civil rights (such as freedom to marry, to acquire property, and to engage in commerce), but denied them the right to worship in public and to organize. Thus the French Revolution brought in its wake full freedom for Calvinists, as well as Jews, to practise their own religion on the same footing as Catholics.

In England, incapacities to which dissenters were subjected were abolished only gradually. The first positive legislation recognizing dissenters was the Toleration Act of 1698, which exempted Protestants who dissented from the Church of England from the penalties of certain laws. Thus Protestant non-conformity was given a legal status, but apart from this the Established Church was maintained, and membership in this Church was an indispensible condition for the holding of public, municipal, military and naval office. The repeal in 1828 of the Test and Corporation Acts put an end to the Established Church in the old sense of that Church enjoying the exclusive confidence of the State as an upholder of the national religious standard. Soon afterwards the Catholic Emancipation Acts of 1829 and 1832 did for Roman Catholic dissenters what had already been done for Protestant dissenters: it made them eligible for seats in Parliament and for such public offices as had not previously been open to them, and gave their churches and charities legal status. In 1846 the Toleration Act was extended to Jews by the Religious Disabilities Act. However, the civil status of dissenters was still inferior to that of members of the Established Church, and the secular and ecclesiastic functions of the parish were almost inextricably mixed. Marriages (except for Jews and Quakers) were legal only when performed by parish clergymen, the parish record of baptisms constituted the only legal record of births, and the parish graveyard was the only place where the dead could be buried. The Established Church also controlled, to a large extent, education, elementary schools, grammar schools, and Oxford and Cambridge Universities. Gradually, over the years, these inequalities have been removed and now, according to the Government of the United Kingdom:

"Religious freedom in modern Britain is complete and a general state of legal equality between the many different religious bodies is well-nigh complete also, with qualified exceptions in the cases of the established Churches of England and Scotland ...

"The marks of the established churches' superiority are perpetuations of the old constitutional forms beyond their active legal significance of a kind very common in Britain: they no longer imply the unmistakable superiority of the established over the non-established churches which marked the 17th and 18th centuries ... No one suffers in conscience or in pocket from the few remaining privileges of the established churches. The existence of the established Churches of England and Scotland must therefore not be taken to make any real inroads upon the rule of religious freedom and equality before the law: the rights and privileges resulting from their establishment are probably smaller than those of any other established churches in the world."

In certain areas the dominant church not only influenced the attitude of public authorities with regard to dissenters, but in turn was used by the State as an instrument for pursuing its own policies, such as an attempt to stamp out the culture of minority groups and to force their members to join the majority group. The State also used discrimination to foster religious and national antagonisms in order to ensure its dominance and to eliminate opposition to the established regime. Thus, according to the Government of the Union of Soviet Socialist Republics:

"In Czarist Russia, the Orthodox Church had occupied a predominant position; it had been the church of the State. All other religious faiths had either been subjected to outright persecution by the State or had at best been tolerated by it. In old Russia citizens of the orthodox faith had enjoyed full rights, whereas members of other denominations were regarded as heretics and their rights were restricted. This applied, for example, to the right to enter government service, to receive an education and to live in certain areas of pre-revolutionary Russia (as in the case of the Jews). The unequal position occupied by different churches in Czarist Russia served to foster religious and national antagonisms and frequently led to conflicts involving bloodshed. The disputes between the Armenians and the Moslems in the Caucasus and the Jewish *pogroms* are a case in point."

After the February Revolution (1917), the Provisional Government enacted the Law of 14 July 1917, guaranteeing freedom of conscience — including the right to profess any religion or to profess none — in the former Russian Empire. After the October Revolution (1917), a decree of the Council of People's Commissars "on the separation of the Church from the State and the School from the Church", reaffirming the guarantee of freedom of conscience and the equality of all religions, was signed by Lenin on 23 January 1918. This was the first legislation enacted by the Soviet State on the subject. It laid down legal provisions governing the relations between the State and religious associations, and abolished the domination over other faiths which the Orthodox Church had exercised in Czarist Russia. Thus the concept of the right to freedom of thought, conscience, and religion was given *de jure* or legal recognition by the Union of Soviet Socialist Republics.

Those European powers which embarked upon colonial enterprises in other continents usually introduced their own Established Church in the overseas territories, and frequently granted this Church even larger privileges than it enjoyed in the mother country. In what is now Peru — to cite

only a single example — the Spanish conquerors introduced Roman Catholicism early in the sixteenth century. It soon became the established official religion to the exclusion of any other. The evolution which followed the emancipation of this and other Ibero-American countries from Spain and Portugal at the beginning of the nineteenth century varied from country to country, especially as regards the relationship of the State with the Roman Catholic Church and other religions or beliefs. In some instances the present-day situation can be understood only in the light of the past, as well as of the more recent interplay of various political forces, either favourable or unfavourable to a privileged position for the church. Various independent countries of Latin America had established religious guarantees at an early date. The constitutions of these countries now recognize the equality of all individuals.

But whereas in certain countries, formerly ruled by Spain and now independent, the Roman Catholic Church is maintained as the official religion, or is declared to be the religion of the nation or of the majority — and enjoys more or less extensive privileges — in others the principle of Separation of State and Church has been proclaimed and all religions enjoy equal treatment. Thus when the Philippines successfully revolted against Spanish rule, its revolutionary Government decreed complete separation of Church and State. The United States of America confirmed that separation, following the war with the Philippines, and the Philippine Bill of Rights ordained that it should be complete and absolute.

During the colonial period of the history of the United States of America the principle of religious freedom was not observed, for the most part, in some of the American colonies. In many of the settlements various

Old World practices and persecutions were repeated. Catholics were hounded and proscribed because of their faith, Quakers were imprisoned, and Baptists were looked down upon by members of other Protestant groups. Dissenters were in some cases punished by fines, imprisonment or banishment, or were required to pay taxes for the support of the clergy and the church; in addition, they were sometimes compelled by law to attend religious services no matter what their belief. In several of the colonies the practice of maintaining one church as the established religion — the usual practice in western and northern Europe at that time — was continued, and frequently no other form of religious expression was tolerated. Only in Rhode Island, Pennsylvania and Delaware did no single church ever attain the status of establishment; in these colonies a large measure of religious freedom not only existed from the beginning, but was actively promoted. But the economic, political and social conditions in the American colonies were not conductive to the survival of an established church. Large sections of the trading class were affiliated with non conformist groups, and clerical authority waned with the growth of business enterprise. The English Act of Toleration of 1689 established a measure of toleration for all except Catholics. The increasing number of groups, and the constant conflict between them, made religious liberty almost imperative. Moreover, the ideological influences of many of the proponents of religious freedom, and of separation of State and Church — such as Roger Williams, William Penn and Issac Backus — were strongly felt. The result of all these factors was a general movement in all the American colonies toward religious freedom — in some cases by granting financial, legal and moral support to several different sects or denominations, and in others by complete separation of State and Church.

As originally drafted in 1787, the Constitution of the United States of America did not contain an article on separation of State and Church or the free exercise of religion. However, the Constitution was immediately amended by the addition of a Bill of Rights, adopted in 1791. The First Amendment forbids the Federal Congress to make any law respecting an establishment of religion, or prohibiting the free exercise thereof. The Fourteenth Amendment, adopted in 1868, was later construed by the United States Supreme Court as having the effect of applying the First Amendment to the Governments of the States.

In India, there have been state religions: Buddhism under Emperor Asoka (274-237 BC) and Islam during the Muslim period (approximately from the end of the tenth to the middle of the eighteenth centuries). However, persecutions and exclusions on the ground of religion were seldom known. Sasanka (approximately 610 AD) was a rare exception in the midst of hosts of understanding and tolerant monarchs, among whom Asoka (mentioned above) and Akbar (1556-1605), stand out. During the British period Christianity became the state religion, but the rulers disclaimed the right and the desire to impose Christianity upon their Indian subjects. In the Queen's Proclamation of 1858 it was declared that none in India should be "in any wise favoured, nor molested or disquieted by reason of their religious faith or observances, but that all shall alike enjoy the equal and impartial protection of the law". Further, authorities were enjoined to "abstain from all interference with religious belief or worship". The Indian Penal Code, enacted in 1860 and still in force, defines a number of offences relating to religion without making any differentiation between the various religions.[5]

This policy of non-intervention in the

religious affairs of groups, embodied in the Queen's Proclamation, was carried to extreme lengths; every religious group was permitted to follow its traditional pattern in all matters regulated by religious custom and usage. The consequence was not only an almost complete absence of control of religious affairs but also — because of the stratification of Indian society — discrimination against members of certain sub-groups. This discrimination was predominantly social in character and reached into all aspects of communal life, including the religious field. It was only toward the end of British rule in India that the Madras Hindu Religious Endowments Act, adopted in 1925, regulated certain important aspects pertaining to the management of the religious affairs of Hindus, with a view, in particular, to attacking discrimination. But this measure — important though it was as a pioneer effort — concerned itself with only one aspect of communal life; furthermore, its application was limited to the Province of Madras.[6]

India achieved independence in 1947 and its present constitution, which came into force on 26 January 1950, guarantees the right to freedom of religion not only to citizens but to every person in India (articles 25 to 28). It abolishes "untouchability" and prohibits its practice in any form (article 17). Further, it includes directives calculated to implement these articles as well as to improve the lot of — and to protect and rehabilitate — persons belonging to scheduled castes and tribes who had suffered from discrimination.

The right to freedom of thought, conscience and religion was examined in the Indian Parliament in 1955, in connexion with a bill calling for the regulation and registration of converts. Mr. Nehru, the Prime Minister, opposing the adoption of the bill, said:

"I fear this bill ... will not help very much in suppressing the evil methods [of gaining converts], but might very well be the cause of great harassment to a large number of people. Also, we have to take into consideration that, however carefully you define these matters, you cannot find really proper phraseology for them. Some members of this House may remember that this very question, in its various aspects, were considered in the Constituent Assembly, [and] before the Constituent Assembly formally met, by various sub-committees ... Ultimately, Sardar Patel got up and said, 'Let there be no heat about this matter — because there was heat — it is obvious that three committees have considered this matter and have not arrived at any conclusion which is generally accepted. After that, they came to the conclusion that it is better not to have any such thing because they could not find a really adequate formula which could not be abused later on.' ...

"The major evils of coercion and deception can be dealt with under the general law. It may be difficult to obtain proof but so is it difficult to obtain proof in the case of many other offences, but to suggest that there should be a licensing system for propagating a faith is not proper. It would lead in its wake to the police having too large a power of interference."

In the same speech, which was an affirmation of public policy, Mr. Nehru pointed out that a faith which had been established for nearly two thousand years in India — Christianity — had a right to enjoy a position of equality with other faiths. The legislature of India, accepting his advice, rejected the bill. It had the support of only one member, the rest of the House being opposed to its adoption.

In the countries of the Near and Middle East — conquered by the Arabs in the seventh century and later incorporated, to a large extent, in the Ottoman Empire — a particular development took place. Although the majority of the indigenous population of the countries had been converted to Islam, various Christian churches and Jewish communities continued to exist. In certain cases there were persecutions, but on the whole the Christians and the Jews enjoyed a large measure of toleration under the Caliphs. Eventually the Islamic States adopted the "millet" system,[7] which not only allowed each non-Muslim community complete autonomy in the administration of its religious affairs but in addition conferred upon it temporal powers over its own members. As the law of the State gradually changed in character from religious to secular, the autonomy of the non-Muslim communities was reduced and generally restricted to matters of personal status such as marriage, divorce, alimony, guardianship, succession, and testaments: and to the administration of religious affairs. Today the "millet" system has evolved, in some countries, into one wherein the recognized religious communities — including in some cases groups other than Christians and Jews — are on a footing similar to the Islamic group, although some traces of former dominance may persist.

These few examples tend to illustrate the considerable progress which has been made in many countries not only in acceptance of the idea of toleration but also in recognition of freedom of thought, conscience and religion as a legal right. However, it cannot be assumed that the principle of non-discrimination in respect of the enjoyment of this right by all individuals and groups has at yet been fully accepted everywhere. An essential fact which should not escape attention is that the forward advance of humanity in this field, as in other fields of human rights, is not in a straight line. Thus, it will be recalled that although the German Constitution of 11 August 1919 assured full freedom of conscience and belief to all inhabitants of that country, and permitted each religious group to administer and control its own affairs, the Nationalist Socialist regime completely reversed the whole attitude of the State towards religion and belief. The Nazis sought to establish a "folk religion", based upon blood, race, and soil. They gradually restricted the activities of the Catholic Church in the sphere of charity, education, sports, and work among youth; and at the same time they made determined efforts to assimilate the Protestant Church into their organization and gradually, through the use of terroristic methods, to gain complete control over it. These doctrines and actions resulted in bitter conflict with both churches, which was partially resolved by the creation of the National Ministry for Church Affairs. The new ministry took over control of Protestant church appointments and finances, and the clergy were forced to take an oath of loyalty to the Führer. Protestant opposition, led by Niemöller, gradually weakened after many of the leaders of the Protestant resistance had been put into concentration camps. At the same time, anti-Semitism, a characteristic of National Socialism, worked towards the destruction of the Jews. A series of enactments gradually closed almost all avenues of education and livelihood to them. The Nürnberg laws deprived them of citizenship. By 1939, they had been forbidden by law to practise a number of professions. In November 1938, a *pogrom* began during which some 1,300 synagogues were burned and thousands of Jewish businesses were

10

destroyed. The Jewish community was fined a billion Reichmarks, and a law was passed forbidding any Jew to own a business or to be an independent craftsman. Before war broke out in September 1939, the Jewish community in Germany had already been deprived of almost every right save that of bare existence. Subsequently, Nazi treatment of the Jews was carried to the point of physical destruction of large sections of the Jewish population in Germany. Nor was this destruction restricted to Germany; it applied also to all the countries of Europe which between 1933 and 1945 came under German occupation or predominant influence. The number of Jews thus exterminated is estimated at more than six million.

INTERNATIONAL RECOGNITION OF THE CONCEPT

Even before the concept of freedom of thought, conscience and religion was recognized in national law — and partly because it had not been so recognized — the practice evolved of making treaty stipulations ensuring certain rights to individuals or groups professing a religion or belief different from that of the majority of the country. Such treaty stipulations date back to the time when law was felt to be personal rather than territorial, and to follow an individual even when he lived in a country other than his own. One of the most important treaties granting such "capitulations" was signed in 1536 by Francis I of France and Suleiman I of the Ottoman Empire, which allowed the establishment of French merchants in Turkey, granted them individual religious freedom, and provided that consuls appointed by the King of France should judge the civil and criminal affairs of French subjects in Turkey according to French law, with the right of appeal to officers of the Sultan for assistance in carrying out their sentences. This treaty became the model for many later treaties of this sort as the capitulation system spread during the seventeenth, eighteenth and early nineteenth centuries.

At a later date, somewhat similar procedures were followed as a means of settling disputes which arose out of the Reformation. For example, the Treaty of Osnabruck, signed in 1648 at the end of the Thirty Years' War, stipulated a certain degree of toleration for Protestants in Catholic States and for Catholics in States which had established a Reformed Church; but it did not go so far as to provide for freedom of thought, conscience and religion for all individuals and groups. Later, under the Treaty of Berlin of 1878, the great European Powers compelled the newly recognized independent and autonomous States of Bulgaria, Montenegro, Romania and Serbia, as well as the Ottoman Empire, to assure religious freedom to all their nationals.

The problem of protection of religious groups and their members came up again at the Paris Peace Conference, after the First World War. Provisions dealing with the protection of minorities, including religious minorities, were either included in peace treaties with some of the defeated countries (Austria, Bulgaria, Hungary and Turkey), or were dealt with in special treaties with certain new or enlarged States (Czechoslovakia, Greece, Poland, Romania and Yugoslavia). Later, some countries (Albania, Estonia, Latvia, Lithuania and Iraq) made declarations to the Council of the League of Nations containing similar provisions. These instruments, while primarily intended to protect minorities, including religious minorities, often contained provisions applicable to all nationals of the country concerned, or even to all its inhabitants. The instruments were placed under the guarantee of the League of Nations; however, it should be noted that the guarantee applied only in respect of members of racial, religious or linguistic minorities.

During the Second World War the need to assure freedom of religion was affirmed in several important statements on the aims of the war. Thus in a joint declaration of 1 January, 1942 the allied leaders stated their conviction "that complete victory over their enemies is essential to defend ... religious freedom and to preserve human rights and justice in their own lands as well as in other lands."

When the Charter of the United Nations was being drafted in San Francisco in 1945, proposals or amendments suggesting the inclusion of detailed provisions on the right to freedom of thought, conscience and religion — or at least certain aspects of this right — were submitted by Chile, Cuba, New Zealand, Norway and Panama. However, the Charter as adopted refers to "human rights and fundamental freedoms for all, without distinction as to race, sex, language or religion", only in general terms. The Universal Declaration of Human Rights, adopted on 10 December 1948, is more explicit: in article 18 it states that "Everyone has the right to freedom of thought, conscience and religion ... "

Certain aspects of this right were recognized in diplomatic instruments concluded at the end of the Second World War: for example, all the treaties of peace concluded in Paris on 10 February 1947 provide that each former enemy country is to take "all measures necessary to secure all persons under its jurisdiction, without distinction as to race, sex, language or religion, the enjoyment of human rights and of the fundamental freedoms, including freedom ... of religious worship ... "[8] Freedom of thought, conscience and religion has also been recognized in international instruments of a regional character, such as the American Declaration of the Rights and Duties of Man, adopted at the ninth International Conference of American States, held in Bogotá in 1948, and the European Convention on Human Rights, adopted and signed at the sixth session of the Committee of Ministers of the Council of Europe in Rome on 4 November 1950. The European Convention is particularly interesting since its provisions — modeled on those of the Universal Declaration of Human Rights — are binding upon the countries which have ratified it, and since it provides for a system of implementation by two organs established by the signatory Powers: the European Commission of Human Rights and the European Court of Human Rights.

CHAPTER I

THE NATURE OF THE RIGHT TO FREEDOM OF THOUGHT, CONSCIENCE AND RELIGION

In order to understand the nature of the right to freedom of thought, conscience and religion — and of discrimination in respect of this right — one cannot do better than take as a basis the Charter of the United Nations and the Universal Declaration of Human Rights. The former affirms that one of the purposes of the United Nations is to promote and encourage respect for human rights and for fundamental freedoms for all without distinction as to race, sex, language or religion. The latter establishes "a common standard of achievement for all peoples and all nations." The relevant provisions of the proposed covenant on civil and political rights are based on those of the Declaration, and represent an attempt to elaborate the latter and to provide guidance to States which become parties to this instrument: however, the covenant is at present only in draft form and these provisions have not yet been examined by the General Assembly.

The basic text of the Declaration on the subject, article 18, reads:

"Article 18

"Everyone has the right to freedom of thought, conscience and religion; this right includes freedom to change his religion or belief, and freedom, either alone or in community with others and in public or private, to manifest his religion or belief in teaching, practice, worship and observance."

This article must be examined in conjunction with articles 29 and 30, which read:

"Article 29

(1) Everyone has duties to the community in which alone the free and full development of his personality is possible.

(2) In the exercise of his rights and freedoms, everyone shall be subject only to such limitations as are determined by law solely for the purpose of securing due recognition and respect for the rights and freedoms of others and of meeting the just requirements of morality, public order and the general welfare in a democratic society.

(3) These rights and freedoms may in no case be exercised contrary to the purposes and principles of the United Nations.

"Article 30

"Nothing in this Declaration may be interpreted as implying for any State, group or person any right to engage in any activity or to perform any act aimed at the destruction of any of the rights and freedoms set forth herein."

Articles 2, 7, and 8, which are also pertinent, read as follows:

"Article 2

"(1) Everyone is entitled to all the rights and freedoms set forth in this Declaration, without distinction of any kind, such as race, colour, sex, language, religion, political or other opinion, national or social origin, property, birth or other status.

"(2) Furthermore, no distinction shall be made on the basis of the political, jurisdictional or international status of the country or territory to which a person belongs, whether this territory be an independent, Trust, Non-Self-Governing territory, or under any other limitation of sovereignty.

"Article 7

"All are equal before the law and are entitled without any discrimination to equal protection of the law. All are entitled to equal protection against any discrimination in violation of this Declaration and against any incitement to such discrimination.

"Article 8

"Everyone has the right to an effective remedy by the competent national tribunals for acts violating the fundamental rights granted him by the constitution or by law."

RECOGNITION OF FREEDOM OF THOUGHT, CONSCIENCE AND RELIGION AS A LEGAL RIGHT

In most areas of the world the right to freedom of thought, conscience and religion is recognized, either by national constitutions or by law. It must therefore be acknowledged to be a fundamental right. The purport of article 18 is that steps should be taken to recognize this right in the few countries which have not already done so. Article 2 of the draft covenant on civil and political rights is somewhat more explicit on this point,[1] and the draft covenant further provides (articles 27-50) for measures of implementation of an international character. When these provisions come into operation, the right will be not only internationally recognized, but also sanctioned.

PROHIBITION OF ANY DISCRIMINATION IN RESPECT OF THE RIGHT

The Declaration prohibits any discrimination in respect of the right to freedom of thought, conscience and religion, and stipulates that all are equal before the law and entitled without any discrimination to equal protection of the law. However, the prohibition of discrimination and the guarantee of equal protection of the law raise special problems in the case of freedom of thought, conscience and religion; since each religion or belief makes different demands on its followers, a mechanical application of the principle of equality which does not take into account these various demands will often lead to injustice and in some cases even to discrimination.

DISTINCTION BETWEEN FREEDOM TO MAINTAIN OR TO CHANGE RELIGION OR BELIEF, AND FREEDOM TO MANIFEST RELIGION OR BELIEF

In describing the nature of the right to freedom of thought, conscience and religion, the Declaration makes a distinction between "freedom to change ... religion or belief" on the one hand and "freedom, either alone or in community with others, and in public or in private, to manifest ... religion or belief in teaching, practice, worship and observance" on the other. The same distinction is made, and appears even more sharply, in the draft covenant on civil and political rights.[2]

Although the Declaration does not explicitly mention freedom to maintain religion or belief, as does the draft covenant, the omission does not appear to involve any question of substance: it would be strange indeed to acknowledge the right to change one's religion or belief without admitting the right to maintain it. But the converse is not correct: it does not follow from the mere acknowledgment of one's right to maintain a religion or belief that the right to change it is also conceded, and there are instances in which a change is prohibited while the right to maintain is recognized.

The essential difference between freedom to maintain or to change a religion or belief and freedom to manifest that religion or belief is that while the former is conceived as admitting of no restriction, the latter is assumed to be subject to limitation by the State for certain defined purposes. Here again the text of the draft covenant is more explicit than that of the Declaration: paragraph 3 of article 18 of the former contains a limitations clause referring only to limitations to be placed on freedom to manifest, while the limitations clauses of the Declaration apply to all the rights and freedoms set forth therein. This may, however, only reflect the different methods of drafting followed in preparing the two instruments: since the limitations clauses of the draft covenant are appended directly to specific articles setting out the substantive right, they naturally can be formulated with greater precision than in the case of the Declaration, where article 29 is placed at the end of the catalogue of rights and freedoms.

THE SCOPE OF FREEDOM TO MAINTAIN OR TO CHANGE RELIGION OR BELIEF

Freedom to maintain or to change religion or belief falls primarily within the domain of the inner faith and conscience of an individual. Viewed from this angle, one would assume that any intervention from outside is not only illegitimate but impossible. None the less, problems do arise and there are even today cases of interference with this freedom — or at least with its outward aspects. In order to understand this apparent contradiction, it must be recollected that the followers of most religions and beliefs are members of some form of organization, such as a church or a community. If it is to be considered that freedom to maintain or to change religion or belief does not admit of any restraint — and it seems to be so rightly considered by the consensus of world opinion — any instance of compelling an individual to join or of preventing him from leaving the organization of a religion or a belief in which he has no faith must be considered to be an infringement of the right to freedom of thought, conscience and religion.

This idea, expressed long ago by Locke, was emphasized in a decision of the Supreme Court of the United States of America made in 1940 and interpreting the First Amendment to the United States Constitution, which read in part as follows:[3]

"The First Amendment forestalls compulsion by law of the acceptance of any creed or the practice of any form of worship. Freedom of conscience and freedom to adhere to such religions organizations or form of worship as the individual may choose cannot be restricted by law ... Thus the amendment embraces two concepts: freedom to believe and freedom to act. The first is absolute, but, in the nature of things, the second cannot be."

The same idea is also brought out succinctly in article 18 of the draft covenant on civil and political rights: "No one shall be subject to coercion which would impair his freedom to maintain or to change his religion or belief." One still has to consider, however, what is to be condemned as "coercion". There may be many border-line cases, particularly when proselytizing activities are being carried on amongst persons or groups more readily susceptible than others to indirect inducements.[4] But the mere existence of certain prescribed procedures for formally joining a religion or belief, or for leaving it, is not necessarily an infringement of the right to maintain or to change: the real test is whether or not in fact these procedures constitute a restraint upon this freedom.

THE SCOPE OF FREEDOM TO MANIFEST RELIGION OR BELIEF

The Universal Declaration of Human Rights states that "Everyone has the right ... to manifest his religion or belief in teaching, practice, worship and observance." The question arises whether the terms "teaching, practice, worship and observance" are intended to circumscribe the freedom, or whether on the contrary they are mentioned only in order to prevent any possible manifestation of a religion or belief from being considered outside the ambit of the freedom. Bearing in mind that on the one hand the Declaration was prepared with a view to bringing all religions or beliefs within its compass, and on the other hand that the forms of manifestation, and the weight attached to each of them, vary considerably from one religion or belief to another, it may safely be assumed that the intention was to embrace all possible manifestations of religion or belief within the terms "teaching, practice, worship and observance."

THE SCOPE OF PERMISSIBLE LIMITATIONS UPON THE RIGHT TO FREEDOM OF THOUGHT, CONSCIENCE AND RELIGION

Article 29 of the Declaration, referred to above, states that "in the exercise of his rights and freedoms, everyone shall be subject only to such limitations as are determined by law solely for the purpose of securing the recognition and respect for the rights and freedoms of others and of meeting the just requirements of morality, public order and the general welfare in a democratic society". The article further states that "everyone has duties to the community", and that the rights and freedoms proclaimed in the Declaration "may in no case be exercised contrary to the purposes and principles of the United Nations". A limitation, therefore, in order to be legitimate, must satisfy two essential criteria: it must be "determined by law," and it must be enforced solely for one or several of the purposes mentioned in the article.

The expression "determined by law" may be thought to be self-explanatory. Its meaning is that the limitations envisaged in the article should he stated in general and objective terms in accordance with the characteristics of the law, as distinct in a sense from individual and concrete legal decisions resulting from decrees of courts or administrative acts. Regulations to control manifestations of religion or belief are normally issued by the executive and executed by subordinate administrative authorities; but these authorities have to take care that their acts are within the scope of the authority given them by law.

The statement that limitations, in order to be legitimate, must be enforced solely for one or several of the purposes mentioned in article 29 means that not only the acts of the executive and of the subordinate authorities, but the law itself, should not be unduly restrictive of the right to freedom of thought, conscience and religion.

The first purpose enumerated in the article, for which a limitation is permitted, is to secure "due recognition and respect for the rights and freedoms of others". This means that, since it has already been recognized that freedom to maintain or to change one's religion or belief should not be impaired, precedence should be given to this freedom whenever it comes into conflict with any practice of a religion or belief which would lead to its disregard. Furthermore, in a multi-religious society, certain limitations on religious practices, or on customs which owe their origin to religious doctrines, may be necessary in order to reconcile the interests of different groups, notably minorities and the majority. Such limitations should not be of such a nature as to sacrifice minorities on the altar of the majority, but to ensure a greater measure of freedom for society as a whole.

A good example of such legislation may be cited. In India, a choice had to be made between acquiescing in a traditional type of discrimination against a minority or eliminating it by measures which, according to a certain group purporting to speak in the name of the majority, were contrary to the religious traditions of the people. The question whether "untouchability" should be abolished, or allowed to remain as part and parcel of religious practice, presented itself in a sharp form to the statesmen of that country. But with the coming into force of the Constitution in January 1950, "untouchability" was abolished by article 17, which reads:

" 'Untouchability' is abolished and its practice in any form is forbidden. The enforcement of any disability arising out of 'untouchability' shall be an offense punishable in accordance with law".

In addition, article 15 provides that:

"No citizen shall, on grounds only of religion, ... be subjected to any disability, liability, restriction or condition with regard to:
"(a)   Access to shops, public restaurants, hotels and places of public entertainment; or
"(b)   The use of wells, tanks, bathing ghats, roads and places of public resort maintained wholly or partly out of State funds or dedicated to the use of the general public".

Where traditional religious practices come into conflict with the basic rights of the individual, it is the former that have to give way. Thus, these limitations by the State on religious practices have increased freedom for Indian society as a whole.

Legitimate limitations upon the right to freedom of thought, conscience and religion can also be imposed, according to article 29, "for the purpose ... of meeting the just requirements of morality, public order and the general welfare in a democratic society". The use of these terms indicates a consensus of opinion that the exercise of the right could be limited only in the interests of the common good of society; great pains were taken in the preparation of the Declaration to avoid the possibility of arbitrary judgment being exercised.

While the legitimate limitations set forth in article 29 apply equally to all rights and freedoms proclaimed in the Declaration, it must be stressed again that the right to freedom of thought, conscience and religion

has a distinctive character because the demands of various religions and beliefs on their followers are so far from identical. As the Supreme Court of India once stated:[5]

"A religion may not only lay down a code of ethical rules for its followers to accept; it might prescribe rituals and observances, ceremonies and modes of worship which are regarded as integral parts of religion, and these forms and observances might extend even to matters of food and dress".

In another decision the same court stated:[6]

"What constitutes the essential part of a religion is primarily to be ascertained with reference to the doctrines of that religion itself. If the tenets of any religious sect of the Hindus prescribe that offerings of food should be given to the idol at particular hours of the day, that periodical ceremonies should be performed in a certain way at certain periods of the year or that there should be daily recital of sacred texts or oblations to the sacred fire, all these would be regarded as parts of religion and the mere fact that they involve expenditure of money or employment of priests and servants or the use of marketable commodities would not make them secular activities partaking of a commercial or economic character ... The freedom [for such religious practices] is guaranteed by the Constitution except when they run counter to public order, health and morality".

Viewed from this angle it may be seen that certain limitations imposed upon particular manifestations of religion or belief, although apparently conceived in general terms, may in fact tend to affect only a particular group, or to affect it more than others. This consideration cannot be ignored when deciding whether or not a particular limitation is legitimate. Only when public authorities refrain from making any adverse distinctions against, or giving undue preferences to, individuals or groups, will they comply with their duty as concerns non-discrimination.

Finally, in any discussion of the permissible limitations on the right to freedom of thought, conscience and religion, account must be taken of the fact that even though each of several limitations taken by itself may be considered to be permissible, the whole complex of limitations when taken together may be such as to render the exercise of the right nugatory. That is why article 29, after setting forth the grounds on which limitations are permissible, uses the term "in a democratic society" — a term which should of course be construed as referring to a society in which human rights and fundamental freedoms are ensured. The same idea is brought out more comprehensively, and in even sharper focus, in article 30, which states that nothing in the Declaration "may be interpreted as implying for any State, group or person any right to engage in any activity or to perform any act aimed at the destruction of any of the rights and freedoms set forth herein". Clearly this article interdicts not only public authorities, but also "any group or person" from engaging in activities aimed at the destruction of a human right or fundamental freedom. Thus the expression "in a democratic society" in article 29 and the provisions of article 30 may be said to constitute restrictions on the permissible limitations.

INDIVIDUAL AND COLLECTIVE ASPECTS OF FREEDOM TO MANIFEST RELIGION OR BELIEF

While for the majority of rights and freedoms set forth in the Universal Declaration of Human Rights only the individual aspect is taken into consideration, article 18 explicitly affirms that freedom to manifest a religion or belief may be exercised either "alone" or "in community with others". The same expressions appear in article 18 of the draft covenant on civil and political rights, and the collective aspect of the right is stressed even more in article 25 of the draft covenant, which states that "persons belonging to [religious] minorities should not be denied the right, in community with other members of their group, ... to profess and practice their own religion".

What do the expressions "in community with others" and "in community with other members of their group" mean? Do they imply simply freedom of assembly exercised from time to time for the purpose of teaching, practice, worship or observance, or do they also imply the right to organize on a permanent basis for these purposes? In other words, do they refer only to freedom of assembly, or also to freedom of association and the right to organize?

It may be argued that freedom of association for the purpose of manifesting a religion or belief is referred to, along with the freedom of peaceful assembly, in article 20 of the Declaration, which provides that "Everyone has the right to freedom of peaceful assembly and association" and that "No one may be compelled to belong to an association". In view of the generality of the terms of this article, there can be no doubt that it extends to the sphere of religion or belief. However, certain facts relating to the two freedoms here involved — freedom of assembly on the one hand and freedom of association and the right to organize on the other — must be pointed out.

History and contemporary practice show a remarkable difference in the attitude of public authorities towards these two freedoms when they are applied in the field of religion or belief, and when they are applied in other fields. In many fields freedom of association and the right to organize have been more readily conceded than freedom of assembly. But in the field of religion, freedom of association and the right to organize have often been, and still are, denied or severely curtailed, whereas freedom of assembly in houses of worship has been recognized first, at least for the dominant religion, and later for a number of recognized — or even all — religions or beliefs. This difference is not accidental; public authorities consider that, in fields other than religion, there is less of a threat to public order and security in the existence of permanent organizations than in the congregation in one place of a large number of people. In the religious field, on the other hand, a meeting held for purposes related purely to matters of religion or belief does not generally present a threat to public order and security, whereas the establishment of a new and permanent organization may be considered dangerous because of the considerable impact which a religion or belief normally has upon its followers. Moreover, as will be seen later, freedom of association and the right to organize may have quite a different meaning in the field of religion from that which they have in other fields: such questions as the structure of the religious organization and the management of its religious affairs are often, to a large extent, questions of dogma and therefore not matters of voluntary choice.

Although freedom of assembly for individuals of a particular faith does not raise such complicated issues as freedom of association and the right to organize, conflicts may arise even here between freedom of assembly and considerations of morality, public order, the general welfare, or respect for the rights and freedoms of others.

Thus it may be seen that the collective aspect of freedom to manifest religion or belief — whether it implies freedom of assembly only, or freedom of association and the right to organize in addition — is of particular importance from the point of view of this study, since intervention by the State to regulate or to limit manifestations of a religion or belief are [sic] more frequent when these manifestations are performed "in community with others" than when they are performed "alone".

PUBLIC AND PRIVATE ASPECTS OF FREEDOM TO MANIFEST RELIGION OR BELIEF

The same observation applies to the reference, in article 18 of the Declaration, to manifestations of religion or belief "in public or private". Intervention by the State is more likely when a manifestation takes place in public than when it takes place in private.

In this connexion, it may be pointed out that limitations upon manifestations of religion or belief are most likely to occur when such manifestations are performed simultaneously "in community with others" and "in public", as in the case of a public procession through the streets of a city, which comes into conflict with certain other aspects of modern life such as urbanization and the flow of traffic.

PROTECTION OF THE FREEDOM OF INDIVIDUALS AND GROUPS TO MANIFEST THEIR RELIGION OR BELIEF AGAINST INFRINGEMENT BY OTHER INDIVIDUALS OR GROUPS

It must be realized that in many cases restraints upon freedom of thought, conscience and religion — and even denials of that freedom — stem not from any governmental action but from pressures within the society in which they occur. Such pressures are usually exercised through subtle methods of exclusion from social life, or other forms of social ostracism. Public authorities have a duty to protect individuals and groups against this kind of discrimination, as is made clear in article 7 of the Universal Declaration of Human Rights. But these authorities do not operate in a vacuum: they cannot overlook the factors which underlie social pressures.

Thus the position which a particular religion or belief enjoys in a country may depend upon the proportion of its adherents to the total population. If the group is relatively small and does not try to expand by converting members of the predominant group, tolerance is the general rule. Conversely, if the group is relatively large and tries not only to gain converts but also to exert political influence, the predominant group often shows impatience which may turn into intolerance.

The origin of the religion or belief may also be a factor: there are "traditional minorities" and groups which have emerged only in recent times. Greater intolerance is usually shown towards the new groups, especially if they are splinters of the predominant religion or belief which attempt to win converts to what the predominant religion considers to be a schism or a heresy. But even "traditional minorities" sometimes arouse the animosity or [sic] the predominant group, which frequently charges them with showing excessive group-consciousness or becoming a "State within a State", with growing more prosperous than other groups in the community, or with practicing secret rites.

Still another factor is the relationship of individuals or groups holding a particular religion or belief to members of that religion or belief residing outside the country. While one such group may have no followers outside the country, another may be merely a local branch of a larger religion or belief. In the latter case, if the same religion or belief is predominant in another State and this State is accused of intervening on behalf of its co-religionists, this may lead to resentment and discrimination.

In a larger context the attitude of a religion or belief, or of its followers, towards the State in which it lives and towards the predominant faith within that State cannot be ignored. Of course no State can turn a blind eye towards activities aimed at its destruction. It should be apparent, however, that in evaluating this particular aspect of the attitude of the State and of the predominant group towards a minority, the greatest caution must be observed; for while the maintenance of social cohesion may be a legitimate aspiration, it has only too often been invoked by States and by predominant groups within the States to justify tyranny and persecution.

Since it is often extremely difficult to disentangle prejudice from such factors, it is not always possible for public authorities to initiate immediately the measures which are necessary to eradicate discrimination against various religions or beliefs. Moreover, where the social pressures are solely the result of unreasoning prejudice and where they are exerted by large and powerful groups, attempts to counter them directly might lead not only to an increase in tension but even to open clashes endangering peace and tranquillity.

Even so, public authorities are under a positive duty to ensure as widely as possible freedom of thought, conscience and religion to all religions and beliefs and to their followers. Further, they have a responsibility to cut at the very roots of intolerance and prejudice by all possible means, such as educational measures and co-operation with groups willing to assist in counteracting prejudice and discrimination. Finally, they must provide adequate protection not only against discrimination itself but also, as mentioned in article 7 of the Declaration, "against any incitement to such discrimination".

All these factors should be borne in mind when assessing the acts of public authorities. A particularly close scrutiny is imperative in determining whether these authorities have used the argument of peace and tranquillity legitimately, or only as a pretext for initiating or perpetuating infringements upon the right to freedom of thought, conscience and religion; in this case more than in any other it is necessary, in assessing the attitude taken by States and public authorities, to take into account whether the infringements are occasional and temporary in nature, or form part of a deliberate and systematic policy.

CHAPTER II

FREEDOM TO MAINTAIN OR TO CHANGE RELIGION OR BELIEF

The right of an individual to freedom of thought, conscience and religion is recognized today in nearly all areas of the world. This right, in the words of the Universal Declaration of Human Rights, "includes freedom to change his religion or belief". It would also seem to include not only the inner freedom of an individual to maintain his religion or belief, but also his freedom to belong, or not to belong, to an organized religion or belief.

Examples of compulsory conversion, or of legislation specifically banning a particular religion or belief — frequent in the past — are nowadays not very much in evidence. However, in certain areas even today the law, which making no distinction — or only relatively minor distinctions — between various theistic religions and their followers, provides for different treatment of non-theistic beliefs and their followers. Conversely, in other areas, non-believers seem to be favoured in comparison with believers. Furthermore, instances may be found of individuals or groups being subjected to pressure to leave their own religion or belief for another. Such pressure ranges from outright persecution of members of a particular group or its spiritual leaders — which may involve denial of their civil and other rights — to measures of an economic character such as exclusion from certain trades and professions. Although it is rare for public authorities to exert such pressure directly nowadays, in many instances they fail to curb sufficiently pressures which are exerted by religions or beliefs enjoying a preferential position in the State.

In some areas of the world, intolerance has been directed not so much against individuals or groups professing a different faith from that of the predominant group, as against heretical or schismatic elements which have broken away from the parent group. Thus in one instance state recognition of such an element as a religious group was denied and its followers were officially considered to be members of the parent group despite the fact that they had withdrawn from it, while in another instance dissenting elements — including their hierarchies as well as their followers — were compelled to merge against their will with the parent group. In both instances individuals were forced not only to give up their religion or belief for another but also to be considered by public authorities as members of a faith which they had not voluntarily accepted.

In other areas law, custom, or social pressure has resulted in the maintenance of a *status quo* in which individuals are restrained — although not actually prevented — from changing their religion or belief. In some instances the limitations thus placed upon a possible change of faith are such as to amount to a total denial of freedom to change.

In this connexion it ought to be realized that while many religions or beliefs welcome — and in some cases even encourage — the conversion of individuals belonging to other faiths, they are reluctant to admit the conversion of individuals of their own faith; apostasy is viewed with disfavour by them and often is prohibited by their religious law or discouraged by social ostracism. While this point of view is understandable, and while almost every religion considers membership in it to be invested with a significance different from that of membership in a civil society, it must none the less be pointed out that the consensus of world opinion, as expressed in the Universal Declaration of Human Rights, is unequivocally in favour of permitting an individual not only to maintain but also to change his religion or belief in accordance with his convictions.

In the past, when State and Church were normally closely associated, the attitude of organized religion towards this ques-tion often found expression in the law, particularly with respect to matters pertaining to membership in the Established Church or the State religion. Whereas conversion to this church or religion was made easy, apostasy often was severely punished by measures such as excommunication, exile, or even death. Today, examples of such harsh treatment are extremely rare. In a few areas, however, the State still recognizes the religious law of a group to be the law of the State. If this religious law does not ensure the right of an individual to leave the group, a change of religion or belief is legally impossible for members of that group; furthermore, the individual who does not submit to the prescriptions of the religious law in such a case is liable to be punished. In other areas, although the State does not deny the right of individuals to change their religion or belief, it enforces that part of the religious law of the various recognized communities which pertains to personal status. Here a change of religion or belief may lead to certain incapacities or to the loss of certain family, inheritance, or other rights. There are also instances of an individual not being permitted to change over from one religious community to another until he receives a formal release from the group to which he had first adhered. If that group, applying its religious law, refuses to grant such a release, the change becomes legally impossible.

In some areas, a change of religion or belief has legal effect only after formal registration by religious or State authorities. Usually this is a remnant of the practice of an Established Church or State religion, which in the past had exercised complete control over its members. Here the formality of registration does not bar an individual from changing his religion or belief, as the facilities for registration are available equally to members of the Established Church or

State religion and to members of the recognized dissident faiths. There is, however, a possibility that such formalities might in fact be employed as a means of dissuading an individual from changing his religion or belief. Moreover, although the conditions which were initially conducive to pressure against, or prohibition of, changes of religion or belief have disappeared, they may have left their pattern on the social attitudes of the community; society still frowns upon certain changes of religion or belief and the individual has to weigh his desire to go over to another group against the ostracism which he can expect to face from the group to which he belongs.

Particular problems arise as to the meaning of freedom to maintain and to change religion or belief in connexion with the upbringing of children. It is generally admitted that children should be brought up in the religion or belief decided upon by their parents. Thus article 14 of the draft covenant on economic, social and cultural rights, as adopted by the Third Committee of the General Assembly, provides (A/3764, para. 50) that the States parties to the covenant will "undertake to have respect for the liberty of parents and, when applicable, legal guardians, to choose for their children schools other than those established by the public authorities which conform to such minimum educational standards as may be laid down or approved by the State and to ensure the religious and moral education of their children in conformity with their own convictions". Further, the Sub-Commission on Prevention of Discrimination and Protection of Minorities, in one of the fundamental principles which it drew up in connextion with its Study of Discrimination in Education, expressed the view (E/CN.4/740, resolution C), that:

"No person or group of persons should be compelled to receive religious or anti-religious instruction inconsistent with his or their convictions, and respect should be paid to the freedom of parents and, when applicable, legal guardians, to ensure the religious education of their children in conformity with their own convictions".

However, the question becomes more complicated in countries where legal recognition is accorded to ante-nuptial agreements concerning the religion or belief in which children are to be educated and — even more important — brought up. Some religions require, as a pre-condition for the marriage of one of their members with a non-member, the conclusion of an ante-nuptial agreement that the children will be brought up in conformity with the religion of the member. Even if the guardian parent wants the child to adhere to another religion, the change cannot be made until the child reaches an age — specified by law — when he can decide for himself. The courts have upheld the validity of such ante-nuptial agreements, thus overruling the wishes of the guardian parent.

The question of the upbringing of children who have been torn from their family environment by events such as serious disturbances of the peace, massacres, or mass migrations — as for example the Jewish orphans living in various countries occupied by Nazi Germany during the Second World War — presents acute problems. While attention should be paid to the expressed or presumed wishes of the deceased or absent parents in such cases, the base interests of the child itself should be the paramount consideration. These interests include not only its material welfare, but spiritual elements, and needless to say they must be ascertained in an objective manner. In each individual case consideration has to be given to all the factors mentioned above, and also the possible inability of the community, or the persons who have taken charge of the child, to bring him up in the religion of his parents. While conceding the unavoidable and sometimes compelling nature of these factors, it must nevertheless be stressed that the child's helplessness and distress should not be exploited for its conversion.

Conflicts also arise between the right of certain individuals to maintain their particular religion or belief and the right of others to disseminate a different faith. The methods of propagation — which sometimes include social ostracism, curtailments of human rights in other fields, or improper inducements through the conferment of various favours, often of a material character — may amount to indirect pressures upon an individual or even upon a group. Improper inducements are particularly difficult to define because even when a line has been drawn between what is proper and what is improper, one must still take into account not only what is given or promised by the missionary but also the receptivity of the individual or group to such inducements.

Another kind of problem arises when educational activities — such as the maintenance of orphanages or schools by missionaries — are considered by some people to be a form of propagation of a faith; in such a situation freedom to disseminate has to be weighed against freedom to maintain, as such propagation operates mainly amongst children — a most impressionable group.[1] It is often argued that children in particular have to be protected against possible conversions which would not be entirely free. This argument has been invoked in many countries in support, if not of an outright ban on educational institutions run by missionaries, at least of a limitation upon their education-al work such as a prohibition against their imparting religious education to children who are not of their faith. Such a limitation is normally considered to be legitimate as long as it does not override the prior right of parents to request such education for their children. However, in fairness to missionaries, it must be pointed out that they have achieved remarkable results in many parts of the world where children would not otherwise have been educated.

Similar arguments have been adduced against certain humanitarian aspects of missionary work, such as the operation of hospitals, dispensaries and workshops, and the distribution of food and clothing. It is said that these services may constitute a material inducement to people to change their faith. While it may be true in certain isolated cases that the provision of such services has amounted to outright bribery intended to induce members of less fortunately placed sections of society to change their faith, it would certainly be improper to generalize from a few instances.

To sum up, it would appear that as a general rule everyone should be free to adhere, or not to adhere, to a religion or belief in accordance with the dictates of his conscience. Parents should have a prior right to decide upon the religion or belief in which their child should be brought up. When a child is torn from its family environment, the decision as to the religion or belief in which that child is to be brought up should be made primarily in accordance with the objectively ascertained interests of the child, due attention being paid to the expressed or presumed wish of the parents. Finally, no one should be subjected to coercion or to improper inducements likely to impair his freedom to maintain or to change his religion or belief.

CHAPTER III

FREEDOM TO MANIFEST RELIGION OR BELIEF

As pointed out above, freedom to manifest a religion or belief may be curtailed legitimately for certain purposes set forth in the Universal Declaration of Human Rights. One cannot examine the various aspects of this freedom without first taking note of these permissible limitations; as a matter of fact, it is above all by a close examination of the conditions and circumstances in which limitations are imposed upon the freedom that conclusions can be drawn as to the existence or absence of discrimination.

The question of which limitations are legitimate ones and which are illegitimate ones amounting to discrimination cannot be fully answered *in abstracto*. One has always to consider the particular nature of the manifestation in question, and the number of ways in which faiths may be manifested is practically limitless. One has also to consider the variety of interpretations which may be given to such terms as those used in article 29 of the Declaration: "the just requirements of morality, public order and the general welfare in a democratic society". All that can be affirmed is that the criteria laid down are intended to exercise a check on arbitrary judgment.

However, there are certain manifestations which are so obviously contrary to morality, public order, or the general welfare that public authorities are always entitled to limit them, or even to prohibit them altogether. Into this category fall such practices as the sacrifice of human beings, self-immolation, mutilation of the self or others, and reduction into slavery or prostitution, if carried out in the service of, or under the pretext of promoting, a religion or belief. In these cases limitations or even prohibitions are not discriminatory since they are founded upon the superior interest of society, or even of the international community.

Nor can public authorities allow activities aimed at the destruction of the State, such as rebellion or subversion, even though undertaken in the name of religion or belief. They are always entitled to restrain or to limit such activities provided that they act in good faith to preserve the security of the State and do not employ the restraints or limitations as a pretext for justifying a policy of repression of a faith.

Measures which may be taken by public authorities against those who refuse to pay taxes on the ground that such payment is contrary to their religion or belief are also justified. This of course does not mean that certain taxes may not themselves be discriminatory; such would be the case if a special tax, earmarked for the support of a particular faith, were to be levied upon individuals who were not members of that faith. Further, it must be borne in mind that a State cannot be precluded from carrying out obligations which it has assumed as a result of taking over property belonging to a religion or belief, nor from contributing funds towards the preservation of religious structures of historic or artistic value, and from using revenue derived from general taxes for these purposes.

Finally, it will be recognized that in the international community, under the Charter of the United Nations, any breach of international peace and security is prohibited. No State or faith may justify such a breach on the ground that it is a manifestation of a religious duty, and limitations upon the right to freedom of thought, conscience and religion imposed in order to prevent such a breach are legitimate and not discriminatory.

Another type of limitation which States may legitimately impose in this field is based not only on considerations of "the just requirements of morality, public order and the general welfare in a democratic society", but also upon the requirement that the State must secure "due recognition and respect for the rights and freedoms of others".

For example, in some areas particular social groups were not permitted until recently to enter temples or other places of worship of their own faith, nor were they allowed access to shops, public restaurants, hotels, or places of public entertainment. They were also prevented from using wells, tanks, and bathing facilities, although these facilities are maintained out of State funds and dedicated to the use of the general public. In recent years constitutional and legislative provisions have been enacted to abolish such prohibitions. There is no doubt that such abolition cannot be considered discriminatory, even though the policy of exclusion was considered by some to be one of the prescriptions of their faith. By enacting such laws, public authorities discharge their duty to establish social justice and equality.

It would seem that similar considerations may be used to justify measures taken against polygamy. In a great number of countries, since time immemorial, polygamy has been considered to be contrary to morality and public order, and consequently has been prohibited for all groups. In some other countries, however, a different view prevailed — at least until recently — and polygamy was permitted at least for members of groups whose religious laws admit this institution. In recent years, in some of these countries, polygamy was banned for members of all groups. Such a prohibition cannot be considered discriminatory; the family being a social institution, a ban on polygamy is justified on considerations of

morality, public order, and general welfare, whether these are determined mainly by the religion or belief of the majority of the population or by other factors. It must be realized that morality, public order and general welfare are not immutable concepts. Further, it has to be borne in mind that polygamy inevitably leads to inequality between the sexes.

In certain areas polygamy, while still permitted for certain groups whose faith allows it, is prohibited for others. When this difference in treatment results from recognition of the differing prescriptions of the religious law of each group in this matter, it cannot be pronounced to be discriminatory as between various religions or beliefs.

There are also countries where the State has prohibited polygamy for members of certain faiths whose religious law permits it, while other groups in the country are still allowed to practice it. This difference in treatment is based on recognition of the difference in social evolution of the groups concerned. The *mores* of one group may have changed so that the group no longer considers the institution of polygamy to be permissible, whereas the *mores* of another group may still allow it. Even in this case the distinction is not discriminatory, as it is based on the difference of *mores* which have prevailed as a result of the evolution of the various groups.

A. FREEDOM TO COMPLY WITH WHAT IS PRESCRIBED OR AUTHORIZED BY A RELIGION OR BELIEF

(i) *Worship*

The individual's right to worship by himself in private does not raise any serious problem; however, worship normally takes place "in community with others" and "in public". In most areas the right to worship in public is not only recognized, but protected, by law; there are, however, notable exceptions. In a few countries the law recognizes the right to worship in public only for followers of the Established Church or the State religion. Members of other faiths do not have this right. In other areas the right to worship in public is denied to certain faiths, either directly, or indirectly by preventing them from using buildings which were erected for purposes of public worship.

The right of a group to manifest its religion or belief through public worship is also sometimes curtailed — and occasionally even negated — by unreasonable regulations. Licenses for the opening of places of worship may be arbitrarily withheld, or permits for the assembling of a group of worshippers arbitrarily refused. Or, if the license or permit is not withheld or refused, it may be granted on terms which are onerous or difficult to comply with, and which may in effect negate — or at least seriously curtail — the right to worship in common.

Two closely related questions are the protection against interference with worship by outsiders, and the protection of places of worship and articles used in the performance of rites. In most areas such protection is provided either by law or by administrative action, and in many cases criminal penalties are visited upon those who disregard such provisions. But if equal protection is not afforded to all faiths, either in law or in fact, discrimination is the result.

Thus while public authorities may legitimately regulate the exercise of the right to freedom of worship "in community with others" and "in public" in the general interest, taking account of rival demands, it must be affirmed that as a general rule everyone should be free to worship in accordance with

the prescriptions of his religion or belief, either alone or in community with others, and in public or in private; and that equal protection should be accorded to all forms of worship, places of worship, and objects necessary for the performance of rites.

(ii) *Processions*

Some religions consider processions to be an integral part of worship, while others use processions as a way of disseminating their faith, in addition, processions may be organized for purely ceremonial purposes, in connexion with such events as funerals and marriages. While all religious processions are prohibited in some areas, only certain types are forbidden in others.

In some areas a distinction is made between traditional and other religious processions. The former can be held without a permit, but for the latter a permit may be granted or refused, subject to the observance of prescribed conditions. At first glance this may appear to involve discrimination, especially if traditional processions are normally organized by long-established groups while the others are planned by relatively new groups. But this difference in treatment is not necessarily discriminatory. Processions present a particular problem because they use the public thoroughfares; when they are held, public authorities not only have to take account of the normal use of that thoroughfare, but also have to maintain order. Processions organized by new groups are more likely to provoke clashes — especially when they are used as a means of propagating a new religion or belief — than traditional ones. Here as elsewhere the public authorities have to maintain order and at the same time protect the participants from interference by rival groups and individuals; hence the need for permitting such processions to be organized only after permission has been granted. But if the permission is unreasonably withheld, or is granted under onerous conditions, one of the important forms of manifestation of a religion or belief is curtailed to the detriment of the group affected.

In view of the fact that particular circumstances have to be taken into account in each case, it is not possible to formulate a rule of non-discrimination having general applicability on this subject. All that can be affirmed is that processions of all religions or beliefs, when legally organized, should enjoy equal protection.

(iii) *Pilgrimages*

While some faiths consider it to be a duty of every follower to undertake pilgrimages to one or more sacred places associated with special events in their history, others favour such pilgrimages without making them obligatory. Pilgrimages may be undertaken by individuals either singly or in groups; in the latter case they sometimes take the form of processions and have to be regulated as such. Frequently they involve not only travel within a country, but also travel to a foreign country where the sacred places are located. Pilgrimages to foreign countries involve not only the possibility for the pilgrim to leave his own country, but also the possibility for him to enter the appropriate foreign country.

Particular circumstances, such as a stare of war or an internal disturbance of the peace, the outbreak of an epidemic, or economic considerations leading to such measures as currency regulations, may necessitate temporary restrictions on the undertaking of pilgrimages to sacred places. But when a pilgrimage is an essential part of a faith, any systematic prohibition or curtailment of the possibility for pilgrims to undertake journeys to sacred places, or of the pos-

sibility for pilgrims to leave their own country or to enter a foreign country where the sacred place is located, would constitute a serious infringement of the right of the individual to manifest his religion or belief. Thus as a general rule the possibility for pilgrims to journey to sacred places as acts of devotion prescribed by their religion or belief — whether inside or outside their own country — should be assured.

(iv) *Equipment and symbols*

When public authorities prohibit or limit the wearing of certain apparel, the use of bells or musical accompaniments, or the display of symbols associated with a religion or belief, they may thereby prevent the observance of an obligatory part of practice, or at least an established custom.

However, in prohibiting the wearing of religious apparel outside places of worship these authorities may only be motivated by a desire to protect the clergy against hostility, which might be great in a period of acute social tension. They might also find it necessary to prevent the exploitation of the wearing of religious apparel outside places of worship. A prohibition of the wearing of religious apparel in certain institutions, such as public schools, may be motivated by the desire to preserve the non-denominational character of these institutions. It would therefore be difficult to formulate a rule of general application as to the right to wear religious apparel, even though it is desirable that persons whose faith prescribes such apparel should not be unreasonably prevented from wearing it.

Regulation by public authorities of the use of symbols, bells, musical accompaniments and amplifiers associated with a religion of belief may be necessary in order to preserve peace and tranquillity, particularly in localities where people of different faiths reside. From such a regulation — or even a temporary prohibition — one cannot necessarily infer a discriminatory practice. In particular, the social climate in which such restrictions are imposed cannot be ignored. If the Government is concerned with curtailing social tensions, the limitations may acquire a special significance. Thus the surrounding circumstances in each case — such as whether or not the display of religious symbols or the use of bells, musical accompaniments or amplifiers is likely to result in a serious breach of the peace — have to be taken into account before an assessment is made. The possibility that other members of the community may be seriously disturbed by the use of such equipment or symbols may also have to be taken into account. When unequal treatment is meted out to various groups as a matter of policy and without valid reason, it is clearly a case of discrimination. But since each case must be considered on its own merits, a rule of general application on this aspect of the question is not formulated. However, it may be asserted that as a general rule the members of a religion or belief should not be prevented from acquiring or producing articles necessary for the performance of the rituals prescribed by their faith, such as prayer books, candles, ritual wine and the like, And in cases where a country has adopted an exonomic [sic] system under which the Government controls means of production and distribution, the public authorities should make such articles, or the means of producing them, available to the groups concerned.

(v) *Arrangements for disposal of the dead*

Burial grounds or cemeteries are normally operated by public authorities, by the Established Church or State religion, by recognized religious groups, or by private individuals. Regulation by public authorities of these grounds and of the burial, cremation, or other methods for the disposal of the dead is legitimate and unavoidable in the interests of morality, public order and the general welfare — including, of course, considerations of public health. However, in certain cases such regulation may lead to abuse, or be so unreasonable as to be discriminatory.

Where public authorities are responsible, burial grounds and cemeteries are usually equally accessible to all. But this very fact of equal accessibility may cause the followers of certain religions or beliefs to complain that such an arrangement is contrary to their faith and hence discriminatory. This objection is met, in many instances, by allotting separate cemeteries or burial grounds to various faiths, and reserving space for those willing to bury their dead in common ground. In addition, in some instances, the families of deceased persons are permitted to display the symbols of their faith. and to participate in their own religious ceremonies, at the common cemeteries or burial grounds.

Where the Established Church or State religion is responsible for the grounds, and its authorities have the discretion to refuse to bury certain individuals in consecrated ground, either because they do not belong to that religion or because of the circumstances of their death, serious discrimination can occur unless alternative facilities for burial are made available. Moreover, where these authorities prohibit the ceremonies of other faiths, or the display of their symbols, discrimination ensues. But such instances are rare. Many countries having an Established Church or State religion provide special cemeteries or burial places for dissidents, where ceremonies according to their own faith may be performed.

Where separate burial grounds or cemeteries are operated by the various recognized religious groups, a problem arises when a person dies who belongs to none of those faiths. This dilemma is sometimes resolved by providing that, where there are no cemeteries or burial grounds available for members of a particular religion or belief, other groups must relax their restrictions. However, such groups may then feel that the prescriptions of their own faith are being disregarded, and that they are being discriminated against.

Where cemeteries or burial grounds are privately operated, religious or non-sectarian groups are usually free to establish and maintain their own, either directly or through a trust or a corporation. Here no problem arises except perhaps in the case of groups so small that they are not in a position to operate a cemetery.

In many areas funeral or commemorative rites are protected, either by law or by administrative action, against interference by outsiders, and cemeteries and burial grounds are protected against desecration. Criminal penalties are often visited upon those who disregard such laws. But if equal protection in this respect is not afforded to all faiths, either in law or in fact, discrimination results.

As a general rule the prescriptions of the religion or belief of a deceased person should be followed in the assignment of places for burial, cremation or other methods of disposal of the dead, in the display in such places of religious or other symbols, and in the performance of funeral or commemorative rites. Equal protection against desecration should be afforded to all places for burial, cremation or other methods of disposal of the dead, as well as to religious and other symbols displayed in these places, and equal protection against interference by outsiders

should be afforded to the funeral or commemorative rites of all religions and beliefs.

(vi) *Observance of holidays and days of rest*

In a multi-religious society, a problem arises in connexion with the observance of holidays and days of rest. No doubt, religious holidays, including periodic days of rest, play an important part in the life of members of every religion. But various faiths attach differing degrees of importance to holidays and days of rest; while for some, strict observance of such days is a categorical imperative, for others it involves only a limited prohibition of certain activities or a prescription to attend services or to perform certain ceremonies.

One of the most common instances of public authorities giving legal effect to the practices of the faith of the majority of the population is in the designation of the holidays and days of rest of that faith as official holidays and days of rest. In many areas special permission is granted to persons of certain faiths to observe a weekly day of rest different from that of the majority, but this is not always possible, since public convenience usually requires some standardization of working days.

When occasional holidays other than the weekly day of rest are considered, the situation may be different. Public authorities are usually in a position to declare holidays for institutions under their control, such as public schools, government offices and defence establishments. But even here, in a multi-religious society, the occasional holidays of all faiths when put together may reach a total which is prohibitive. This may not only preclude the granting of all religious holidays to members of all faiths, but may even lead to a reduction in the number of holidays granted to the members of each group, including the predominant one. However, public authorities must take care to mete out approximately equal treatment to all faiths. As a general rule the prescriptions of each religion or belief relating to holidays and days of rest should be taken into account, subject to the overriding consideration of the interest of society as a whole.

(vii) *Dietary practices*

Although dietary regulations prescribed by various religions and beliefs are usually followed in private, they nevertheless give rise to some problems which the public authorities cannot overlook. It may not be possible, for example, to conform to such regulations in preparing food for members of a mixed group for example in schools, hospitals, prisons or the armed forces — unless the number of people observing a particular regulation is sufficiently large. Moreover, certain dietary practices are dependent upon the performance of certain other acts of a preparatory nature, and these acts may not be permitted. Thus, according to the Jewish religion, only meat prepared by the ritual slaughtering of animals (*Shehitah*) may be eaten; and in some countries the law precludes this form of slaughter. Such laws may not expressly prohibit *Shehitah*, being phrased in general terms, but their intent as well as their effect may be to prevent the observance of this rite; and this is felt to be discriminatory by the group affected, even though public authorities take measures to mitigate their difficulties by permitting the importation of ritually prepared meat from abroad. Moreover, in countries where the entire economy — or at least the provision of food — is government-controlled or government-operated, the observance of such dietary practices may be difficult if not impossible unless special provisions are made.

Although it would not seem possible to impose upon the public authorities a duty of securing by positive measures the observance of dietary practices of all faiths in all circumstances, the general rule should be that no one should be prevented from observing the dietary practices prescribed by his religion or belief. In the case of a country which has an economic system under which the Government controls the means of production and distribution, this rule would imply that its public authorities are under an obligation to place the object necessary for observing dietary practices prescribed by particular faiths, or the means of producing them, at the disposal of members of those faiths.

(viii) *Celebration of marriage and its dissolution by divorce*

A particularly fertile ground for conflicts between the prescriptions of religious law and those of secular law is to be found in questions pertaining to the celebration and dissolution of marriage. These conflicts occur because most religions or beliefs consider these questions to be within their competence, whereas the modern State assumes the right to regulate family relationships on the ground that the family is the basic unit of society.

(ix) *Celebration of marriage*

Most countries prescribe or recognize one or more forms of celebration of marriage. Some recognize only marriage performed by the civil authorities, others give equal recognition to civil and to religious marriage and leave the parties free to make a choice between the two, while still others permit only a religious celebration of marriage either for all or for certain groups of the population. The problems to which each of these systems give rise are somewhat different.

In countries which recognize only civil marriage, there would appear to be equal treatment for all. But if this rule were to be coupled with a prohibition of religious marriage ceremonies, this would undoubtedly be considered discriminatory by persons belonging to religious groups. Actually there is no such general prohibition in any country of this category; in all of them individuals are free to celebrate their marriage in the form prescribed by their religion, although no legal effects may be attached in such a ceremony. In such countries the law usually prescribes that religious ceremonies should take place only after civil marriage, and sometimes it imposes penalties upon clergymen who perform religious ceremonies in disregard of this provision.

In countries where individuals are free to choose between a marriage according to secular law or one with religious rites, there is no discrimination if legal recognition is accorded to the marriage rites of all faiths.

In countries where only civil marriages and marriages performed in accordance with the rites of certain recognized religions are valid, individuals who do not belong to such religions are precluded from celebrating a marriage in accordance with the prescriptions of their faith, and having legal effect. Since, however, such individuals may contract a civil marriage — and in addition are not precluded from celebrating their marriage in accordance with the rites of their own religion or belief — this inequality does not have serious consequences.

In some countries which permit the celebration of marriage only in accordance with the rites of certain recognized religions, and in which there is no secular law of marriage, individuals who do not belong to one of the recognized religions have no choice except to be married by a ceremony prescribed by

one of the recognized groups, although it may not be in conformity with their own convictions. In other countries members of certain recognized religions are compelled to celebrate their marriage in accordance with the prescriptions of those religions, while civil marriage is available to those who belong to other religions, or to none at all. In either case considerable difficulties arise for individuals who belong to a faith which does not admit the right of a member to break away. Even though the individual considers himself to be a dissenter, he is sometimes not permitted to contract a marriage except in the form prescribed by the faith to which he is nominally attached. Furthermore, in the second group of countries the performance of a civil marriage may be conditional upon proof that the individual has left his former religion or belief; difficulties and delays may arise because of the reluctance of the ecclesiastical authorities to recognize the break. In addition, some clergymen in these countries may refuse to celebrate a marriage between a member of their own religion and one who belongs to another faith, or may agree to celebrate the marriage only upon the promise to fulfill certain conditions, such as an undertaking to bring up any children of the marriage in their religion.

To sum up, in countries where there is no civil form of marriage, those who do not belong to a recognized religion or belief are compelled to celebrate marriage in accordance with religious rites not in conformity with their convictions. In countries where only religious marriage is available to members of certain groups, persons who withdraw from these groups are sometimes compelled to celebrate marriage in accordance with rites prescribed by a faith of which they no longer consider themselves to be members. Both cases involve discrimination.

As a general rule, it may be said that no one should be prevented from having marriage rites performed in accordance with the prescriptions of his religion or belief, nor be compelled to undergo a religious marriage ceremony not in conformity with his convictions.

(x) *Dissolution of marriage by divorce*

The possibility of and the grounds for dissolution of marriage by divorce vary from area to area, and are influenced by social as well as religious considerations. In some areas divorce is not permitted. Countries which permit divorce fall into two main categories: those in which divorce can be granted only by civil courts which apply the same law to all irrespective of their faith, and those in which civil or religious authorities apply the religious law of each community to members of that community.

Where divorce is not permitted, this policy normally stems from the concept which society entertains of the family and its protection. Often this concept reflects the prescriptions of the faith of the majority, and in such cases the fact that the country has adopted the principle of separation of State from religion or belief makes no difference. In such countries, persons whose faith permits the dissolution of marriage by divorce are precluded from the possibility of obtaining one. It must be noted, however, that in prohibiting a divorce a State does not prohibit any mandatory prescription of a religion or belief, but only a practice which is considered permissible.

In countries where divorce is granted only by civil courts, which apply the same law to all, irrespective of their religion or belief, the procedure for granting a divorce, or the grounds on which it may be granted, need not necessarily be in conformity with the prescriptions of a particular faith. Here members of a religion or belief, the concepts of which do not coincide with — or opposed to — those of the law of the land, may feel aggrieved. However, since the State is entitled to regulate marriage and its dissolution in conformity with the views entertained by society, and since in such cases the law reflects the concept which society as a whole entertains of the family and its protection, it would not be proper to consider the result as discriminatory. Even when the prescriptions of the law are identical with those of the faith of the majority, the result cannot be considered discriminatory, and for the same reason.

In countries where civil or religious authorities apply the religious law of each faith to members of that faith, the results again can hardly be considered discriminatory, since each individual is governed by the prescriptions of his own religion or belief. However, problems may arise, mainly in three types of cases. First, individuals who are not members of a recognized group cannot effect a dissolution of their marriage, since no authority has the competence to grant it. Secondly, individuals who do not consider themselves as belonging to a particular faith may nevertheless be compelled to submit to its religious law in areas where religious authorities, rather than the individuals concerned, have the power to determine who is a member of their faith. Thirdly, individuals may find it impossible to effect a dissolution of their marriage in cases where they have been married in accordance with the religious law of a recognized community, because of a stipulation in that religious law that it would govern marital relations between the parties irrespective of any change of faith by either of the parties.

Because of the great variety of policies followed by States in this matter — some recognizing the dissolution of marriage by divorce and others not recognizing it — it is impossible to frame a rule covering all countries and all legal systems. However, in countries which recognize the dissolution of marriage by divorce, the right to seek and to obtain a divorce should not be denied to anyone whose convictions admit divorce, solely on the ground that he professes a particular religion or belief.

(xi) Dissemination of religion or belief

While some faiths do not attempt to win new converts, many of them make it mandatory for their followers to spread their message to all, and to attempt to convert others. For the latter, dissemination is an important aspect of the right to manifest their religion or belief.

The problems raised by dissemination, although in the main the same as those raised by other forms of manifestation, present an intensity and a sharpness not to be found in any of the others. The attempt to convert individuals from one faith to another may conflict with their freedom to maintain their own religion or belief, and tends to meet with resistance not only from the individual concerned but from groups as well. And even the propagation of a message may affect the peaceful coexistence of various faiths and lead to clashes between them, either because of the contents of the message or the methods used in spreading it. In such instances the State may have to intervene, but any such intervention should not be more than what is justified in order to ensure peace and tranquillity.

In some areas cultural factors determine, at least to a large extent, the attitude of society and of the State towards dissemination of a faith. For example, where a religion or belief, introduced from outside a country or territory, propagates its faith through foreign missionaries, a fresh culture

is introduced which may not harmonize with the existing order. It was probably with this is mind that the work of missionaries has often been curtailed by the powers administering non-self-governing territories, either in the territory as a whole or in certain regions. This action was taken in many cases despite the fact that the religion of the missionaries was that of the administering authorities.[1] Here the hostility of the local population was not based so much upon antagonism to a new religion as upon the fear of the introduction of a fresh cultural impact, and this fear had to be recognized by the authorities. The rival claims of competing faiths, social stability, and national security all had to be taken into account in determining the extent to which the right to disseminate religion or belief had to be limited. But it is clear that sometimes concepts of social stability and national security were over-emphasized, with the result that the right to disseminate was unduly limited.

It is sometimes argued that educational and social activities such as the maintenance by a faith or by its missionaries of hospitals, schools and orphanages, constitute an unfair form of dissemination, since such activities are carried on amongst children — undoubtedly a particularly impressionable group. But where the prior right of parents or guardians to decide whether or not their children shall attend religious instruction is conceded, and where the institutions in question advance social welfare, the advantages obtained by such educational and humanitarian activities can hardly be considered to constitute a material inducement to a change of religion or belief. This is not, however, to overlook the fact that in certain isolated cases improper inducements — amounting even to out-right bribes offered to members of the less fortunately placed sections of society — may bring about a change of faith which does not spring from genuine conviction. Here the State has a right to limit such activities in order to protect individuals from conversion by unfair means.

Where missionaries come from another country, the attitude of the State towards them is determined not only by their own conduct but also by the relations subsisting between the two countries. Sometimes in periods of acute international tension exceptional measure — curtailing missionary activity or even prohibiting it entirely in certain regions such as frontier areas — may be necessary. It is clear that dissemination of a faith cannot be allowed to cloak the pursuit of political aims calculated to impair the security of the State.

The need for upholding morality and the general welfare, and for promoting health, may also at times necessitate a limitation upon the right to disseminate a faith. But while recognizing the inherent right of the State to protect the morals of its society and the rights of all faiths and their followers, one cannot overlook the fact that sometimes the prescriptions of the predominant religion or belief have been incorporated in the laws of the State, and that these may restrict the emergence of new competitive faiths.

Dissemination of a religion or belief has two facets: the substance of the message and the method by which it is spread. Members of other faiths may object to the message, or to the manner in which it is propagated, or to both, and these objections may lead to clashes between the groups. It is to prevent the dissemination of a faith in a manner offensive to others that special laws, such as laws against blasphemy, have been enacted in some areas; and even in countries where freedom of anti-religious propaganda is recognized, it is considered necessary to caution against methods of dissemination

calculated to wound the religious feelings of the faithful or of the clergy. Unfortunately, in some cases the laws against blasphemy have been framed in such a manner that they characterize any pronouncement not in conformity with the predominant faith as blasphemous. Under such laws, censorship of books, pamphlets and newspapers, as well as control of the media of mass communications such as films, radio, television and the like, have sometimes been used to limit unduly — or even to prohibit altogether — the dissemination of beliefs other than those of the predominant religion or philosophy. However, in some countries the laws against blasphemy — although still on the statute books — are no longer applied because the times have changed and society is stronger than before; in modern times reasonable men do not foresee the dissolution or downfall of society because a religion or belief is publicly criticized "by methods not scandalous".

To sum up: in this difficult field where the dividing line between justifiable and not-so-justifiable restraints is thin, it is more than ever necessary to emphasize the objectives which should influence the policies of States. Firstly, although the right to disseminate a faith must be safeguarded, this should be done within the framework of ensuring to everyone freedom to maintain his religion or belief. Secondly, any limitations on the dissemination of a faith should be such as will maintain peace and tranquillity both inside and outside the country or territory, failing which no religious freedom is possible. Thirdly, although certain limitations upon particular forms of dissemination are permissible in the interest of morals as conceived by society as a whole, such limitations as may be temporarily imposed should be removed as quickly as possible — even though gradually — in order that the largest possible measure of freedom may be assured.

Apart from these considerations, it may be stated as a general rule that everyone should be free to disseminate a religion or belief, in so far as his actions do not impair the right of any other individual to maintain his religion or belief.

(xii) *Training of personnel*

Freedom to manifest a religion or belief implies the right to train personnel such as ministers, priests, rabbis, mullahs and imams, since the lack of adequately trained leaders may make the performance of many practices and observances difficult, if not impossible. Arrangements for such training vary from area to area. In some countries personnel of the predominant religious group are trained in state-operated or state-supported institutions. In others, the State provides facilities for several different faiths to train their personnel. In still others, each religion or belief has to provide the facilities for training its personnel at its own expense. As long as a State does not hinder or prevent any faith from training the personnel required, the unequal treatment which results from some of these arrangements is not serious, except in so far as it involves favoured financial treatment of certain religions or beliefs. This aspect is considered later.

If the facilities to train the personnel required by a faith are available only abroad — either because the group is too small to maintain an appropriate institution in its own country or because its prescriptions call for training at particular places outside the country — the withholding of permission for prospective trainees to travel abroad would affect the manifestation of the religion or belief. Whether or not such treatment is discriminatory can be determined only after a full consideration of all the facts. If it is

based on a systematic policy of preventing or hindering the training of personnel of a particular faith or of all faiths, then it is clearly discriminatory. But if it is genuinely based upon other grounds, such as external or internal security or a shortage of foreign currency, it cannot be pronounced to be discriminatory.

As a general rule, no group professing a religion or belief should be prevented from training the personnel required for the performance of practices or observances prescribed by that religion or belief. When such training is available only outside the country, no permanent limitations should be placed upon travel abroad for the purpose of undergoing such training.

B. FREEDOM FROM PREFORMING ACTS INCOMPATIBLE WITH THE PRESCRIPTIONS OF A RELIGION OR BELIEF

(i) *Taking of an oath*

In most countries the law requires that an individual, before testifying in court or giving information to specified public authorities, should take an oath. Usually provision is made that anyone whose religion or belief does not permit him to take an oath may make a solemn declaration of affirmation instead; in some cases this question is left entirely to the discretion of the individual and anyone may substitute a solemn declaration or an affirmation for an oath, whether or not he invokes religious grounds. In some countries permission to substitute a declaration or an affirmation for an oath is granted either to members of specified religions, or to the followers of any faith who object to taking an oath, but no corresponding provision is made for atheists, agnostics, or rationalists. There are also a few countries when the law does not provide for the substitution of a declaration or an affirmation for an oath under any circumstances.

When the law compels an individual to take an oath in disregard of the prescriptions of his religion or belief, there is discrimination. Even though refusal to take an oath may not be punishable, it may nevertheless give rise to problems as when, for example, an individual is impeded in his defense in criminal proceedings or prevented from proving his case in civil matters by his failure to take an oath. A second and similar issue arises in countries where individuals are obliged to take an oath before exercising certain rights or assuming certain public or other offices. A special problem presents itself if a particular oath is prescribed by the State for clerics before they can enter upon their clerical duties and the taking of that oath is contrary to the prescriptions of their religion. Here not only is the cleric himself excluded from access to office, but the group to which he belongs may also be deprived of having spiritual leaders and thereby penalized.

Thus it may be said that as a general rule no one should be compelled to take an oath contrary to the prescriptions of his religion or belief.

(ii) *Military service*

There is no uniform solution to the problem of conscientious objection to military service based on the ground that such service is contrary to the prescriptions of a religion or belief; it varies considerably from country to country, and even in various parts of the same country, according to circumstances and the state of public opinion. Normally recognition of the claim of conscientious objectors to full or partial exemption from military service is left to the discretion of the State. This arrangement has been rec-

ognized in article 8 of the draft covenant on civil and political rights, recently adopted by the Third Committee of the General Assembly, which deals with forced or compulsory labour and which specifically lays down that this term shall not include: "... any service of a military character and, in countries where conscientious objection is recognized, any national service required by law of conscientious objectors ... "

Some countries do not exempt any individual from military service on the ground that such service is contrary to the prescriptions of his faith, others exempt anyone who genuinely objects to military service for conscientious reasons, and still others exempt only those who are members of certain religions or beliefs. In addition, in a few countries exemption is granted but only to specified categories of individuals, such as the clerics of all religions or of one or several particular religions. Further, countries excusing conscientious objectors from military service differ in the extent of the exemption which they grant. While some exempt only from combatant duties, others exempt even from non-combatant duties those whose faith prohibits any participation in the armed forces. However, it must be realized that even though the right to conscientious objection is recognized by law, impediments may be placed in the way of conscientious objectors by the public, particularly in regard to their access to employment and to social life.

Some conscientious objectors do not believe in performing any services which are even remotely connected with a military effort: in the present circumstances hardly any society can afford to recognize this stand. Others are prepared and even willing to perform alternative compensatory national services, often in conditions of considerable hardship and of danger to their lives;

and wherever possible such alternative avenues of service should be explored. But whether an individual belongs to the first or the second category, the population of the country as a whole may feel that any exemption creates a privilege entailing discriminatory treatment of others.

As a rule, it may be stated that where the principle of conscientious objection to military service is recognized, exemptions should be granted to genuine objectors in a manner ensuring that no adverse distinction based upon religion or belief may result.

(iii) Participation in religious or civic ceremonies

Certain ceremonies or observances sponsored by public authorities, which individuals such as schoolchildren, hospital patients and members of the armed forces are required to attend, may be objected to by some on the ground that participation in them is contrary to a prescription of their religion or belief. Such ceremonies may be those prescribed by a faith to which the objectors do not belong, or they may be purely civic in character, such as pledging allegiance to a country's flag or singing its national anthem.

A variety of approaches to this problem has been adopted in different countries and even in different parts of a single country. Particular circumstances such as the climate of public opinion, the need to strengthen the common bonds of citizenship, or the existence of a state of war, may have a decisive influence. But it is clear that States cannot give up the sponsoring of such ceremonies and observances altogether, and therefore it is not possible to decide in the absolute whether or not a particular solution is justified.

What can be affirmed is that, as a rule, in a country where exemptions from partici-

pation in certain or all public ceremonies are granted to individuals who object to such participation on the ground that it is contrary to a prescription of their religion or belief, such exemptions should be granted in such a manner that no adverse distinction based upon religion or belief may result.

(iv) Secrecy of the confession

Some religions require their followers to confess their sins to a cleric and prohibit him from divulging such information. In many countries the confidential nature of such confessions is protected by law — even to the extent of forbidding the cleric, under penalty, to divulge the information thus obtained. But in countries where the confidential nature of such confessions is not recognized, clerics may be compelled to divulge information obtained in confessions at the request of public authorities. In the latter group of countries an important duty prescribed by religion cannot be discharged.

It would appear, therefore, that as a general rule no cleric who receives information in confidence, in accordance with the prescriptions of his religion, should be compelled by public authorities to divulge such information.

(v) Compulsory prevention or treatment of disease

Some individuals object to certain measures for preventing disease — such as the fluoridation of water supplies, vaccination, or inoculation — and others object to certain or any forms of medical treatment on the ground that such measures are contrary to the prescription of their religion or belief. What value should public authorities attach to such objections?

Certainly where there is any likelihood of an epidemic endangering the welfare of the whole community, public authorities are under an obligation to take all possible preventive and curative measures: they cannot therefore exempt the members of any particular faith from the operation of these measures. Further, they may consider it proper to insist upon what are considered to be scientifically proven methods of preventing and curing disease, and in so doing may have to overrule the prescriptions of an individual's religion or belief. A particular problem arises in the case of refusal by parents to apply such preventive or curative measures to their children. Here a conflict arises between what the parents on the one hand, and society on the other, consider to be in the child's interest. In such a case that State is entitled, on behalf of society, to impose its decision upon the parents.

But where there is no danger of an epidemic, and where adults are concerned, the attitude of the public authorities varies greatly from country to country, although it would seem that everywhere it is admitted that the public has to be protected against abuses such as witchcraft and quackery. While in some countries the authorities are not willing to interfere with the freedom of an individual to follow the method of treatment prescribed by his faith, unless this method is considered to be contrary to accepted standards of morality, in other countries they consider it proper to insist upon what is considered to be scientifically proven medical treatment even though individuals or groups object on the ground that such treatment is contrary to the prescriptions of their religion or belief.

For these reasons it would seem impossible to formulate a rule of general applicability on this subject. But generally it would be conceded that where an individual's refusal of scientific medical treatment, or his resort to unscientific treatment, endangers

his life, public authorities may intervene just as they would intervene to prevent an individual from taking his own life.

CHAPTER IV

THE STATUS OF RELIGIONS IN RELATION TO THE STATE

JURIDICAL RELATIONSHIP BETWEEN THE STATE AND RELIGION

From a juridical point of view countries may be classified broadly into three categories: those which have an Established Church or State religion, those in which several religions are recognized by the State, and those in which the State and religion are separate.

It is sometimes contended that the mere fact of separation of the State and religion ensures non-discrimination and that other arrangements — particularly the establishment of a religion by the State — necessarily give rise to discrimination. Actually, the situation is not so simple. For one thing, where the law does not explicitly define the relationship between the State and religion, it may be difficult to determine into which of the three categories a country falls. And even when the law defines the relationship and several countries fall into the same broad category, their interpretation of the relationship in practice may be quite different, resulting in discrimination in some and not in others. Conversely, when several countries fall into different categories, the actual arrangements made in respect of religions may be found to be so similar that it is difficult to suggest that one type of relationship leads to discrimination while the other does not.

Established Church or State religion

For centuries, a close relationship existed in almost all countries between the State and the predominant religion. This religion enjoyed a special status, either because it had been recognized as the Established Church or because it had been accepted as the State religion. Not infrequently recognition of the predominant religion led to the total exclusion of all other religions, or at least to their reduction to a subordinate position. Thus in the past the mere existence in a country of an Established Church or of a State religion usually connoted severe discrimination — and sometimes even outright persecution — directed against dissenters. But is it correct today to suggest that wherever there is an Established Church or a State religion, there is necessarily discrimination against all other religions or their followers?

An examination of the present-day situation in various countries which have either an Established Church or a State religion reveals that in a few of them there is as still a more or less pronounced discrimination against other faiths-and sometimes even against their followers as individuals — not only in the matter of religious rights and practices but also in other fields. But in other countries of this group, as a result of evolution, a number of other religions — or even all of them — have achieved a status identical in almost all respects to that of the Established Church or the State religion. Thus the survival of an Established Church or of a State religion in a country may today be not much more than a mere historic relic.

Nor can it be inferred, from the mere fact of a State recognizing a single religion, that other religions or their followers are necessarily treated in a discriminatory manner. In some countries, for example, concordats assure certain rights and privileges to the Roman Catholic Church, but these do not preclude non-discriminatory treatment of other religions or of their followers, since equal rights and privileges may be accorded to them by the State.

Recognition of several religions

There is no strict dividing line between countries having an Established Church or a State religion and those where several religions are recognized: in many Muslim countries, for example, Islam is the State religion, but recognition is accorded to a number of other religious communities as well. In the countries of this group a considerable variety of arrangements may be found. In some of them only two — or a few — religions have a status in law. In others, any religion may be granted recognition upon application and the completion of certain formalities. But even in countries where only a limited number of religions are recognized, this fact does not necessarily imply that there is discrimination against the unrecognized religions or their followers, since in many cases such religions can avail themselves of the general law of association and since, in addition, their followers, as citizens, are equal under the law.

But of course if the State has discretionary power to grant or to refuse recognition, and if the privileges accorded to recognized religions, or to their followers, are very different from those accorded to unrecognized ones, this may lead to discrimination. Where the cumulative impact of such arrangements is severe — as in countries where to a large extent the personal status of each individual is regulated by the religious law of his community — even the basic right of an individual to change his religion or belief may be seriously impaired. This right may also be curtailed more directly — or even nullified — where religious leaders are entitled to prevent, or to refuse to recognize, the withdrawal of a member from his religion.

Separation of State and religion

There is no doubt that historically the principle of separation of State and religion emerged as a reaction against the privileged position of the Established Church or the State religion, and that its purpose was to assure a large measure of equality to the members of various religions. Within the framework of this principle of separation, however, *de facto* preeminence is sometimes achieved by a particular religion and the law of the country — although equally applicable to everyone — reflects in certain important matters the concepts of the predominant group. Thus rules regulating marriage and its dissolution are often taken over from the religious law of the predominant group. Similarly, official holidays and days of rest in many countries correspond to a large extent to the religious holidays and days of rest of the predominant group.

The State, even when applying the principle of separation, may accord a special status to religious organizations, distinct from that accorded to other kinds of associations. But such a status may be granted only on condition that the religious group satisfies certain specified conditions — a possibility for some but not for others. Even if a State maintains strict neutrality as between various faiths, inequality of treatment is not necessarily excluded. The demands of various religions are different, and a law prohibiting certain acts, or enjoining the performance of others, may prevent one religious group from performing an essential rite or from following a basic observance, but be of no importance at all to another group.

It would seem therefore that the mere fact that a country falls into one of the three categories mentioned above is not in itself a sufficient basis upon which to determine whether or not discrimination with respect to freedom of thought, conscience and religion exists in that country. It is necessary to probe more deeply into the actual situation in each case in order to reach a conclusion in this matter. Thus it is impossible to draft a rule of general applicability, recommending a particular form of juridical relationship between the State and religion.

MANAGEMENT OF RELIGIOUS AFFAIRS

The term "management of religious affairs", which is variously interpreted by practically every religion, is used here as referring to such essential matters as the determination of the membership of a religion, its organizational structure, and its spiritual administration. These usually fall within the province of dogma, since they pertain to matters of faith, ritual and doctrine.

If we examine first the example of an oecumenical religion, it will be found that the essential rules concerning these matters are determined by supranational organs. However, in some cases, agreements between the State and the supranational religion, or its local hierarchy, give the State a voice in such matters as the appointment of the local clergy, the use of buildings for religious purposes, and the expenditure of funds. Some of these agreements impose upon the clergy the obligation to take an oath of allegiance to the State before they enter upon their religious duties, and stipulate their removal from office by ecclesiastical authorities at the request of the State. Such agreements have to take into account the fact that the religion is precluded from accepting what is contrary to its dogma. They also normally imply a recognition by the State of the juridical personality of the religion for various purposes, such as the acquisition and management of property and the operation of various institutions.

Where there is an Established Church, the relationship between the State and that Church is usually so intimate that the political organs of the State are clothed with power to decide questions relating to faith, doctrine and ritual, including rules for the management of religious affairs. But this does not mean that public authorities can intervene at will in the management of religious affairs. For example, although theoretically they have the power to appoint any member to the clergy, actually their choice is limited since they cannot appoint a person who does not possess the requirements laid down by the Church. In addition, today, in a large number of countries having an Established Church, the State concedes considerable autonomy to elected church bodies in several fields, including not only day-to-day administration but also the organization of the church. For example, the appointment of the clergy, including members of the hierarchy, often must be recommended by church assemblies or other ecclesiastical authorities, and the State exercises only the right to formal approval of the appointment.

Where the State recognizes several religions, either along with or without an Established Church or a State religion, a similar situation prevails. The degree of autonomy which each faith enjoys in the management of its religious affairs is determined by the State. The recognition of each religion takes into account the important prescriptions of that religion.

It will be realized that in none of the three cases is there absolute freedom for the management of religious affairs. In particular, there is no freedom of association in the ordinary sense of this term because, to a large extent, the form of organization of a religious group is determined by dogma.

It is sometimes contended that, at least in one important respect, maximum freedom in the management of religious affairs is assured to all faiths in those countries where the State and religion are separate. According to this view, all religions are automatically treated equally in such countries; and the very idea of separation implies at least a minimum of intervention — if not complete non-intervention — in the management of religious affairs.

However, it must be borne in mind that since the demands made by various religions upon their members are different and since varying degrees of importance are attached to different manifestations, uniformity of treatment may in reality lead to discrimination against some religions. Thus, if the State prescribes a certain pattern of religious organization — in which, for example, all members of each religious group have an equal voice in some aspects of its management, such as the selection of its leaders — this would be detrimental to those groups whose religions prescribe a hierarchical organization and submission to a supranational authority, and would therefore be discriminatory. Or, in a case where the law prescribes a minimum membership for forming a religious association, but the religion itself considers fewer members to be sufficient for this purpose, a small group may be handicapped in its desire to organize. In a country where the right to organize a religious group is recognized only if the sole purpose of the group is to hold religious services, this would constitute a severe limitation upon those religions for whom propagation of their faith, social, cultural or humanitarian activities, or the distribution of alms, are essential. Similarly, a prohibition of monastic orders would adversely affect religions maintaining such institutions, or a limitation on the right to correspond with co-religionists abroad would be resented as a grievous discrimination by a group which considers it an obligatory duty on the part of its clergy to correspond with spiritual leaders outside the country.

Regarding the notion that separation of State and religion somehow guarantees a minimum of State intervention in the management of religious affairs, it must be pointed out that even in countries where the principle of separation is in effect, the State cannot afford to dissociate itself completely from what is happening in the religious sphere. Freedom ensured to one religion may at some point conflict with freedom assured to another. Or a conflict may arise between the right of a religion to determine its membership and the right of an individual to follow the dictates of his conscience, since religions often do not recognize the right of a member to leave the faith into which he was born, or at least view such a change with extreme disfavour. In such a situation the State cannot remain indifferent and may have to limit the authority of the group to determine its membership, even though this might result in some curtailment of its right to manage its religious affairs.

Certain practices of a religion or of its followers may also conflict with the requirement of public order and national security. One cannot, for instance, allow subversive acts to be committed from a place of worship. As has been pointed out, if such subversive action should be attempted by a cleric, neither his robe nor his pulpit will be a defense.

In some instances such authorities have to adjudicate between rival elements within a religion, each of which claims the right to conduct services, to perform religious rites in a place of worship, or to appoint religious leaders. When such matters come before civil courts, lay judges must decide between the conflicting claims; and not infrequently they can do this only after taking cognizance of, and interpreting, the provisions of the religious law. This necessarily implies some interference in the management of religious affairs, but is inevitable in the circumstances.

Therefore it should be realized that however strong the desire of a Government to refrain from interfering in the management of religious affairs, circumstances can compel such authorities to take a stand, not only on questions of internal administration, but sometimes also on matters of faith, ritual or doctrine. This has occurred in countries of all types, including those in which the State and religion are separate. But it is clear that not all interventions by the State in the management of religious affairs can be considered proper.

The line between legitimate interference and undue pressure is in many cases extremely thin. When there are rival claimants to the headship of a religion, or where two or more elements of a single faith claim the exclusive right to perform a certain ritual and there is a possibility that the organization may be torn by strife, or that a breach of the peace may occur, the State assuredly has the right to intervene at a certain stage, and even to pronounce its views on matters of internal administration, faith, ritual or doctrine. However, when such a situation arises because the public authorities themselves have created the conflict or have sponsored one or more elements in the dispute in order to achieve extra-religious ends — even though the real nature of their action is thinly veiled — this might not only be a serious case of discrimination but might even amount to a denial of religious and other human rights and fundamental freedoms.

In view of the variety of considerations involved, it is difficult to formulate a rule of general applicability, even though it would be desirable to affirm once more the principle that every religion should be accorded the greatest possible freedom in the management of its religious affairs.

FINANCIAL RELATIONSHIP BETWEEN THE STATE AND RELIGION

Public authorities may — and sometimes do — use their financial powers as a potent weapon of discrimination against various religions or their followers; in some cases these measures severely restrict the enjoyment of the right to freedom of thought, conscience and religion.

From the point of view of the individual, certain fiscal measures may be discriminatory because they compel him to support a religion to which he does not belong. An extreme case is that of a special tax levied upon all citizens to support an Established Church or a State religion. This situation was much more in evidence in the past than it is today, when religious tax laws normally exempt dissenters or permit them to pay a lower rate. In the latter case the reduced tax is justified on the ground that it compensates for services rendered to dissenters on behalf of the community — as for example when ministers of the established religion or of the State Church keep records of births, marriages and deaths, and issue official documents based on these records.

A tax intended solely for the support of a particular religion, levied upon everyone irrespective of his faith, would be discriminatory. On the other hand, compulsory contributions by an individual to his own religious community or organization are not usually considered discriminatory, and in a large number of countries — particularly those having an Established Church or a State religion and those recognizing several religions — civil authorities assist in the collection of these contributions. So long as the right of the individual to change his religion or belief is not impaired, either in law or in fact, and so long as he is not compelled to remain a member of any particular faith against his will, the practice of levying contributions from him for the support of his own religion may not be discriminatory.

Where certain religions are subsidized or exempted from paying taxes by the State, the others — and individual taxpayers as well — may consider that they are being discriminated against and object to State funds being used in this way. These objections appear to have a *prima facie* justification; however, they cannot always be accepted at their face value. In some instances the subsidies or exemptions from taxation are the result of arrangements made to compensate the religious organization for property taken over by sequestration or otherwise. Or they may result from the interest of society in the maintenance of religious structures not so much because of their religious significance, as because they constitute monuments of historic or artistic value. Or they may simply be a method of compensating clergy of the Established Church or the State religion for performing duties on behalf of the community which the dissident clergy do not have to perform.

A problem arises when educational or humanitarian enterprises, operated by a religious group on a non-commercial basis mainly for the benefit of its own members, receive subsidies from the exchequer or are granted exemption of payment of certain taxes. It is contended, on the one hand, that this policy of financial assistance is justified since the community is thus provided with facilities for which the State would otherwise have to pay the full cost. On the other hand, it is argued that the sole function of the State is to provide equal facilities for all citizens without in the least taking account of their religion, and that it should not promote — even indirectly — the establishment of separate facilities for members of a particular religion. In considering this problem, it is necessary to take into account the benefits that accrue to the whole community. Where the enterprise in question is on such a scale that it amounts to a public service benefiting the population as a whole — and this is so in many cases — subsidies and even exemption from the payment of taxes may be justified, provided of course that any other religious group which wishes to undertake similar activities is accorded equal treatment. On the other hand, where such an enterprise benefits exclusively the members of the particular religion which sponsors it, and is run with the sole aim of providing facilities to its members, a subsidy or exemption from taxation would be discriminatory if other groups were not entitled to equal treatment.

Another problem arises where enterprises are run by a religious organization for profit, and are exempted from the payment of certain taxes. It is contended by some that these enterprises should not be exempted from the payment of taxes even though they are of an educational or humanitarian character, since such exemption would constitute an indirect form of propagation of that faith. However, this argument does not seem to have much substance since instances of conversion as a result of such activity are rare.

Where the State is separated from religion, the situation appears to be simpler and indeed to present no problems. But here too

complications arise, mainly because the demands of various religions are different. In certain countries where the principle of separation is recognized, the State puts the necessary buildings and other physical facilities at the disposal of followers of various religions. If the State has a monopoly of printing presses, factories, and workshops, it may likewise assume the responsibility for producing various religious accessories and placing them at the disposal of the appropriate religion. The sameness of treatment meted out to all faiths is considered to be non-discriminatory by the State. But it is possible that public authorities may in fact disregard — or may not take into account as fully as they should — the needs of a particular religion or its followers while providing fully for the needs of other faiths.

The very fact that the State and religion are separate may be felt by some religions, in certain cases, to be discriminatory — as for example where public authorities, applying the general rule that no religion should be subsidized or exempted from taxes, refuse any support to religious schools out of the public treasury. The members of these religions suggest that their children's education costs twice as much as it normally would, since they have to maintain religious schools in accordance with the prescriptions of their faith, and still pay taxes to support public schools. Other religions of course maintain that this refusal of the State to support religious schools stems from a correct application of the principle of separation of State and religion. Thus differing interpretations of the principle lead to precisely opposite results.

Strictly speaking, it may be argued that the question of the financial relationship between State and religion falls outside the province of the right to freedom of thought, conscience and religion. Nevertheless, this question is an extremely important one for this study since financial measures, such as subsidies or exemption from taxation, may easily be abused by public authorities and used as a means of discriminating against certain religions or their followers.

To sum up, it may be stated that as a general rule no adverse distinctions between various religions or their followers in such matters as subsidization or exemption from taxation should be made by public authorities. Nevertheless the State is not precluded from levying general taxes, nor from carrying out obligations which it assumed as a result of arrangements made to compensate a religious organization for property taken over by sequestration or otherwise, nor from contributing funds towards the preservation of religious structures recognized to be monuments of historic or artistic value.

DUTIES OF PUBLIC AUTHORITIES

Throughout this study references have been made to various duties devolving upon public authorities in connection with the question of ensuring to everyone without discrimination the right to freedom of thought, conscience and religion. It may be useful to summarize these duties at this point.

Firstly, public authorities must themselves refrain from making any adverse distinction against, or giving undue preference to, individuals or groups of individuals with regard to this right. Secondly, they must prevent any individual, or group of individuals, from making such adverse distinctions or giving such undue preferences. They may discharge these duties through the adoption of appropriate legal provisions of a preventive or remedial character — including, when necessary, penal sanctions — as well as by administrative action. In addition, they should make every effort to educate public

opinion to an acceptance of the principle of non-discrimination in respect of the right to freedom of thought, conscience and religion, and to create proper leadership for this purpose.

In discharging these duties certain considerations ought to be borne in mind by the public authorities. For example, in case of a conflict between the requirements of two or more religions or beliefs, they should endeavor to find a solution assuring the greatest measure of freedom to society as a whole, while giving preference to the freedom of everyone to maintain or to change his religion or belief over any practice or observance tending to restrict this freedom.

Primarily, public authorities have to ensure that the freedom of everyone to maintain or change his religion or belief is not impaired. Secondarily, they must ensure as widely as possible the freedom of everyone to manifest his religion or belief, either alone or in community with others, and in public or in private. In this connection they must see to it that any limitation imposed upon that freedom is exceptional; that it is confined within the narrowest possible bounds; that it is prescribed by law solely for the purpose of securing due recognition and respect for the rights and freedoms of others and of meeting the just requirements of morality, public order and the general welfare in a democratic society; and that it is not exercised in a manner contrary to the purposes and principles of the United Nations. In addition, they are under a duty not to make any adverse distinctions against, or to give undue preference to, religions or their followers in the granting of subsidies or exemptions from taxation; however, this does not preclude the State from levying general taxes or from carrying out obligations assumed as a result of arrangements made to compensate a religious organization for property taken over by sequestration or otherwise, or from contributing funds for the preservation of religious structures recognized as monuments of historic or artistic value.

*   *   *

CHAPTER VI

A PROGRAMME FOR ACTION

*   *   *

ENUNCIATION OF BASIC RULES

This study reveals that the principles of the Universal Declaration of Human Rights with regard to non-discrimination in respect of the right to freedom of thought, conscience and religion have not as yet been fully implemented in all countries. In order to assist Governments in eradicating discriminatory measures in this field, it may be useful as a first step to enunciate basic rules for dealing with concrete problems which have emerged from the study.

The rules presented below are intended to show how the goals proclaimed in the Declaration may be reached. If followed, they would ensure the achievement of these goals. But even if not followed immediately in all cases, they might nevertheless be useful in educating world opinion.

Once the international community has examined, debated, and accepted these rules, their meaning and significance will be brought forcefully to the attention of Governments. Not only will they be awakened to an awareness of concrete aspects of discrimination in this sphere, but their attention will be directed to measures calculated to overcome such discrimination. More important, individuals, groups, and public authorities who still practice or condone discrimination will feel the impact of crystalliz-ing world opinion. Furthermore, new forces will emerge in each country, and those who practice or condone discrimination will be placed on the defensive.

It must be realized that even those who are the victims of discrimination are often unaware of the wrong that is being done them. Long-standing habits sometimes lead people to believe that the existing order is the best possible one, and to accept its evils together with its virtues. Particularly the education of the young in the principles of non-discrimination will help to widen the ambit of freedom in this sphere, for they will be in a position, once aroused, to expose more clearly and forcefully the evils that lie shrouded in their social system.

Underlying most discriminatory practices are prejudices which have crystallized into *mores* of a society. In the particular case of attitudes towards religions or beliefs, perhaps more than in any other field, *mores* are slow to change since they stem from deeply held convictions. It is therefore all the more important that forces within a society holding non-discrimination to be a basic tenet should consider ways and means of educating public opinion. Legal techniques may also hasten the process of eradicating discrimination, particularly when they involve the imposition of penal sanctions. The very process of adoption of laws may in itself constitute an educational measure. Individuals are inclined to consider wrong what the law prohibits, and right what it enjoins them to do. The new things learned in the forward march of humanity, the pressures of new hopes and even new fears, the consciousness that discrimination tends to narrow public spirit and to pervert the noble ideal of citizenship, may lead, sooner than many realize, to a change of values and a consequent removal of stains that mar present-day society.

THE BASIC RULES

I. FREEDOM TO MAINTAIN OR TO CHANGE RELIGION OR RELIEF

Rule 1

1. Everyone should be free to adhere, or not to adhere, to a religion or belief, in accordance with the dictates of his conscience.

2. Parents should have a prior right to decide upon the religion or belief in which their child should be brought up. When a child is torn from its family environment, the decision as to the religion or belief in which that child is to be brought up should be made primarily in accordance with the objectively ascertained interests of the child, due attention being paid to the expressed or presumed wish of the parents.

3. No one should be subjected to coercion or to improper inducements likely to impair his freedom to maintain or to change his religion or belief.

II. FREEDOM TO MANIFEST RELIGION OR BELIEF

Rule 2

Everyone should be free to comply with what is prescribed or authorized by his religion or belief, and free from performing acts incompatible with the prescriptions of his religion or belief.

Rule 3

1. Everyone should be free to worship in accordance with the prescriptions of his religion or belief, either alone or in community with others, and in public or in private.

2. Equal protection should be accorded to all forms of worship, places of worship, and objects necessary for the performance of rites.

Rule 4

The possibility for pilgrims to journey to sacred places as acts of devotion prescribed by their religion or belief, whether inside or outside their own country, should be assured.

Rule 5

1. The members of a religion or belief should not be prevented from acquiring or producing articles necessary for the performance of the rituals prescribed by their religion or belief, such as prayer books, candles, and ritual wine.

2. Where the Government controls the means of production and distribution, it should make such articles, or the means for producing them, available to the groups concerned.

Rule 6

1. The prescriptions of the religion or belief of a deceased person should be followed in the assignment of places for burial, cremation or other methods of disposal of the dead, the display in such places of religious or other symbols, and the performance of funeral or commemorative rites.

2. Equal protection against desecration should be afforded to all places for burial, cremation or other methods of disposal of the dead, as well as to religious and other symbols displayed in these places; and equal protection against interference by outsiders should be afforded to the funeral or commemorative rites of all religions and beliefs.

Rule 7

The prescriptions of each religion or belief relating to holidays and days of rest should be taken into account, subject to the overriding consideration of the interest of society as a whole.

48

Rule 8

1.   No one should be prevented from observing the dietary practices prescribed by his religion or belief.

2.   Where the Government controls the means of production and distribution, it should place the objects necessary for observing dietary practices prescribed by particular religions or beliefs, or the means of producing them, at the disposal of members of those religions or beliefs.

Rule 9

1.   No one should be prevented from having marriage rites performed in accordance with the prescriptions of his religion or belief, nor compelled to undergo a religious marriage ceremony not in conformity with his convictions.

2.   The right to seek and to obtain a divorce should not be denied to anyone whose convictions admit divorce, solely on the ground that he professes a particular religion or belief.

Rule 10

Everyone should be free to disseminate a religion or belief, in so far as his actions do not impair the right of any other individual to maintain his religion or belief.

Rule 11

1.   No group professing a religion or belief should be prevented from training the personnel required for the performance of practices or observances prescribed by that religion or belief.

2.   When such training is available only outside the country, no permanent limitations should be placed upon travel abroad for the purpose of undergoing such training.

Rule 12

No one should be compelled to take an oath contrary to the prescriptions of his religion or belief.

Rule 13

In a country where the principle of conscientious objection to military service is recognized, exemptions should be granted to genuine objectors in a manner ensuring that no adverse distinction based upon religion or belief may result.

Rule 14

In a country where exemptions from participation in certain or all public ceremonies are granted to individuals who object to such participation on the ground that it is contrary to a prescription of their religion or belief, such exemptions should be granted in such a manner that no adverse distinction based upon religion or belief may result.

Rule 15

No cleric who receives information in confidence, in accordance with the prescriptions of his religion, should be compelled by public authorities to divulge such information.

III. DUTIES OF PUBLIC AUTHORITIES

Rule 16

1.   Public authorities should refrain from making any adverse distinction against, or giving preference to individuals or groups of individuals with regard to the right to freedom of thought, conscience and religion; and should prevent any individual or group of individuals from making such adverse

distinctions or giving such undue preferences.

2. These duties must be discharged through the adoption of appropriate legal provisions of a preventive or remedial character, including penal sanctions when necessary, as well as by administrative action.

3. Public authorities should make every effort to educate public opinion to an acceptance of the principle of non-discrimination in respect of the right to freedom of thought, conscience and religion and to create proper leadership for this purpose.

4. In discharging these duties, public authorities should be guided by the following considerations:

(a) The freedom of everyone to maintain or change his religion or belief must be ensured;

(b) The freedom of everyone to manifest his religion or belief, either alone or in community with others, and in public or in private, must be ensured as widely as possible. Any limitation imposed upon that freedom should be exceptional, should be confined within the narrowest possible bound, should be prescribed by law solely for the purpose of securing due recognition and respect for the rights and freedoms of others and of meeting the just requirements of morality, public order and the general welfare in a democratic society; and should not be exercised in a manner contrary to the purposes and principles of the United Nations;

(c) In case of a conflict between the requirements of two or more religions or beliefs, public authorities should endeavour to find a solution assuring the greatest measure of freedom to society as a whole, while giving preference to the freedom of everyone to maintain or to change his religion or belief over any practice or observance tending to restrict this freedom;

(d) Public authorities should make no adverse distinctions against, or give undue preference to religions or their followers in the granting of subsidies or exemptions from taxation. The State is, however, not precluded from levying general taxes or from carrying out obligations assumed as a result of arrangements made to compensate a religious organization for property taken over by sequestration or otherwise, nor from contributing funds for the preservation of religious structures recognized as monuments of historic or artistic value.

* * *

ANNEXES
ANNEX I

DRAFT PRINCIPLES ON FREEDOM AND NON-DISCRIMINATION IN THE MATTER OF RELIGIOUS RIGHTS AND PRACTICES

Preamble

Whereas the peoples of the United Nations have, in the Charter, reaffirmed their faith in human rights and fundamental freedoms, and have taken a stand against all forms of discrimination, including discrimination on the ground of religion or belief,

Whereas the principle of non-discrimination and the right to freedom of thought, conscience and religion have been proclaimed in the Universal Declaration of Human Rights,

Whereas the disregard of human rights and fundamental freedoms and in particular of the right to freedom of thought, conscience and religion has brought in the past untold sorrow to mankind,

Whereas it is therefore the duty of Governments, organizations and private persons to promote through education, as well as through other means, respect for the dignity of man and a spirit of understanding, tolerance and friendship among all religious and racial groups, as well as among all nations,

Whereas the efforts of Governments, organizations and private persons to eradicate discrimination in respect of the right to freedom of thought, conscience and religion should be supported by elaborating the provisions relating to these freedoms with a view to ensuring their protection and furtherance,

Now therefore the following provisions are proclaimed to promote the freedom of thought, conscience and religion and the eradication of discrimination on the ground of religion or belief:

Part I

1. Everyone shall be free to adhere, or not to adhere, to a religion or belief, in accordance with the dictates of his conscience.

2. Parents or, when applicable, legal guardians, shall have the prior right to decide upon the religion or belief in which their child should be brought up. In the case of a child who has been deprived of its parents, their expressed or presumed wish shall be duly taken into account, the best interests of the child being the guiding principle.

3. No one shall be subjected to material or moral coercion likely to impair his freedom to maintain or to change his religion or belief.

4. Anyone professing any religious or non-religious belief shall be free to do so openly without suffering any discrimination on account of his religion or belief.

Part II

Everyone shall be free to comply with what is prescribed or authorized by his religion or belief, and free from performing acts incompatible with the prescriptions of his religion or belief, particularly in the following respects, subject to the interests of society as a whole as provided in parts III and IV:

1. *(a)* Everyone shall be free to worship, either alone or in community with others, and in public or in private.

(b) Equal protection shall be accorded to all forms of worship, places of worship, and objects necessary for the performance of rites.

2. Everyone shall have the freedom, as acts of devotion, to journey to sacred places, whether inside or outside his country.

3. No one shall be prevented from observing the dietary practices prescribed by his religion or belief.

4. *(a)* The members of a religion or belief shall not be prevented from acquiring or producing all materials and objects necessary for the performance or observance of prescribed rituals or practices, including dietary practices.

(b) Where the Government controls the means of production and distribution, it shall make such materials or objects, or the means of producing them, available to the members of the religion or belief concerned.

5. *(a)* Without prejudice to the right of the State to lay down the conditions of a valid marriage, no one shall be prevented from having marriage rites performed in accordance with the prescriptions of his religion or belief.

(b) No one shall be compelled to undergo a religious marriage ceremony not in conformity with his convictions.

(c) The right to seek and to obtain a dissolution of marriage shall be determined solely in accordance with the provisions of

the law applicable to it without any adverse distinction being based upon the religion or belief of the parties.

6. *(a)* The prescriptions of the religion or belief of a deceased person shall be followed in all matters affecting burial, cremation or other methods of disposal of the dead, particularly in the assignment of places of such disposal, the display in such places of religious or other symbols, and the performance of funeral or commemorative rites.

(b) Equal protection against desecration shall be afforded to all places for burial, cremation or other methods of disposal of the dead, as well as to religious or other symbols displayed in these places; and equal protection against interference by outsiders shall be afforded to the funeral or commemorative rites of all religions and beliefs.

7. Due account shall be taken of the prescriptions of each religion or belief relating to holidays or days of rest.

8. *(a)* Everyone shall be free to teach or to disseminate his religion or belief, either in public or in private.

(b) No one shall be compelled to receive religious or atheistic instruction, contrary to his convictions or, in the case of children, contrary to the wishes of their parents and, when applicable, legal guardians.

9. *(a)* No group professing a religion or belief shall be prevented from training the personnel intending to devote themselves to the performance of its practices or observances, or from bringing teachers from abroad necessary for this purpose.

(b) When such training is available only outside the country, no permanent limitations shall be placed upon travel abroad for the purpose of undergoing such training.

10. No one shall be compelled to take an oath of a religious nature contrary to his convictions.

11. In countries where conscientious objection to military service is recognized, exemptions shall be granted to genuine objectors in a manner ensuring that no adverse distinction based upon religion or belief may result.

12. In countries where exemptions from participation in certain or all public ceremonies are granted to individuals who object to such participation on the ground that it is contrary to their conscience, such exemptions shall be granted in such a manner that no adverse distinction based upon religion or belief may result.

13. No priest or minister of religion who receives information in confidence in the performance of his duties as prescribed by his religion or belief shall be compelled to divulge such information.

Part III

1. The freedom set out in part I and in paragraphs 10 and 13 of part II shall not be subject to any restrictions.

2. *(a)* The freedoms and rights set out in the other paragraphs of part II shall be subject only to the limitations prescribed by law solely for the purpose of securing due recognition and respect for the rights and freedoms of others and of meeting the just requirements of morality, health, public order and the general welfare in a democratic society. Any limitations which may be imposed shall be consistent with the purposes and principles of the United Nations.

(b) These freedoms and rights may in no case be exercised contrary to the purposes and principles of the United Nations.

Part IV

Public authorities shall refrain from making any adverse distinctions against, or giving undue preference to, individuals or groups of individuals with respect to the right to freedom of thought, conscience and religion; and shall endeavour to prevent any individual or group of individuals from doing so. In particular:

1. In the event of a conflict between the demands of two or more religions or beliefs, public authorities shall endeavour to find a solution reconciling these demands in a manner such as to ensure the greatest measure of freedom to society as a whole.

2. In the granting of subsidies or exemptions from taxation, no adverse distinction shall be made between, and no undue preference shall be given to, any religion or belief or its followers. However, public authorities shall not be precluded from levying general taxes or from carrying out obligations assumed as a result of arrangements made to compensate a religious organization for property taken over by the State or from contributing funds for the preservation of religious structure recognized as monuments of historic or artistic value.

*   *   *

Notes

INTRODUCTION

1. In view of the difficulty of defining "religion", the term "religion or belief" is used in this study to include, in addition to various theistic creeds, such other beliefs as agnosticism, free thought, atheism and rationalism.

2. *Summa Theologica*, II, II, q. 10, a. 11.

3. *De Fide*, Disp. 18, sect. 4, No. 10.

4. Quoted in Khairallah, Ibrahim A., *The Law of Inheritance in the Republics of Syria and Lebanon*, American Press, Beirut, 1941, p. 316.

5. See, for example, sections 295, 295A, 296, 297 and 298.

6. A detailed analysis may be found in Pannikar, K.M.: *The Working of Dyarchy in India*, London, Longmans Green, pp. 32-35.

7. Under this system various religious communities recognized by the State enjoy a measure of autonomy in their religious and civil affairs.

8. Treaty of Peace with Bulgaria, article 2; Treaty of Peace with Finland, article 6; Treaty of Peace with Hungary, article 2, para.1; Treaty of Peace with Italy, article 15; Treaty of Peace with Romania, article 3, para. 1. An identical provision is to be found in the Treaty for the re-establishment of an independent and democratic Austria of 15 May 1955, article 8. The treaties with Hungary and Romania, as well as the Austrian Treaty, contain also certain non-discrimination clauses which prohibit, *inter alia*, discrimination on the ground of religion. The Peace Treaty with Japan of 8 September 1951 does not contain similar provisions. However, the preamble to the Treaty includes a clause under which "Japan for its part declares its intention ... in all circumstances, to conform to the principles of the Charter of the United Nations; to strive to realize the objectives of the Universal Declaration of Human Rights ... "

CHAPTER I

1. Article 2, as adopted by the Commission on Human Rights at its tenth session, reads (E/2573, annex I B):

"1. Each State Party hereto undertakes to respect and to ensure to all individuals within its territory and subject to its jurisdiction the rights recognized in this Covenant, without distinction of any kind such as race, colour, sex, language, religion, political or other opinion, national or social origin, property, birth or other status.

"2. Where not already provided for by existing legislative or other measures, each State undertakes to take the necessary steps, in accordance with its constitutional processes and with the provisions of this Covenant, to adopt such legislative or other measures as may be necessary to give effect to the rights recognized in this Covenant.

"3. Each State Party hereto undertakes:

"(a) To ensure that any person whose rights or freedoms as herein recognized are violated shall have an effective remedy, notwithstanding that the violation has been committed by persons acting in an official capacity;

"(b) To develop the possibilities of judicial remedy and to ensure that any person claiming such a remedy shall have his right thereto determined by competent authorities, political, administrative or judicial;

"(c) To ensure that the competent authorities shall enforce such remedies when granted."

2. Article 18 of the draft convention on civil and political rights,as adopted by the Commission on Human Rights at its tenth session, reads (E/2573, annex I B):

"1. Everyone shall have the right to freedom of thought, conscience and religion. This rights shall include freedom to maintain or to change his religion, or belief, and freedom, either individually or in community with others and in public or private, to manifest his religion or belief in worship,observance, practice and teaching.

"2. No one shall be subject to coercion which would impair his freedom to maintain or to change his religion or belief.

"3. Freedom to manifest one's religion or beliefs may be subject only to such limitations as are prescribed by law and are necessary to protect public safety, order, health, or morals or the fundamental rights and freedoms of others".

The draft covenant on civil and political rights also contains, in article 25, a special provision relating to minorities. This provision reads:
"In those States in which ... religious ... minorities exist, persons belonging to such minorities shall not be denied the right, in community with other members of their group ... to profess and practise their own religion ... "

3. *Cantwell v. Connecticut*, 310 U.S. 296.

4. See page 24 and 35 of this report.

5. *The Commissioner, H.R.E. Madras v. Sir L.T. Swamiar* (1955), S.C.R. 1005, at 1023-4

6. *Commr. H.R.E. v. Lakshmindra* (1954), S.C.A. 415 (432).

CHAPTER II

1. The importance of the right to teach co-religionists is admitted; indeed, it is the exercise of this right that helps to keep many religious organizations alive. One of the basic rules suggested later deals with the right of a group to train its personnel in the performance of practices or observances prescribed by its religion or belief. Since other aspects of religious teaching have been dealt with in the *Study of Discrimination in Education*, they are not examined in this study.

CHAPTER III

1. Thus the Government of the United Kingdom, in a memorandum submitted on 1 October 1957 on the subject of "Religious Discrimination in British Non-Self-Governing Territories", stated that:
" ... Generally speaking, immigrant missionaries are treated in the same way as other immigrants under the Immigration Law. In the early years of this century, however, there was some friction in Northern Nigeria and in the Sudan between the British authorities and the various Christian Missionary Societies. The Christian Missionaries claimed that as these lands were not under effective British rule, they should be free to travel there and to preach Christianity to any of the people who wished to listen. The government, on the other hand, took the line that since Northern Nigeria and the Sudan were Islamic Countries and the indigenous rulers were unwilling to permit Christian preaching, it would be wrong for them to permit Christian missionary work until public opinions should change. This applies also to the Somaliland Protectorate."

PART I
THE INTERNATIONAL BILL OF RIGHTS

UNIVERSAL DECLARATION OF HUMAN RIGHTS

Adopted and Proclaimed by
United Nations General Assembly Resolution 217A (III)
on 10 December 1948.

PREAMBLE

Whereas recognition of the inherent dignity and of the equal and inalienable rights of all members of the human family is the foundation of freedom, justice and peace in the world,

Whereas disregard and contempt for human rights have resulted in barbarous acts which have outraged the conscience of mankind, and the advent of a world in which human beings shall enjoy freedom of speech and belief and freedom from fear and want has been proclaimed as the highest aspiration of the common people,

Whereas it is essential, if man is not to be compelled to have recourse, as a last resort, to rebellion against tyranny and oppression, that human rights should be protected by the rule of law,

Whereas it is essential to promote the development of friendly relations between nations,

Whereas the peoples of the United Nations have in the Charter reaffirmed their faith in fundamental human rights, in the dignity and worth of the human person and in the equal rights of men and women and have determined to promote social progress and better standards of life in larger freedom,

Whereas Member States have pledged themselves to achieve, in co-operation with the United Nations, the promotion of universal respect for and observance of human rights and fundamental freedoms,

Whereas a common understanding of these rights and freedoms is of the greatest importance for the full realisation of this pledge,

Now, therefore,
The General Assembly

Proclaims this Universal Declaration of Human Rights as a common standard of achievement for all peoples and all nations, to the end that every individual and every organ of society, keeping this Declaration constantly in mind, shall strive by teaching and education to promote respect for these rights and freedoms and by progressive measures, national and international, to secure their universal and effective recognition and observance, both among the peoples of Member States themselves and among the peoples of territories under their jurisdiction.

Article 1

All human beings are born free and equal in dignity and rights. They are endowed with reason and conscience and should act towards one another in a spirit of brotherhood.

Article 2

Everyone is entitled to all the rights and freedoms set forth in this Declaration, without distinction of any kind, such as race, colour, sex, language, religion, political or other opinion, national or social origin, property, birth or other status.

Furthermore, no distinction shall be made on the basis of the political, jurisdictional or international status of the country or territory to which a person belongs, whether it be independent, trust, non-self-governing or under any other limitation of sovereignty.

Article 3
Everyone has the right to life, liberty and security of person.

Article 4
No one shall be held in slavery or servitude; slavery and the slave trade shall be prohibited in all their forms.

Article 5
No one shall be subjected to torture or to cruel, inhuman or degrading treatment or punishment.

Article 6
Everyone has the right to recognition everywhere as a person before the law.

Article 7
All are equal before the law and are entitled without any discrimination to equal protection of the law. All are entitled to equal protection against any discrimination in violation of this Declaration and against any incitement to such discrimination.

Article 8
Everyone has the right to an effective remedy by the competent national tribunals for acts violating the fundamental rights granted him by the constitution or by law.

Article 9
No one shall be subjected to arbitrary arrest, detention or exile.

Article 10
Everyone is entitled in full equality to a fair and public hearing by an independent and impartial tribunal, in the determination of his rights and obligations and of any criminal charge against him.

Article 11
1. Everyone charged with a penal offence has the right to be presumed innocent until proved guilty according to law in a public trial at which he has had all the guarantees necessary for his defence.
2. No one shall be held guilty of any penal offence on account of any act or omission which did not constitute a penal offence, under national or international law, at the time when it was committed. Nor shall a heavier penalty be imposed than the one that was applicable at the time the penal offence was committed.

Article 12
No one shall be subjected to arbitrary interference with his privacy, family, home or correspondence, nor to attacks upon his honour and reputation. Everyone has the right to the protection of the law against such interference or attacks.

Article 13
1. Everyone has the right to freedom of movement and residence within the borders of each State.
2. Everyone has the right to leave any country, including his own, and to return to his country.

Article 14
1. Everyone has the right to seek and to enjoy in other countries asylum from persecution.
2. This right may not be invoked in the case of prosecutions genuinely arising from nonpolitical crimes or from acts contrary to the purposes and principles of the United Nations.

Article 15

1. Everyone has the right to a nationality.

2. No one shall be arbitrarily deprived of his nationality nor denied the right to change his nationality.

Article 16

1. Men and women of full age, without any limitation due to race, nationality or religion, have the right to marry and to found a family. They are entitled to equal rights as to marriage, during marriage and at its dissolution.

2. Marriage shall be entered into only with the free and full consent of the intending spouses.

3. The family is the natural and fundamental group unit of society and is entitled to protection by society and the State.

Article 17

1. Everyone has the right to own property alone as well as in association with others.

2. No one shall be arbitrarily deprived of his property.

Article 18

Everyone has the right to freedom of thought, conscience and religion; this right includes freedom to change his religion or belief, and freedom, either alone or in community with others and in public or private, to manifest his religion or belief in teaching, practice, worship and observance.

Article 19

Everyone has the right to freedom of opinion and expression; this right includes freedom to hold opinions without interference and to seek, receive and impart information and ideas through any media and regardless of frontiers.

Article 20

1. Everyone has the right to freedom of peaceful assembly and association.

2. No one may be compelled to belong to an association.

Article 21

1. Everyone has the right to take part in the government of his country, directly or through freely chosen representatives.

2. Everyone has the right of equal access to public service in his country.

3. The will of the people shall be the basis of the authority of government; this will shall be expressed in periodic and genuine elections which shall be by universal and equal suffrage and shall be held by secret vote or by equivalent free voting procedures.

Article 22

Everyone, as a member of society, has the right to social security and is entitled to realization, through national effort and international co-operation and in accordance with the organization and resources of each State, of the economic, social and cultural rights indispensable for his dignity and the free development of his personality.

Article 23

1. Everyone has the right to work, to free choice of employment, to just and favourable conditions of work and to protection against unemployment.

2. Everyone, without any discrimination, has the right to equal pay for equal work.

3. Everyone who works has the right to just and favourable remuneration ensuring for himself and his family an existence worthy of human dignity, and supplemented, if necessary, by other means of social protection.

4. Everyone has the right to form

and to join trade unions for the protection of his interests.

Article 24
Everyone has the right to rest and leisure, including reasonable limitation of working hours and periodic holidays with pay.

Article 25
1. Everyone has the right to a standard of living adequate for the health and well-being of himself and of his family, including food, clothing, housing and medical care and necessary social services, and the right to security in the event of unemployment, sickness, disability, widowhood, old age or other lack of livelihood in circumstances beyond his control.

2. Motherhood and childhood are entitled to special care and assistance. All children, whether born in or out of wedlock, shall enjoy the same social protection.

Article 26
1. Everyone has the right to education. Education shall be free, at least in the elementary and fundamental stages. Elementary education shall be compulsory. Technical and professional education shall be made generally available and higher education shall be equally accessible to all on the basis of merit.

2. Education shall be directed to the full development of the human personality and to the strengthening of respect for human rights and fundamental freedoms. It shall promote understanding, tolerance and friendship among all nations, racial or religious groups, and shall further the activities of the United Nations for the maintenance of peace.

3. Parents have a prior right to choose the kind of education that shall be given to their children.

Article 27
1. Everyone has the right freely to participate in the cultural life of the community, to enjoy the arts and to share in scientific advancement and its benefits.

2. Everyone has the right to the protection of the moral and material interests resulting from any scientific, literary or artistic production of which he is the author.

Article 28
Everyone is entitled to a social and international order in which the rights and freedoms set forth in this Declaration can be fully realized.

Article 29
1. Everyone has duties to the community in which alone the free and full development of his personality is possible.

2. In the exercise of his rights and freedoms, everyone shall be subject only to such limitations as are determined by law solely for the purpose of securing due recognition and respect for the rights and freedoms of others and of meeting the just requirements of morality, public order and the general welfare in a democratic society.

3. These rights and freedoms may in no case be exercised contrary to the purposes and principles of the United Nations.

Article 30
Nothing in this Declaration may be interpreted as implying for any State, group or person any right to engage in any activity or to perform any act aimed at the destruction of any of the rights and freedoms set forth herein.

INTERNATIONAL COVENANT ON ECONOMIC, SOCIAL AND CULTURAL RIGHTS

Adopted and Opened for Signature by United Nations General Assembly Resolution 2200A (XXI) on 16 December 1966. Entered into Force 3 January 1976.

PREAMBLE

The States Parties to the present Covenant,

Considering that, in accordance with the principles proclaimed in the Charter of the United Nations, recognition of the inherent dignity and of the equal and inalienable rights of all members of the human family is the foundation of freedom, justice and peace in the world,

Recognizing that these rights derive from the inherent dignity of the human person,

Recognizing that, in accordance with the Universal Declaration of Human Rights, the ideal of free human beings enjoying freedom from fear and want can only be achieved if conditions are created whereby everyone may enjoy his economic, social and cultural rights, as well as his civil and political rights,

Considering the obligation of States under the Charter of the United Nations to promote universal respect for, and observance of, human rights and freedoms,

Realizing that the individual, having duties to other individuals and to the community to which he belongs, is under a responsibility to strive for the promotion and observance of the rights recognized in the present Covenant,

Agree upon the following articles:

PART I

Article 1

1.   All peoples have the right of self-determination. By virtue of that right they freely determine their political status and freely pursue their economic, social and cultural development.

2.   All peoples may, for their own ends, freely dispose of their natural wealth and resources without prejudice to any obligations arising out of international economic cooperation, based upon the principle of mutual benefit, and international law. In no case may a people be deprived of its own means of subsistence.

3.   The States Parties to the present Covenant, including those having responsibility for the administration of Non-Self-Governing and Trust Territories, shall promote the realization of the right of self-determination, and shall respect that right, in conformity with the provisions of the Charter of the United Nations.

PART II

Article 2

1.   Each State Party to the present Covenant undertakes to take steps, individually and through international assistance and co-operation, especially economic and technical, to the maximum of its available resources, with a view to achieving

progressively the full realization of the rights recognized in the present Covenant by all appropriate means, including particularly the adoption of legislative measures.

2. The States Parties to the present Covenant undertake to guarantee that the rights enunciated in the present Covenant will be exercised without discrimination of any kind as to race, colour, sex, language, religion, political or other opinion, national or social origin, property, birth or other status.

3. Developing countries, with due regard to human rights and their national economy, may determine to what extent they would guarantee the economic rights recognized in the present Covenant to non-nationals.

Article 3

The States Parties to the present Covenant undertake to ensure the equal right of men and women to the enjoyment of all economic, social and cultural rights set forth in the present Covenant.

Article 4

The States Parties to the present Covenant recognize that, in the enjoyment of those rights provided by the State in conformity with the present Covenant, the State may subject such rights only to such limitations as are determined by law only in so far as this may be compatible with the nature of these rights and solely for the purpose of promoting the general welfare in a democratic society.

Article 5

1. Nothing in the present Covenant may be interpreted as implying for any State, group or person any right to engage in any activity or to perform any act aimed at the destruction of any of the rights or freedoms recognized herein, or at their limitation to a greater extent than is provided for in the present Covenant.

2. No restriction upon or derogation from any of the fundamental human rights recognized or existing in any country in virtue of law, conventions, regulations or custom shall be admitted on the pretext that the present Covenant does not recognize such rights or that it recognizes them to a lesser extent.

PART III

Article 6

1. The States Parties to the present Covenant recognize the right to work, which includes the right of everyone to the opportunity to gain his living by work which he freely chooses or accepts, and will take appropriate steps to safeguard this right.

2. The steps to be taken by a State Party to the present Covenant to achieve the full realization of this right shall include technical and vocational guidance and training programmes, policies and techniques to achieve steady economic, social and cultural development and full and productive employment under conditions safeguarding fundamental political and economic freedoms to the individual.

Article 7

The States Parties to the present Covenant recognize the right of everyone to the enjoyment of just and favourable conditions of work which ensure, in particular:

(a) Remuneration which provides all workers, as a minimum, with:

(i) Fair wages and equal remuneration for work of equal value without distinction of any kind, in particular women being guaranteed conditions of work not inferior to those enjoyed by men, with equal pay for equal work;

(ii) A decent living for themselves and their families in accordance with the provisions of the present Covenant;

(b) Safe and healthy working conditions;

(c) Equal opportunity for everyone to be promoted in his employment to an appropriate higher level, subject to no considerations other than those of seniority and competence;

(d) Rest, leisure and reasonable limitation of working hours and periodic holidays with pay, as well as remuneration for public holidays.

Article 8

1. The States Parties to the present Covenant undertake to ensure:

(a) The right of everyone to form trade unions and join the trade union of his choice, subject only to the rules of the organization concerned, for the promotion and protection of his economic and social interests. No restrictions may be placed on the exercise of this right other than those prescribed by law and which are necessary in a democratic society in the interests of national security or public order or for the protection of the rights and freedoms of others;

(b) The right of trade unions to establish national federations or confederations and the right of the latter to form or join international trade-union organizations;

(c) The right of trade unions to function freely subject to no limitations other than those prescribed by law and which are necessary in a democratic society in the interests of national security or public order or for the protection of the rights and freedoms of others;

(d) The right to strike, provided that it is exercised in conformity with the laws of the particular country.

2. This article shall not prevent the imposition of lawful restrictions on the exercise of these rights by members of the armed forces or of the police or of the administration of the State.

3. Nothing in this article shall authorize States Parties to the International Labour Organisation Convention of 1948 concerning Freedom of Association and Protection of the Right to Organize to take legislative measures which would prejudice, or apply the law in such a manner as would prejudice, the guarantees provided for in that Convention.

Article 9

The States Parties to the present Covenant recognize the right of everyone to social security, including social insurance.

Article 10

The States Parties to the present Covenant recognize that:

1. The widest possible protection and assistance should be accorded to the family, which is the natural and fundamental group unit of society, particularly for its establishment and while it is responsible for the care and education of dependent children. Marriage must be entered into with the free consent of the intending spouses.

2. Special protection should be accorded to mothers during a reasonable period before and after childbirth. During such period working mothers should be accorded paid leave or leave with adequate social security benefits.

3. Special measures of protection and assistance should be taken on behalf of all children and young persons without any discrimination for reasons of parentage or other conditions. Children and young persons should be protected from economic and social exploitation. Their employment in work harmful to their morals or health or dangerous to life or likely to hamper their normal development should be punishable by law. States should also set age limits below which the paid employment of child labour should be prohibited and punishable by law.

Article 11

1.   The States Parties to the present Covenant recognize the right of everyone to an adequate standard of living for himself and his family, including adequate food, clothing and housing, and to the continuous improvement of living conditions. The States Parties will take appropriate steps to ensure the realization of this right, recognizing to this effect the essential importance of international co-operation based on free consent.

2.   The States Parties to the present Covenant, recognizing the fundamental right of everyone to be free from hunger, shall take, individually and through international co-operation, the measures, including specific programmes, which are needed:

(a)   To improve methods of production, conservation and distribution of food by making full use of technical and scientific knowledge, by disseminating knowledge of the principles of nutrition and by developing or reforming agrarian systems in such a way as to achieve the most efficient development and utilization of natural resources;

(b)   Taking into account the problems of both food-importing and food-exporting countries, to ensure an equitable distribution of world food supplies in relation to need.

Article 12

1.   The States Parties to the present Covenant recognize the right of everyone to the enjoyment of the highest attainable standard of physical and mental health.

2.   The steps to be taken by the States Parties to the present Covenant to achieve the full realization of this right shall include those necessary for:

(a)   The provision for the reduction of the stillbirth-rate and of infant mortality and for the healthy development of the child;

(b)   The improvement of all aspects of environmental and industrial hygiene;

(c)   The prevention, treatment and control of epidemic, endemic, occupational and other diseases;

(d)   The creation of conditions which would assure to all medical service and medical attention in the event of sickness.

Article 13

1.   The States Parties to the present Covenant recognize the right of everyone to education. They agree that education shall be directed to the full development of the human personality and the sense of its dignity, and shall strengthen the respect for human rights and fundamental freedoms. They further agree that education shall enable all persons to participate effectively in a free society, promote understanding, tolerance and friendship among all nations and all racial, ethnic or religious groups, and further the activities of the United Nations for the maintenance of peace.

2.   The States Parties to the present Covenant recognize that, with a view to achieving the full realization of this right:

(a)   Primary education shall be compulsory and available free to all;

(b)   Secondary education in its different forms, including technical and vocational secondary education, shall be made generally available and accessible to all by every appropriate means, and in particular by the progressive introduction of free education;

(c)   Higher education shall be made equally accessible to all, on the basis of capacity, by every appropriate means, and in particular by the progressive introduction of free education;

(d)   Fundamental education shall be encouraged or intensified as far as possible for those persons who have not received or completed the whole period of their primary education;

(e)   The development of a system of schools at all levels shall be actively pursued, an adequate fellowship system shall be established, and the material conditions of teaching staff shall be continuously improved.

3. The States Parties to the present Covenant undertake to have respect for the liberty of parents and, when applicable, legal guardians to choose for their children schools, other than those established by the public authorities, which conform to such minimum educational standards as may be laid down or approved by the State and to ensure the religious and moral education of their children in conformity with their own convictions.

4. No part of this article shall be construed so as to interfere with the liberty of individuals and bodies to establish and direct educational institutions, subject always to the observance of the principles set forth in paragraph 1 of this article and to the requirement that the education given in such institutions shall conform to such minimum standards as may be laid down by the State.

Article 14

Each State Party to the present Covenant which, at the time of becoming a Party, has not been able to secure in its metropolitan territory or other territories under its jurisdiction compulsory primary education, free of charge, undertakes, within two years, to work out and adopt a detailed plan of action for the progressive implementation, within a reasonable number of years, to be fixed in the plan, of the principle of compulsory education free of charge for all.

Article 15

1. The States Parties to the present Covenant recognize the right of everyone:

(a) To take part in cultural life;

(b) To enjoy the benefits of scientific progress and its applications;

(c) To benefit from the protection of the moral and material interests resulting from any scientific, literary or artistic production of which he is the author.

2. The steps to be taken by the States Parties to the present Covenant to achieve the full realization of this right shall include those necessary for the conservation, the development and the diffusion of science and culture.

3. The States Parties to the present Covenant undertake to respect the freedom indispensable for scientific research and creative activity.

4. The States Parties to the present Covenant recognize the benefits to be derived from the encouragement and development of international contacts and cooperation in the scientific and cultural fields.

PART IV

Article 16

1. The States Parties to the present Covenant undertake to submit in conformity with this part of the Covenant reports on the measures which they have adopted and the progress made in achieving the observance of the rights recognized herein.

2. (a) All reports shall be submitted to the Secretary-General of the United Nations, who shall transmit copies to the Economic and Social Council for consideration in accordance with the provisions of the present Covenant;

(b) The Secretary-General of the United Nations shall also transmit to the specialized agencies copies of the reports, or any relevant parts therefrom, from States Parties to the present Covenant which are also members of these specialized agencies in so far as these reports, or parts therefrom, relate to any matters which fall within the responsibilities of the said agencies in accordance with their constitutional instruments.

Article 17

1. The States Parties to the present Covenant shall furnish their reports in

stages, in accordance with a programme to be established by the Economic and Social Council within one year of the entry into force of the present Covenant after consultation with the States Parties and the specialized agencies concerned.

2. Reports may indicate factors and difficulties affecting the degree of fulfillment of obligations under the present Covenant.

3. Where relevant information has previously been furnished to the United Nations or to any specialized agency by any State Party to the present Covenant, it will not be necessary to reproduce that information, but a precise reference to the information so furnished will suffice.

Article 18

Pursuant to its responsibilities under the Charter of the United Nations in the field of human rights and fundamental freedoms, the Economic and Social Council may make arrangements with the specialized agencies in respect of their reporting to it on the progress made in achieving the observance of the provisions of the present Covenant falling within the scope of their activities. These reports may include particulars of decisions and recommendations on such implementation adopted by their competent organs.

Article 19

The Economic and Social Council may transmit to the Commission on Human Rights for study and general recommendation or, as appropriate, for information the reports concerning human rights submitted by States in accordance with articles 16 and 17, and those concerning human rights submitted by the specialized agencies in accordance with article 18.

Article 20

The States Parties to the present Covenant and the specialized agencies concerned may submit comments to the Economic and Social Council on any general recommendation under article 19 or reference to such general recommendation in any report of the Commission on Human Rights or any documentation referred to therein.

Article 21

The Economic and Social Council may submit from time to time to the General Assembly reports with recommendations of a general nature and a summary of the information received from the States Parties to the present Covenant and the specialized agencies on the measures taken and the progress made in achieving general observance of the rights recognized in the present Covenant.

Article 22

The Economic and Social Council may bring to the attention of other organs of the United Nations, their subsidiary organs and specialized agencies concerned with furnishing technical assistance any matters arising out of the reports referred to in this part of the present Covenant which may assist such bodies in deciding, each within its field of competence, on the advisability of international measures likely to contribute to the effective progressive implementation of the present Covenant.

Article 23

The States Parties to the present Covenant agree that international action for the achievement of the rights recognized in the present Covenant includes such methods as the conclusion of conventions, the adoption of recommendations, the furnishing of technical assistance and the holding of regional meetings and technical meetings for the purpose of consultation and study organized in conjunction with the Governments concerned.

Article 24

Nothing in the present Covenant shall be interpreted as impairing the provisions of the Charter of the United Nations and of the constitutions of the specialized agencies which define the respective responsibilities of the various organs of the United Nations and of the specialized agencies in regard to the matters dealt with in the present Covenant.

Article 25

Nothing in the present Covenant shall be interpreted as impairing the inherent right of all peoples to enjoy and utilize fully and freely their natural wealth and resources.

PART V

Article 26

1.   The present Covenant is open for signature by any State Member of the United Nations or member of any of its specialized agencies, by any State Party to the Statute of the International Court of Justice, and by any other State which has been invited by the General Assembly of the United Nations to become a party to the present Covenant.

2.   The present Covenant is subject to ratification. Instruments of ratification shall be deposited with the Secretary-General of the United Nations.

3.   The present Covenant shall be open to accession by any State referred to in paragraph 1 of this article.

4.   Accession shall be effected by the deposit of an instrument of accession with the Secretary-General of the United Nations.

5.   The Secretary-General of the United Nations shall inform all States which have signed the present Covenant or acceded to it of the deposit of each instrument of ratification or accession.

Article 27

1.   The present Covenant shall enter into force three months after the date of the deposit with the Secretary-General of the United Nations of the thirty-fifth instrument of ratification or instrument of accession.

2.   For each State ratifying the present Covenant or acceding to it after the deposit of the thirty-fifth instrument of ratification or instrument of accession, the present Covenant shall enter into force three months after the date of the deposit of its own instrument of ratification or instrument of accession.

Article 28

The provisions of the present Covenant shall extend to all parts of federal States without any limitations or exceptions.

Article 29

1.   Any State Party to the present Covenant may propose an amendment and file it with the Secretary-General of the United Nations.   The Secretary-General shall thereupon communicate any proposed amendments to the States Parties to the present Covenant with a request that they notify him whether they favour a conference of States Parties for the purpose of considering and voting upon the proposals. In the event that at least one third of the States Parties favours such a conference, the Secretary-General shall convene the conference under the auspices of the United Nations.   Any amendment adopted by a majority of the States Parties present and voting at the conference shall be submitted to the General Assembly of the United Nations for approval.

2.   Amendments shall come into force when they have been approved by the General Assembly of the United Nations and accepted by a two-thirds majority of the States Parties to the present Covenant in accordance with their respective constitutional processes.

3.   When amendments come into force they shall be binding on those States

Parties which have accepted them, other States Parties still being bound by the provisions of the present Covenant and any earlier amendment which they have accepted.

Article 30

Irrespective of the notifications made under article 26, paragraph 5, the Secretary-General of the United Nations shall inform all States referred to in paragraph 1 of the same article of the following particulars:

1. Signatures, ratifications and accessions under article 26;

2. The date of the entry into force of the present Covenant under article 27 and the date of the entry into force of any amendments under article 29.

Article 31

1. The present Covenant, of which the Chinese, English, French, Russian and Spanish texts are equally authentic, shall be deposited in the archives of the United Nations.

2. The Secretary-General of the United Nations shall transmit certified copies of the present Covenant to all States referred to in article 26.

INTERNATIONAL COVENANT ON CIVIL AND POLITICAL RIGHTS

Adopted and Opened for Signature by United Nations General Assembly
Resolution 2200A (XXI) on 16 December 1966.
Entered into Force 23 March 1976.

PREAMBLE

The States Parties to the present Covenant,

Considering that, in accordance with the principles proclaimed in the Charter of the United Nations, recognition of the inherent dignity and of the equal and inalienable rights of all members of the human family is the foundation of freedom, justice and peace in the world,

Recognizing that these rights derive from the inherent dignity of the human person,

Recognizing that, in accordance with the Universal Declaration of Human Rights, the ideal of free human beings enjoying civil and political freedom and freedom from fear and want can only be achieved if conditions are created whereby everyone may enjoy his civil and political rights, as well as his economic, social and cultural rights,

Considering the obligation of States under the Charter of the United Nations to promote universal respect for, and observance of, human rights and freedoms,

Realizing that the individual, having duties to other individuals and to the community to which he belongs, is under a responsibility to strive for the promotion and observance of the rights recognized in the present Covenant,

Agree upon the following articles:

PART I

Article 1

1. All peoples have the right of self-determination. By virtue of that right they freely determine their political status and freely pursue their economic, social and cultural development.

2. All peoples may, for their own ends, freely dispose of their natural wealth and resources without prejudice to any obligations arising out of international economic co-operation, based upon the principle of mutual benefit, and international law. In no case may a people be deprived of its own means of subsistence.

3. The States Parties to the present Covenant, including those having responsibility for the administration of Non-Self-Governing and Trust Territories, shall promote the realization of the right of self-determination, and shall respect that right, in conformity with the provisions of the Charter of the United Nations.

PART II

Article 2

1. Each State Party to the present Covenant undertakes to respect and to ensure to all individuals within its territory and subject to its jurisdiction the rights recognized in the present Covenant, without distinction of any kind, such as race, colour, sex, language, religion, political or other

opinion, national or social origin, property, birth or other status.

2. Where not already provided for by existing legislative or other measures, each State Party to the present Covenant undertakes to take the necessary steps, in accordance with its constitutional processes and with the provisions of the present Covenant, to adopt such legislative or other measures as may be necessary to give effect to the rights recognized in the present Covenant.

3. Each State Party to the present Covenant undertakes:

(a) To ensure that any person whose rights or freedoms as herein recognized are violated shall have an effective remedy, notwithstanding that the violation has been committed by persons acting in an official capacity;

(b) To ensure that any person claiming such a remedy shall have his right thereto determined by competent judicial, administrative or legislative authorities, or by any other competent authority provided for by the legal system of the State, and to develop the possibilities of judicial remedy;

(c) To ensure that the competent authorities shall enforce such remedies when granted.

Article 3

The States Parties to the present Covenant undertake to ensure the equal right of men and women to the enjoyment of all civil and political rights set forth in the present Covenant.

Article 4

1. In time of public emergency which threatens the life of the nation and the existence of which is officially proclaimed, the States Parties to the present Covenant may take measures derogating from their obligations under the present Covenant to the extent strictly required by the exigencies of the situation, provided that such measures are not inconsistent with their other obligations under international law and do not involve discrimination solely on the ground of race, colour, sex, language, religion or social origin.

2. No derogation from articles 6, 7, 8 (paragraphs 1 and 2), 11, 15, 16 and 18 may be made under this provision.

3. Any State Party to the present Covenant availing itself of the right of derogation shall immediately inform the other States Parties to the present Covenant, through the intermediary of the Secretary-General of the United Nations, of the provisions from which it has derogated and of the reasons by which it was actuated. A further communication shall be made, through the same intermediary, on the date on which it terminates such derogation.

Article 5

1. Nothing in the present Covenant may be interpreted as implying for any State, group or person any right to engage in any activity or perform any act aimed at the destruction of any of the rights and freedoms recognized herein or at their limitation to a greater extent than is provided for in the present Covenant.

2. There shall be no restriction upon or derogation from any of the fundamental human rights recognized or existing in any State Party to the present Covenant pursuant to law, conventions, regulations or custom on the pretext that the present Covenant does not recognize such rights or that it recognizes them to a lesser extent.

PART III

Article 6

1. Every human being has the inherent right to life. This right shall be protected by law. No one shall be arbitrarily deprived of his life.

2. In countries which have not abolished the death penalty, sentence of death may be imposed only for the most serious crimes in accordance with the law in force at the time of the commission of the crime and not contrary to the provisions of the present Covenant and to the Convention on the Prevention and Punishment of the Crime of Genocide. This penalty can only be carried out pursuant to a final judgement rendered by a competent court.

3. When deprivation of life constitutes the crime of genocide, it is understood that nothing in this article shall authorize any State Party to the present Covenant to derogate in any way from any obligation assumed under the provisions of the Convention on the Prevention and Punishment of the Crime of Genocide.

4. Anyone sentenced to death shall have the right to seek pardon or commutation of the sentence. Amnesty, pardon or commutation of the sentence of death may be granted in all cases.

5. Sentence of death shall not be imposed for crimes committed by persons below eighteen years of age and shall not be carried out on pregnant women.

6. Nothing in this article shall be invoked to delay or to prevent the abolition of capital punishment by any State Party to the present Covenant.

Article 7

No one shall be subjected to torture or to cruel, inhuman or degrading treatment or punishment. In particular, no one shall be subjected without his free consent to medical or scientific experimentation.

Article 8

1. No one shall be held in slavery; slavery and the slave-trade in all their forms shall be prohibited.

2. No one shall be held in servitude.

3. (a) No one shall be required to perform forced or compulsory labour;

(b) Paragraph 3 (a) shall not be held to preclude, in countries where imprisonment with hard labour may be imposed as a punishment for a crime, the performance of hard labour in pursuance of a sentence to such punishment by a competent court;

(c) For the purpose of this paragraph the term "forced or compulsory labour" shall not include:

(i) Any work or service, not referred to in sub-paragraph (b), normally required of a person who is under detention in consequence of a lawful order of a court, or of a person during conditional release from such detention;

(ii) Any service of a military character and, in countries where conscientious objection is recognized, any national service required by law of conscientious objectors;

(iii) Any service exacted in cases of emergency or calamity threatening the life or well-being of the community;

(iv) Any work or service which forms part of normal civil obligations.

Article 9

1. Everyone has the right to liberty and security of person. No one shall be subjected to arbitrary arrest or detention. No one shall be deprived of his liberty except on such grounds and in accordance with such procedure as are established by law.

2. Anyone who is arrested shall be informed, at the time of arrest, of the reasons for his arrest and shall be promptly informed of any charges against him.

3. Anyone arrested or detained on a criminal charge shall be brought promptly before a judge or other officer authorized by law to exercise judicial power and shall be

entitled to trial within a reasonable time or to release. It shall not be the general rule that persons awaiting trial shall be detained in custody, but release may be subject to guarantees to appear for trial, at any other stage of the judicial proceedings, and, should occasion arise, for execution of the judgement.

4. Anyone who is deprived of his liberty by arrest or detention shall be entitled to take proceedings before a court, in order that that court may decide without delay on the lawfulness of his detention and order his release if the detention is not lawful.

5. Anyone who has been the victim of unlawful arrest or detention shall have an enforceable right to compensation.

Article 10

1. All persons deprived of their liberty shall be treated with humanity and with respect for the inherent dignity of the human person.

2. (a) Accused persons shall, save in exceptional circumstances, be segregated from convicted persons and shall be subject to separate treatment appropriate to their status as unconvicted persons;

(b) Accused juvenile persons shall be separated from adults and brought as speedily as possible for adjudication.

3. The penitentiary system shall comprise treatment of prisoners the essential aim of which shall be their reformation and social rehabilitation. Juvenile offenders shall be segregated from adults and be accorded treatment appropriate to their age and legal status.

Article 11

No one shall be imprisoned merely on the ground of inability to fulfil a contractual obligation.

Article 12

1. Everyone lawfully within the territory of a State shall, within that territory, have the right to liberty of movement and freedom to choose his residence.

2. Everyone shall be free to leave any country, including his own.

3. The above-mentioned rights shall not be subject to any restrictions except those which are provided by law, are necessary to protect national security, public order (*ordre public*), public health or morals or the rights and freedoms of others, and are consistent with the other rights recognized in the present Covenant.

4. No one shall be arbitrarily deprived of the right to enter his own country.

Article 13

An alien lawfully in the territory of a State Party to the present Covenant may be expelled therefrom only in pursuance of a decision reached in accordance with law and shall, except where compelling reasons of national security otherwise require, be allowed to submit the reasons against his expulsion and to have his case reviewed by, and be represented for the purpose before, the competent authority or a person or persons especially designated by the competent authority.

Article 14

1. All persons shall be equal before the courts and tribunals. In the determination of any criminal charge against him, or of his rights and obligations in a suit at law, everyone shall be entitled to a fair and public hearing by a competent, independent and impartial tribunal established by law. The Press and the public may be excluded from all or part of a trial for reasons of morals, public order (*ordre public*) or national security in a democratic society, or when the interest of the private lives of the parties so requires, or to the extent strictly necessary in the opinion of the court in special circumstances where publicity would prejudice the

interests of justice; but any judgement rendered in a criminal case or in a suit at law shall be made public except where the interest of juvenile persons otherwise requires or the proceedings concern matrimonial disputes or the guardianship of children.

2. Everyone charged with a criminal offence shall have the right to be presumed innocent until proved guilty according to law.

3. In the determination of any criminal charge against him, everyone shall be entitled to the following minimum guarantees, in full equality:

(a) To be informed promptly and in detail in a language which he understands of the nature and cause of the charge against him;

(b) To have adequate time and facilities for the preparation of his defence and to communicate with counsel of his own choosing;

(c) To be tried without undue delay;

(d) To be tried in his presence, and to defend himself in person or through legal assistance of his own choosing; to be informed, if he does not have legal assistance, of this right; and to have legal assistance assigned to him, in any case where the interests of justice so require, and without payment by him in any such case if he does not have sufficient means to pay for it;

(e) To examine, or have examined, the witnesses against him and to obtain the attendance and examination of witnesses on his behalf under the same conditions as witnesses against him;

(f) To have the free assistance of an interpreter if he cannot understand or speak the language used in court;

(g) Not to be compelled to testify against himself or to confess guilt.

4. In the case of juvenile persons, the procedure shall be such as will take account of their age and the desirability of promoting their rehabilitation.

5. Everyone convicted of a crime shall have the right to his conviction and sentence being reviewed by a higher tribunal according to law.

6. When a person has by a final decision been convicted of a criminal offence and when subsequently his conviction has been reversed or he has been pardoned on the ground that a new or newly discovered fact shows conclusively that there has been a miscarriage of justice, the person who has suffered punishment as a result of such conviction shall be compensated according to law, unless it is proved that the non-disclosure of the unknown fact in time is wholly or partly attributable to him.

7. No one shall be liable to be tried or punished again for an offence for which he has already been finally convicted or acquitted in accordance with the law and penal procedure of each country.

Article 15

1. No one shall be held guilty of any criminal offence on account of any act or omission which did not constitute a criminal offence, under national or international law, at the time when it was committed. Nor shall a heavier penalty be imposed than the one that was applicable at the time when the criminal offence was committed. If, subsequent to the commission of the offence, provision is made by law for the imposition of the lighter penalty, the offender shall benefit thereby.

2. Nothing in this article shall prejudice the trial and punishment of any person for any act or omission which, at the time when it was committed, was criminal according to the general principles of law recognized by the community of nations.

Article 16

Everyone shall have the right to recognition everywhere as a person before the law.

Article 17

1. No one shall be subjected to arbitrary or unlawful interference with his privacy, family, home or correspondence, nor to unlawful attacks on his honour and reputation.

2. Everyone has the right to the protection of the law against such interference or attacks.

Article 18

1. Everyone shall have the right to freedom of thought, conscience and religion. This right shall include freedom to have or to adopt a religion or belief of his choice, and freedom, either individually or in community with others and in public or private, to manifest his religion or belief in worship, observance, practice and teaching.

2. No one shall be subject to coercion which would impair his freedom to have or to adopt a religion or belief of his choice.

3. Freedom to manifest one's religion or beliefs may be subject only to such limitations as are prescribed by law and are necessary to protect public safety, order, health, or morals or the fundamental rights and freedoms of others.

4. The States Parties to the present Covenant undertake to have respect for the liberty of parents and, when applicable, legal guardians to ensure the religious and moral education of their children in conformity with their own convictions.

Article 19

1. Everyone shall have the right to hold opinions without interference.

2. Everyone shall have the right to freedom of expression; this right shall include freedom to seek, receive and impart information and ideas of all kinds, regardless of frontiers, either orally, in writing or in print, in the form of art, or through any other media of his choice.

3. The exercise of the rights provided for in paragraph 2 of this article carries with it special duties and responsibilities. It may therefore be subject to certain restrictions, but these shall only be such as are provided by law and are necessary:

(a) For respect of the rights or reputations of others;

(b) For the protection of national security or of public order (*ordre public*), or of public health or morals.

Article 20

1. Any propaganda for war shall be prohibited by law.

2. Any advocacy of national, racial or religious hatred that constitutes incitement to discrimination, hostility or violence shall be prohibited by law.

Article 21

The right of peaceful assembly shall be recognized. No restrictions may be placed on the exercise of this right other than those imposed in conformity with the law and which are necessary in a democratic society in the interests of national security or public safety, public order (*ordre public*), the protection of public health or morals or the protection of the rights and freedoms of others.

Article 22

1. Everyone shall have the right to freedom of association with others, including the right to form and join trade unions for the protection of his interests.

2. No restrictions may be placed on the exercise of this right other than those which are prescribed by law and which are necessary in a democratic society in the interests of national security or public safety, public order (*ordre public*), the protection of public health or morals or the protection of the rights and freedoms of others. This article shall not prevent the imposition of lawful restrictions on members of the armed forces and of the police in their exercise of this right.

3. Nothing in this article shall authorize States Parties to the International

Labour Organisation Convention of 1948 concerning Freedom of Association and Protection of the Right to Organize to take legislative measures which would prejudice, or to apply the law in such a manner as to prejudice, the guarantees provided for in that Convention.

Article 23

1. The family is the natural and fundamental group unit of society and is entitled to protection by society and the State.

2. The right of men and women of marriageable age to marry and to found a family shall be recognized.

3. No marriage shall be entered into without the free and full consent of the intending spouses.

4. States Parties to the present Covenant shall take appropriate steps to ensure equality of rights and responsibilities of spouses as to marriage, during marriage and at its dissolution. In the case of dissolution, provision shall be made for the necessary protection of any children.

Article 24

1. Every child shall have, without any discrimination as to race, colour, sex, language, religion, national or social origin, property or birth, the right to such measures of protection as are required by his status as a minor, on the part of his family, society and the State.

2. Every child shall be registered immediately after birth and shall have a name.

3. Every child has the right to acquire a nationality.

Article 25

Every citizen shall have the right and the opportunity, without any of the distinctions mentioned in article 2 and without unreasonable restrictions:

(a) To take part in the conduct of public affairs, directly or through freely chosen representatives;

(b) To vote and to be elected at genuine periodic elections which shall be by universal and equal suffrage and shall be held by secret ballot, guaranteeing the free expression of the will of the electors;

(c) To have access, on general terms of equality, to public service in his country.

Article 26

All persons are equal before the law and are entitled without any discrimination to the equal protection of the law. In this respect, the law shall prohibit any discrimination and guarantee to all persons equal and effective protection against discrimination on any ground such as race, colour, sex, language, religion, political or other opinion, national or social origin, property, birth or other status.

Article 27

In those States in which ethnic, religious or linguistic minorities exist, persons belonging to such minorities shall not be denied the right, in community with the other members of their group, to enjoy their own culture, to profess and practice their own religion, or to use their own language.

PART IV

Article 28

1. There shall be established a Human Rights Committee (hereafter referred to in the present Covenant as the Committee). It shall consist of eighteen members and shall carry out the functions hereinafter provided.

2. The Committee shall be composed of nationals of the States Parties to the present Covenant who shall be persons of high moral character and recognized competence in the field of human rights, con-

sideration being given to the usefulness of the participation of some persons having legal experience.

3. The members of the Committee shall be elected and shall serve in their personal capacity.

Article 29

1. The members of the Committee shall be elected by secret ballot from a list of persons possessing the qualifications prescribed in article 28 and nominated for the purpose by the States Parties to the present Covenant.

2. Each State Party to the present Covenant may nominate not more than two persons. These persons shall be nationals of the nominating State.

3. A person shall be eligible for renomination.

Article 30

1. The initial election shall be held no later than six months after the date of the entry into force of the present Covenant.

2. At least four months before the date of each election to the Committee, other than an election to fill a vacancy declared in accordance with article 34, the Secretary-General of the United Nations shall address a written invitation to the States Parties to the present Covenant to submit their nominations for membership of the Committee within three months.

3. The Secretary-General of the United Nations shall prepare a list in alphabetical order of all the persons thus nominated, with an indication of the States Parties which have nominated them, and shall submit it to the States Parties to the present Covenant no later than one month before the date of each election.

4. Elections of the members of the Committee shall be held at a meeting of the States Parties to the present Covenant convened by the Secretary-General of the

United Nations at the Headquarters of the United Nations. At that meeting, for which two thirds of the States Parties to the present Covenant shall constitute a quorum, the persons elected to the Committee shall be those nominees who obtain the largest number of votes and an absolute majority of the votes of the representatives of States Parties present and voting.

Article 31

1. The Committee may not include more than one national of the same State.

2. In the election of the Committee, consideration shall be given to equitable geographical distribution of membership and to the representation of the different forms of civilization and of the principal legal systems.

Article 32

1. The members of the Committee shall be elected for a term of four years. They shall be eligible for re-election if renominated. However, the terms of nine of the members elected at the first election shall expire at the end of two years; immediately after the first election, the names of these nine members shall be chosen by lot by the Chairman of the meeting referred to in article 30, paragraph 4.

2. Elections at the expiry of office shall be held in accordance with the preceding articles of this part of the present Covenant.

Article 33

1. If, in the unanimous opinion of the other members, a member of the Committee has ceased to carry out his functions for any cause other than absence of a temporary character, the Chairman of the Committee shall notify the Secretary-General of the United Nations, who shall then declare the seat of that member to be vacant.

2. In the event of the death or the resignation of a member of the Committee, the Chairman shall immediately notify the Secretary-General of the United Nations, who shall declare the seat vacant from the date of death or the date on which the resignation takes effect.

Article 34

1. When a vacancy is declared in accordance with article 33 and if the term of office of the member to be replaced does not expire within six months of the declaration of the vacancy, the Secretary-General of the United Nations shall notify each of the States Parties to the present Covenant, which may within two months submit nominations in accordance with article 29 for the purpose of filling the vacancy.

2. The Secretary-General of the United Nations shall prepare a list in alphabetical order of the persons thus nominated and shall submit it to the States Parties to the present Covenant. The election to fill the vacancy shall then take place in accordance with the relevant provisions of this part of the present Covenant.

3. A member of the Committee elected to fill a vacancy declared in accordance with article 33 shall hold office for the remainder of the term of the member who vacated the seat on the Committee under the provisions of that article.

Article 35

The members of the Committee shall, with the approval of the General Assembly of the United Nations, receive emoluments from United Nations resources on such terms and conditions as the General Assembly may decide, having regard to the importance of the Committee's responsibilities.

Article 36

The Secretary-General of the United Nations shall provide the necessary staff and facilities for the effective performance of the functions of the Committee under the present Covenant.

Article 37

1. The Secretary-General of the United Nations shall convene the initial meeting of the Committee at the Headquarters of the United Nations.

2. After its initial meeting, the Committee shall meet at such times as shall be provided in its rules of procedure.

3. The Committee shall normally meet at the Headquarters of the United Nations or at the United Nations Office at Geneva.

Article 38

Every member of the Committee shall, before taking up his duties, make a solemn declaration in open committee that he will perform his functions impartially and conscientiously.

Article 39

1. The Committee shall elect its officers for a term of two years. They may be re-elected.

2. The Committee shall establish its own rules of procedure, but these rules shall provide, *inter alia*, that:

(a) Twelve members shall constitute a quorum;

(b) Decisions of the Committee shall be made by a majority vote of the members present.

Article 40

1. The States Parties to the present Covenant undertake to submit reports on the measures they have adopted which give effect to the rights recognized herein and on the progress made in the enjoyment of those rights:

(a) Within one year of the entry into

force of the present Covenant for the States Parties concerned;

(b) Thereafter whenever the Committee so requests.

2. All reports shall be submitted to the Secretary-General of the United Nations, who shall transmit them to the Committee for consideration. Reports shall indicate the factors and difficulties, if any, affecting the implementation of the present Covenant.

3. The Secretary-General of the United Nations may, after consultation with the Committee, transmit to the specialized agencies concerned copies of such parts of the reports as may fall within their field of competence.

4. The Committee shall study the reports submitted by the States Parties to the present Covenant. It shall transmit its reports, and such general comments as it may consider appropriate, to the States Parties. The Committee may also transmit to the Economic and Social Council these comments along with the copies of the reports it has received from States Parties to the present Covenant.

5. The States Parties to the present Covenant may submit to the Committee observations on any comments that may be made in accordance with paragraph 4 of this article.

Article 41

1. A State Party to the present Covenant may at any time declare under this article that it recognizes the competence of the Committee to receive and consider communications to the effect that a State Party claims that another State Party is not fulfilling its obligations under the present Covenant. Communications under this article may be received and considered only if submitted by a State Party which has made a declaration recognizing in regard to itself the competence of the Committee. No communication shall be received by the Committee if it concerns a State Party which has not made such a declaration. Communications received under this article shall be dealt with in accordance with the following procedure:

(a) If a State Party to the present Covenant considers that another State Party is not giving effect to the provisions of the present Covenant, it may, by written communication, bring the matter to the attention of that State Party. Within three months after the receipt of the communication, the receiving State shall afford the State which sent the communication an explanation or any other statement in writing clarifying the matter, which should include, to the extent possible and pertinent, reference to domestic procedures and remedies taken, pending, or available in the matter;

(b) If the matter is not adjusted to the satisfaction of both States Parties concerned within six months after the receipt by the receiving State of the initial communication, either State shall have the right to refer the matter to the Committee, by notice given to the Committee and to the other State;

(c) The Committee shall deal with a matter referred to it only after it has ascertained that all available domestic remedies have been invoked and exhausted in the matter, in conformity with the generally recognized principles of international law. This shall not be the rule where the application of the remedies is unreasonably prolonged;

(d) The Committee shall hold closed meetings when examining communications under this article;

(e) Subject to the provisions of subparagraph (c), the Committee shall make available its good offices to the States Parties concerned with a view to a friendly solution of the matter on the basis of respect for human rights and fundamental freedoms as recognized in the present Covenant;

(f) In any matter referred to it, the Committee may call upon the States Parties concerned, referred to in sub-paragraph (b), to supply any relevant information;

(g) The States Parties concerned, referred to in sub-paragraph (b), shall have the right to be represented when the matter is being considered in the Committee and to make submissions orally and/or in writing;

(h) The Committee shall, within twelve months after the date of receipt of notice under sub-paragraph (b), submit a report:

(i) If a solution within the terms of sub-paragraph (e) is reached, the Committee shall confine its report to a brief statement of the facts and of the solution reached;

(ii) If a solution within the terms of sub-paragraph (e) is not reached, the Committee shall confine its report to a brief statement of the facts; the written submissions and record of the oral submissions made by the States Parties concerned shall be attached to the report. In every matter, the report shall be communicated to the States Parties concerned.

2. The provisions of this article shall come into force when ten States Parties to the present Covenant have made declarations under paragraph 1 of this article. Such declarations shall be deposited by the States Parties with the Secretary-General of the United Nations, who shall transmit copies thereof to the other States Parties. A declaration may be withdrawn at any time by notification to the Secretary-General. Such a withdrawal shall not prejudice the consideration of any matter which is the subject of a communication already transmitted under this article; no further communication by any State Party shall be received after the notification of withdrawal of the declaration has been received by the Secretary-General, unless the State Party concerned has made a new declaration.

Article 42

1. (a) If a matter referred to the Committee in accordance with article 41 is not resolved to the satisfaction of the States Parties concerned, the Committee may, with the prior consent of the States Parties concerned, appoint an *ad hoc* Conciliation Commission (hereinafter referred to as the Commission). The good offices of the Commission shall be made available to the States Parties concerned with a view to an amicable solution of the matter on the basis of respect for the present Covenant;

(b) The Commission shall consist of five persons acceptable to the States Parties concerned. If the States Parties concerned fail to reach agreement within three months on all or part of the composition of the Commission, the members of the Commission concerning whom no agreement has been reached shall be elected by secret ballot by a two-thirds majority vote of the Committee from among its members.

2. The members of the Commission shall serve in their personal capacity. They shall not be nationals of the States Parties concerned, or of a State not Party to the present Covenant, or of a State Party which has not made a declaration under article 41.

3. The Commission shall elect its own Chairman and adopt its own rules of procedure.

4. The meetings of the Commission shall normally be held at the Headquarters of the United Nations or at the United Nations Office at Geneva. However, they may be held at such other convenient places as the Commission may determine in consultation with the Secretary-General of the United Nations and the States Parties concerned.

5. The secretariat provided in accordance with article 36 shall also service the commissions appointed under this article.

6. The information received and collated by the Committee shall be made

available to the Commission and the Commission may call upon the States Parties concerned to supply any other relevant information.

7. When the Commission has fully considered the matter, but in any event not later than twelve months after having been seized of the matter, it shall submit to the Chairman of the Committee a report for communication to the States Parties concerned:

(a) If the Commission is unable to complete its consideration of the matter within twelve months, it shall confine its report to a brief statement of the status of its consideration of the matter;

(b) If an amicable solution to the matter on the basis of respect for human rights as recognized in the present Covenant is reached, the Commission shall confine its report to a brief statement of the facts and of the solution reached;

(c) If a solution within the terms of sub-paragraph (b) is not reached, the Commission's report shall embody its findings on all questions of fact relevant to the issues between the States Parties concerned, and its views on the possibilities of an amicable solution of the matter. This report shall also contain the written submissions and a record of the oral submissions made by the States Parties concerned;

(d) If the Commission's report is submitted under sub-paragraph (c), the States Parties concerned shall, within three months of the receipt of the report, notify the Chairman of the Committee whether or not they accept the contents of the report of the Commission.

8. The provisions of this article are without prejudice to the responsibilities of the Committee under article 41.

9. The States Parties concerned shall share equally all the expenses of the members of the Commission in accordance with estimates to be provided by the Secretary-General of the United Nations.

10. The Secretary-General of the United Nations shall be empowered to pay the expenses of the members of the Commission, if necessary, before reimbursement by the States Parties concerned, in accordance with paragraph 9 of this article.

Article 43

The members of the Committee, and of the *ad hoc* conciliation commissions which may be appointed under article 42, shall be entitled to the facilities, privileges and immunities of experts on mission for the United Nations as laid down in the relevant sections of the Convention on the Privileges and Immunities of the United Nations.

Article 44

The provisions for the implementation of the present Covenant shall apply without prejudice to the procedures prescribed in the field of human rights by or under the constituent instruments and the conventions of the United Nations and of the specialized agencies and shall not prevent the States Parties to the present Covenant from having recourse to other procedures for settling a dispute in accordance with general or special international agreements in force between them.

Article 45

The Committee shall submit to the General Assembly of the United Nations, through the Economic and Social Council, an annual report on its activities.

PART V

Article 46

Nothing in the present Covenant shall be interpreted as impairing the provisions of the Charter of the United Nations and of the constitutions of the specialized agencies which define the respective responsibilities of the various organs of the United Nations and of the specialized agencies in regard to the matters dealt within the present Covenant.

Article 47

Nothing in the present Covenant shall be interpreted as impairing the inherent right of all peoples to enjoy and utilize fully and freely their natural wealth and resources.

PART VI

Article 48

1. The present Covenant is open for signature by any State Member of the United Nations or member of any of its specialized agencies, by any State Party to the Statute of the International Court of Justice, and by any other State which has been invited by the General Assembly of the United Nations to become a party to the present Covenant.

2. The present Covenant is subject to ratification. Instruments of ratification shall be deposited with the Secretary-General of the United Nations.

3. The present Covenant shall be open to accession by any State referred to in paragraph 1 of this article.

4. Accession shall be effected by the deposit of an instrument of accession with the Secretary-General of the United Nations.

5. The Secretary-General of the United Nations shall inform all States which have signed this Covenant or acceded to it of the deposit of each instrument of ratification or accession.

Article 49

1. The present Covenant shall enter into force three months after the date of the deposit with the Secretary-General of the United Nations of the thirty-fifth instrument of ratification or instrument of accession.

2. For each State ratifying the present Covenant or acceding to it after the deposit of the thirty-fifth instrument of ratification or instrument of accession, the present Covenant shall enter into force three months after the date of the deposit of its own instrument of ratification or instrument of accession.

Article 50

The provisions of the present Covenant shall extend to all parts of federal States without any limitations or exceptions.

Article 51

1. Any State Party to the present Covenant may propose an amendment and file it with the Secretary-General of the United Nations. The Secretary-General of the United Nations shall thereupon communicate any proposed amendments to the States Parties to the present Covenant with a request that they notify him whether they favour a conference of States Parties for the purpose of considering and voting upon the proposals. In the event that at least one third of the States Parties favours such a conference, the Secretary-General shall convene the conference under the auspices of the United Nations. Any amendment adopted by a majority of the States Parties present and voting at the conference shall be submitted to the General Assembly of the United Nations for approval.

2. Amendments shall come into force when they have been approved by the General Assembly of the United Nations and accepted by a two-thirds majority of the States Parties to the present Covenant in accordance with their respective constitutional processes.

3. When amendments come into force, they shall be binding on those States Parties which have accepted them, other States Parties still being bound by the provisions of the present Covenant and any earlier amendment which they have accepted.

Article 52

Irrespective of the notifications made under article 48, paragraph 5, the Secretary-General of the United Nations shall inform all States referred to in paragraph 1 of the same article of the following particulars:

(a) Signatures, ratifications and accessions under article 48;

(b) The date of the entry into force of the present Covenant under article 49 and the date of the entry into force of any amendments under article 51.

Article 53

1. The present Covenant, of which the Chinese, English, French, Russian and Spanish texts are equally authentic, shall be deposited in the archives of the United Nations.

2. The Secretary-General of the United Nations shall transmit certified copies of the present Covenant to all States referred to in article 48.

OPTIONAL PROTOCOL TO THE INTERNATIONAL COVENANT ON CIVIL AND POLITICAL RIGHTS

Adopted and Opened for Signature by United Nations General Assembly Resolution 2200A (XXI) on 16 December 1966. Entered into Force 23 March 1976.

The States Parties to the present Protocol,

Considering that in order further to achieve the purposes of the Covenant on Civil and Political Rights (hereinafter referred to as the Covenant) and the implementation of its provisions it would be appropriate to enable the Human Rights Committee set up in part IV of the Covenant (hereinafter referred to as the Committee) to receive and consider, as provided in the present Protocol, communications from individuals claiming to be victims of violations of any of the rights set forth in the Covenant,

Have agreed as follows:

Article 1

A State Party to the Covenant that becomes a party to the present Protocol recognizes the competence of the Committee to receive and consider communications from individuals subject to its jurisdiction who claim to be victims of a violation by that State Party of any of the rights set forth in the Covenant. No communication shall be received by the Committee if it concerns a State Party to the Covenant which is not a Party to the present Protocol.

Article 2

Subject to the provisions of article 1, individuals who claim that any of their rights enumerated in the Covenant have been violated and who have exhausted all available domestic remedies may submit a written communication to the Committee for consideration.

Article 3

The Committee shall consider inadmissible any communication under the present Protocol which is anonymous, or which it considers to be an abuse of the right of submission of such communications or to be incompatible with the provisions of the Covenant.

Article 4

1. Subject to the provisions of article 3, the Committee shall bring any communications submitted to it under the present Protocol to the attention of the State Party to the present Protocol alleged to be violating any provision of the Covenant.

2. Within six months, the receiving State shall submit to the Committee written explanations or statements clarifying the matter and the remedy, if any, that may have been taken by that State.

Article 5

1. The Committee shall consider communications received under the present Protocol in the light of all written information made available to it by the individual and by the State Party concerned.

2. The Committee shall not consider any communication from an individual unless it has ascertained that:

(a) The same matter is not being examined under another procedure of international investigation or settlement;

(b) The individual has exhausted all available domestic remedies. This shall not be the rule where the application of the remedies is unreasonably prolonged.

3. The Committee shall hold closed meetings when examining communications under the present Protocol.

4. The Committee shall forward its views to the State Party concerned and to the individual.

Article 6

The Committee shall include in its annual report under article 45 of the Covenant a summary of its activities under the present Protocol.

Article 7

Pending the achievement of the objectives of resolution 1514 (XV) adopted by the General Assembly of the United Nations on 14 December 1960 concerning the Declaration on the Granting of Independence to Colonial Countries and Peoples, the provisions of the present Protocol shall in no way limit the right of petition granted to these peoples by the Charter of the United Nations and other international conventions and instruments under the United Nations and its specialized agencies.

Article 8

1. The present Protocol is open for signature by any State which has signed the Covenant.

2. The present Protocol is subject to ratification by any State which has ratified or acceded to the Covenant. Instruments of ratification shall be deposited with the Secretary-General of the United Nations.

3. The present Protocol shall be open to accession by any State which has ratified or acceded to the Covenant.

4. Accession shall be effected by the deposit of an instrument of accession with the Secretary-General of the United Nations.

5. The Secretary-General of the United Nations shall inform all States which have signed the present Protocol or acceded to it of the deposit of each instrument of ratification or accession.

Article 9

1. Subject to the entry into force of the Covenant, the present Protocol shall enter into force three months after the date of the deposit with the Secretary-General of the United Nations of the tenth instrument of ratification or instrument of accession.

2. For each State ratifying the present Protocol or acceding to it after the deposit of the tenth instrument of ratification or instrument of accession, the present Protocol shall enter into force three months after the date of the deposit of its own instrument of ratification or instrument of accession.

Article 10

The provisions of the present Protocol shall extend to all parts of federal States without any limitations or exceptions.

Article 11

1. Any State Party to the present Protocol may propose an amendment and file it with the Secretary-General of the United Nations. The Secretary-General shall thereupon communicate any proposed amendments to the States Parties to the present Protocol with a request that they notify him whether they favour a conference of States Parties for the purpose of considering and voting upon the proposal. In the event that at least one third of the States Parties favours such a conference, the Secretary-General shall convene the conference under the auspices of the United Nations. Any amendment adopted by a majority of the

States Parties present and voting at the conference shall be submitted to the General Assembly of the United Nations for approval.

2. Amendments shall come into force when they have been approved by the General Assembly of the United Nations and accepted by a two-thirds majority of the States Parties to the present Protocol in accordance with their respective constitutional processes.

3. When amendments come into force, they shall be binding on those States Parties which have accepted them, other States Parties still being bound by the provisions of the present Protocol and any earlier amendment which they have accepted.

Article 12

1. Any State Party may denounce the present Protocol at any time by written notification addressed to the Secretary-General of the United Nations. Denunciation shall take effect three months after the date of receipt of the notification by the Secretary-General.

2. Denunciation shall be without prejudice to the continued application of the provisions of the present Protocol to any communication submitted under article 2 before the effective date of denunciation.

Article 13

Irrespective of the notifications made under article 8, paragraph 5, of the present Protocol, the Secretary-General of the United Nations shall inform all States referred to in article 48, paragraph 1, of the Covenant of the following particulars:

(a) Signatures, ratifications and accessions under article 8;

(b) The date of the entry into force of the present Protocol under article 9 and the date of the entry into force of any amendments under article 11;

(c) Denunciations under article 12.

Article 14

1. The present Protocol, of which the Chinese, English, French, Russian and Spanish texts are equally authentic, shall be deposited in the archives of the United Nations.

2. The Secretary-General of the United Nations shall transmit certified copies of the present Protocol to all States referred to in article 48 of the Covenant.

PART II
INTERNATIONAL STANDARDS OF HUMAN RIGHTS RELATED TO RELIGION AND BELIEF

THE UNITED NATIONS HUMAN RIGHTS COMMITTEE

The Human Rights Committee periodically issues general comments in order to assist states parties to the International Covenant on Civil and Political Rights (ICCPR) in the implementation of their obligations under the Covenant.

The documents of the Human Rights Committee contain a wealth of information on the status in states parties of human rights related to religion or belief. The Committee prepares an annual report for the General Assembly, published as Supplement 40 to the *Official Records of the General Assembly*. This report includes summaries of the Committee's consideration of reports by states parties and the consideration of individual communications submitted under the Optional Protocol to the ICCPR, as well as the texts of any general comments issued and the views or decisions of the Committee with respect to individual communications. More extensive documentation of the work of the Human Rights Committee, including summary records of their meetings, the texts of states parties' reports submitted to the Committee as well as the annual reports to the General Assembly are periodically published as the *Official Records of the Human Rights Committee* (formerly entitled the *Yearbook of the Human Rights Committee*).

As of its fifty-fourth session in 1995, the Human Rights Committee has not adopted the view, in response to an individual communication, that a state party has violated human rights related to religion and belief protected under the Covenant (esp. Arts. 2(1), 18, 20(2), 26 and 27), although a number of decisions have addressed these rights.

UNITED NATIONS HUMAN RIGHTS COMMITTEE
GENERAL COMMENT NO. 18 (37)
(NON-DISCRIMINATION)

Adopted by the U.N. Human Rights Committee on 9 November 1989.
U.N. Doc. CCPR/C/21/Rev.1/Add.1 (1989),
reprinted in U.N. Doc. HRI/GEN/1/ Rev.1 at 26 (1994).

1.   Non-discrimination, together with equality before the law and equal protection of the law without any discrimination, constitute a basic and general principle relating to the protection of human rights. Thus, article 2, paragraph 1, of the International Covenant on Civil and Political Rights obligates each State party to respect and ensure to all persons within its territory and subject to its jurisdiction the rights recognized in the Covenant without distinction of any kind, such as race, colour, sex, language, religion, political or other opinion, national or social origin, property, birth or other status. Article 26 not only entitles all persons to equality before the law as well as equal protection of the law but also prohibits any discrimination under the law and guarantees to all persons equal and effective protection against discrimination on any ground such as race, colour, sex, language, religion, political or other opinion, national or social origin, property, birth or other status.

2.   Indeed, the principle of non-discrimination is so basic that article 3 obligates each State party to ensure the equal right of men and women to the enjoyment of the rights set forth in the Covenant. While article 4, paragraph 1, allows States parties to take measures derogating from certain obligations under the Covenant in time of public emergency, the same article requires, *inter alia*, that those measures should not involve discrimination solely on the ground of race, colour, sex, language, religion or social origin. Furthermore, article 20, paragraph 2, obligates States parties to prohibit, by law, any advocacy of national, racial or religious hatred which constitutes incitement to discrimination.

3.   Because of their basic and general character, the principle of non-discrimination as well as that of equality before the law and equal protection of the law are sometimes expressly referred to in articles relating to particular categories of human rights. Article 14, paragraph 1, provides that all persons shall be equal before the courts and tribunals, and paragraph 3 of the same article provides that, in the determination of any criminal charge against him, everyone shall be entitled, in full equality, to the minimum guarantees enumerated in sub-paragraphs (a) to (g) of paragraph 3. Similarly, article 25 provides for the equal participation in public life of all citizens, without any of the distinctions mentioned in article 2.

4.   It is for the States parties to determine appropriate measures to implement the relevant provisions. However, the Committee is to be informed about the nature of such measures and their conformity with the principles of non-discrimination and equality before the law and equal protection of the law.

5.   The Committee wishes to draw the attention of States parties to the fact that the Covenant sometimes expressly requires them to take measures to guarantee the equality of rights of the persons concerned. For example, article 23, paragraph 4, stipulates that States parties shall take appropriate steps to ensure equality of rights as well as responsibilities of spouses as to marriage, during marriage and at its dissolution. Such steps may take the form of legislative, administrative or other measures, but it is a positive duty of States parties to make certain that spouses have equal rights as required by the Covenant. In relation to children, article 24 provides that all children, without any discrimination as to race, colour, sex, language, religion, national or social origin, property or birth, have the right to such measures of protection as are required by their status as minors, on the part of their family, society and the State.

6.   The Committee notes that the Covenant neither defines the term "discrimination" nor indicates what constitutes discrimination. However, article 1 of the International Convention on the Elimination of All Forms of Racial Discrimination provides that the term "racial discrimination" shall mean any distinction, exclusion, restriction or preference based on race, colour, descent, or national or ethnic origin which has the purpose or effect of nullifying or impairing the recognition, enjoyment or exercise, on an equal footing, of human rights and fundamental freedoms in the political, economic, social, cultural or any other field of public life. Similarly, article 1 of the Convention on the Elimination of All Forms of Discrimination against Women provides that "discrimination against women" shall mean any distinction, exclusion or restriction made on the basis of sex which has the effect or purpose of impairing or nullifying the recognition, enjoyment or exercise by women, irrespective of their marital status, on a basis of equality of men and women, of human rights and fundamental freedoms in the political, economic, social, cultural, civil or any other field.

7.   While these conventions deal only with cases of discrimination on specific grounds, the Committee believes that the term "discrimination" as used in the Covenant should be understood to imply any distinction, exclusion, restriction or preference which is based on any ground such as race, colour, sex, language, religion, political or other opinion, national or social origin, property, birth or other status, and which has the purpose or effect of nullifying or impairing the recognition, enjoyment or exercise by all persons, on an equal footing, of all rights and freedoms.

8.   The enjoyment of rights and freedoms on an equal footing, however, does not mean identical treatment in every instance. In this connection, the provisions of the Covenant are explicit. For example, article 6, paragraph 5, prohibits the death sentence from being imposed on persons below 18 years of age. The same paragraph prohibits that sentence from being carried out on pregnant women. Similarly, article 10, paragraph 3, requires the segregation of juvenile offenders from adults. Furthermore, article 25 guarantees certain political rights, differentiating on grounds of citizenship.

9.   Reports of many States parties contain information regarding legislative as well as administrative measures and court decisions which relate to protection against discrimination in law, but they very often lack information which would reveal discrimination in fact. When reporting on articles 2 (1), 3 and 26 of the Covenant, States parties usually cite provisions of their constitution or equal opportunity laws with respect to equality of persons. While such information is of course useful, the Committee wishes to know if there remain any problems of discrimination in fact, which may be practised either by

public authorities, by the community, or by private persons or bodies. The Committee wishes to be informed about legal provisions and administrative measures directed at diminishing or eliminating such discrimination.

10.   The Committee also wishes to point out that the principle of equality sometimes requires States parties to take affirmative action in order to diminish or eliminate conditions which cause or help to perpetuate discrimination prohibited by the Covenant. For example, in a State where the general conditions of a certain part of the population prevent or impair their enjoyment of human rights, the State should take specific action to correct those conditions. Such action may involve granting for a time to the part of the population concerned certain preferential treatment in specific matters as compared with the rest of the population. However, as long as such action is needed to correct discrimination in fact, it is a case of legitimate differentiation under the Covenant.

11.   Both article 2, paragraph 1, and article 26 enumerate grounds of discrimination such as race, colour, sex, language, religion, political or other opinion, national or social origin, property, birth or other status. The Committee has observed that in a number of constitutions and laws not all the grounds on which discrimination is prohibited, as cited in article 2, paragraph 1, are enumerated. The Committee would therefore like to receive information from States par-

ties as to the significance of such omissions.

12.   While article 2 limits the scope of the rights to be protected against discrimination to those provided for in the Covenant, article 26 does not specify such limitations. That is to say, article 26 provides that all persons are equal before the law and are entitled to equal protection of the law without discrimination, and that the law shall guarantee to all persons equal and effective protection against discrimination on any of the enumerated grounds. In the view of the Committee, article 26 does not merely duplicate the guarantee already provided for in article 2 but provides in itself an autonomous right. It prohibits discrimination in law or in fact in any field regulated and protected by public authorities. Article 26 is therefore concerned with the obligations imposed on States parties in regard to their legislation and the application thereof. Thus, when legislation is adopted by a State party, it must comply with the requirement of article 26 that its content should not be discriminatory. In other words, the application of the principle of non-discrimination contained in article 26 is not limited to those rights which are provided for in the Covenant.

13.   Finally, the Committee observes that not every differentiation of treatment will constitute discrimination, if the criteria for such differentiation are reasonable and objective and if the aim is to achieve a purpose which is legitimate under the Covenant.

UNITED NATIONS HUMAN RIGHTS COMMITTEE
GENERAL COMMENT NO. 22 (48)
(ARTICLE 18)
Adopted by the U.N. Human Rights Committee on 20 July 1993.
U.N. Doc. CCPR/C/21/Rev.1/Add.4 (1993),
reprinted in U.N. Doc. HRI/GEN/1/ Rev.1 at 35 (1994).

1.   The right to freedom of thought, conscience and religion (which includes the freedom to hold beliefs) in article 18(1) is far-reaching and profound; it encompasses freedom of thoughts on all matters, personal conviction and the commitment to religion or belief, whether manifested individually or in community with others. The Committee draws the attention of States parties to the fact that the freedom of thought and the freedom of conscience are protected equally with the freedom of religion and belief. The fundamental character of these freedoms is also reflected in the fact that this provision cannot be derogated from, even in time of public emergency, as stated in article 4(2) of the Covenant.

2.   Article 18 protects theistic, non-theistic and atheistic beliefs, as well as the right not to profess any religion or belief. The terms belief and religion are to be broadly construed. Article 18 is not limited in its application to traditional religions or to religions and beliefs with institutional characteristics or practices analogous to those of traditional religions. The Committee therefore views with concern any tendency to discriminate against any religion or belief for any reasons, including the fact that they are newly established, or represent religious minorities that may be the subject of hostility by a predominant religious community.

3.   Article 18 distinguishes the free-dom of thought, conscience, religion or belief from the freedom to manifest religion or belief. It does not permit any limitations whatsoever on the freedom of thought and conscience or on the freedom to have or adopt a religion or belief of one's choice. These freedoms are protected unconditionally, as is the right of everyone to hold opinions without interference in article 19(1). In accordance with articles 18(2) and 17, no one can be compelled to reveal his thoughts or adherence to a religion or belief.

4.   The freedom to manifest religion or belief may be exercised "either individually or in community with others and in public or private". The freedom to manifest religion or belief in worship, observance, practice and teaching encompasses a broad range of acts. The concept of worship extends to ritual and ceremonial acts giving direct expression to belief, as well as various practices integral to such acts, including the building of places of worship, the use of ritual formulae and objects, the display of symbols, and the observance of holidays and days of rest. The observance and practice of religion or belief may include not only ceremonial acts but also such customs as the observance of dietary regulations, the wearing of distinctive clothing or headcoverings, participation in rituals associated with certain stages of life, and the use of a particular language customarily spoken by a group. In addition, the practice and teaching of reli-

gion or belief includes acts integral to the conduct by religious groups of their basic affairs, such as, *inter alia*, the freedom to choose their religious leaders, priests and teachers, the freedom to establish seminaries or religious schools and the freedom to prepare and distribute religious texts or publications.

5. The Committee observes that the freedom to "have or to adopt" a religion or belief necessarily entails the freedom to choose a religion or belief, including, *inter alia*, the right to replace one's current religion or belief with another or to adopt atheistic views, as well as the right to retain one's religion or belief. Article 18(2) bars coercion that would impair the right to have or adopt a religion or belief, including the use of threat of physical force or penal sanctions to compel believers or non-believers to adhere to their religious beliefs and congregations, to recant their religion or belief or to convert. Policies or practices having the same intention or effect, such as for example those restricting access to education, medical care, employment or the rights guaranteed by article 25 and other provisions of the Covenant are similarly inconsistent with article 18(2). The same protection is enjoyed by holders of all beliefs of a non-religious nature.

6. The Committee is of the view that article 18(4) permits public school instruction in subjects such as the general history of religions and ethics if it is given in a neutral and objective way. The liberty of parents or legal guardians to ensure that their children receive a religious and moral education in conformity with their own convictions, set forth in article 18(4), is related to the guarantees of the freedom to teach a religion or belief stated in article 18(1). The Committee notes that public education that includes instruction in a particular religion or belief is inconsistent with article 18(4) unless provision is made for non-discriminatory exemptions or alternatives that would accommodate the wishes of parents and guardians.

7. In accordance with article 20, no manifestation of religions or beliefs may amount to propaganda for war or advocacy of national, racial or religious hatred that constitutes incitement to discrimination, hostility or violence. As stated by the Committee in its General Comment 11 [19], States parties are under the obligation to enact laws to prohibit such acts.

8. Article 18(3) permits restrictions on the freedom to manifest religion or belief only if limitations are prescribed by law and are necessary to protect public safety, order, health or morals, or the fundamental rights and freedoms of others. The freedom from coercion to have or to adopt a religion or belief and the liberty of parents and guardians to ensure religious and moral education cannot be restricted. In interpreting the scope of permissible limitation clauses, States parties should proceed from the need to protect the rights guaranteed under the Covenant, including the right to equality and non-discrimination on all grounds specified in articles 2, 3 and 26. Limitations imposed must be established by law and must not be applied in a manner that would vitiate the rights guaranteed in article 18. The Committee observes that paragraph 3 of article 18 is to be strictly interpreted: restrictions are not allowed on grounds not specified there, even if they would be allowed as restrictions to other rights protected in the Covenant, such as national security. Limitations may be applied only for those purposes for which they were prescribed and must be directly related and proportionate to the specific need on which they are predicated. Restrictions may not be imposed for dis-

criminatory purposes or applied in a discriminatory manner. The Committee observes that the concept of morals derives from many social, philosophical and religious traditions; consequently, limitations on the freedom to manifest a religion or belief for the purpose of protecting morals must be based on principles not deriving exclusively from a single tradition. Persons already subject to certain legitimate constraints, such as prisoners, continue to enjoy their rights to manifest their religion or belief to the fullest extent compatible with the specific nature of the constraint. States parties' reports should provide information on the full scope and effects of limitations under article 18(3), both as a matter of law and of their application in specific circumstances.

9.   The fact that a religion is recognized as a state religion or that it is established as official or traditional or that its followers comprise the majority of the population, shall not result in any impairment of the enjoyment of any of the rights under the Covenant, including articles 18 and 27, nor in any discrimination against adherents of other religions or non-believers. In particular, certain measures discriminating against the latter, such as measures restricting eligibility for government service to members of the predominant religion or giving economic privileges to them or imposing special restrictions on the practice of other faiths, are not in accordance with the prohibition of discrimination based on religion or belief and the guarantee of equal protection under article 26. The measures contemplated by article 20, paragraph 2, of the Covenant constitute important safeguards against infringement of the rights of religious minorities and of other religious groups to exercise the rights guaranteed by articles 18 and 27, and against acts of violence or persecution directed toward those groups. The Committee wishes to be informed of measures taken by States parties concerned to protect the practices of all religions or beliefs from infringement and to protect their followers from discrimination. Similarly, information as to respect for the rights of religious minorities under article 27 is necessary for the Committee to assess the extent to which the freedom of thought, conscience, religion and belief has been implemented by States parties. States parties concerned should also include in their reports information relating to practices considered by their laws and jurisprudence to be punishable as blasphemous.

10.   If a set of beliefs is treated as official ideology in constitutions, statutes, proclamations of the ruling parties, etc., or in actual practice, this shall not result in any impairment of the freedoms under article 18 or any other rights recognized under the Covenant nor in any discrimination against persons who do not accept the official ideology or who oppose it.

11.   Many individuals have claimed the right to refuse to perform military service (conscientious objection) on the basis that such right derives from their freedoms under article 18. In response to such claims, a growing number of States have in their laws exempted from compulsory military service citizens who genuinely hold religious or other beliefs that forbid the performance of military service and replaced it with alternative national service. The Covenant does not explicitly refer to a right of conscientious objection, but the Committee believes that such a right can be derived from article 18, inasmuch as the obligation to use lethal force may seriously conflict with the freedom of conscience and the right to manifest one's religion or belief. When this right is recognized by law or practice, there shall be no differentiation among conscientious objectors on the basis of the nature of their particular beliefs; like-

wise, there shall be no discrimination against conscientious objectors because they have failed to perform military service. The Committee invites States parties to report on the conditions under which persons can be exempted from military service on the basis of their rights under article 18 and on the nature and length of alternative national service.

UNITED NATIONS HUMAN RIGHTS COMMITTEE
GENERAL COMMENT NO. 11 (19)
(ARTICLE 20)

Adopted by the U.N. Human Rights Committee on 29 July 1983.
U.N. Doc. CCPR/C/21/Add.2 (1983),
reprinted in U.N. Doc. HRI/GEN/1/ Rev.1 at 12 (1994).

1.   Not all reports submitted by States parties have provided sufficient information as to the implementation of article 20 of the Covenant. In view of the nature of article 20, States parties are obliged to adopt the necessary legislative measures prohibiting the actions referred to therein. However, the reports have shown that in some States such actions are neither prohibited by law nor are appropriate efforts intended or made to prohibit them. Furthermore, many reports failed to give sufficient information concerning the relevant national legislation and practice.

2.   Article 20 of the Covenant states that any propaganda for war and any advocacy of national, racial or religious hatred that constitutes incitement to discrimination, hostility or violence shall be prohibited by law. In the opinion of the Committee, these required prohibitions are fully compatible with the right of freedom of expression as contained in article 19 the exercise of which carries with it special duties and responsibilities. The prohibition under paragraph 1 extends to all forms of propaganda threatening or resulting in an act of aggression or breach of the peace contrary to the Charter of the United Nations, while paragraph 2 is directed against any advocacy of national, racial or religious hatred that constitutes incitement to discrimination, hostility or violence, whether such propaganda or advocacy has aims which are internal or external to the State concerned. The provisions of article 20, paragraph 1, do not prohibit advocacy of the sovereign right of self-defence or the right of peoples to self-determination and independence in accordance with the Charter of the United Nations. For article 20 to become fully effective there ought to be a law making it clear that propaganda and advocacy as described therein are contrary to public policy and providing for an appropriate sanction in case of violation. The Committee, therefore, believes that States parties which have not yet done so should take the measures necessary to fulfil the obligations contained in article 20, and should themselves refrain from any such propaganda or advocacy.

United Nations Human Rights Committee
General Comment No. 23 (50)
(Article 27)

Adopted by the U.N. Human Rights Committee on 6 April 1994.
U.N. Doc. CCPR/C/21/Rev.1/Add.5 (1994),
reprinted in U.N. Doc. HRI/GEN/1/ Rev.1 at 38 (1994).

1.   Article 27 of the Covenant provides that, in those States in which ethnic, religious or linguistic minorities exist, persons belonging to such minorities shall not be denied the right, in community with the other members of their group, to enjoy their own culture, to profess and practice their own religion, or to use their own language. The Committee observes that this article establishes and recognizes a right which is conferred on individuals belonging to minority groups and which is distinct from, and additional to, all the other rights which, as individuals in common with everyone else, they are already entitled to enjoy under the Covenant.

2.   In some communications submitted to the Committee under the Optional Protocol, the right protected under article 27 has been confused with the right of peoples to self-determination proclaimed in article 1 of the Covenant. Further, in reports submitted by States parties under article 40 of the Covenant, the obligations placed upon States parties under article 27 have sometimes been confused with their duty under article 2(1) to ensure the enjoyment of the rights guaranteed under the Covenant without discrimination and also with equality before the law and equal protection of the law under article 26.

3.1.   The Covenant draws a distinc-

tion between the right to self-determination and the rights protected under article 27. The former is expressed to be a right belonging to peoples and is dealt with in a separate part (part I) of the Covenant. Self-determination is not a right cognizable under the Optional Protocol. Article 27, on the other hand, relates to rights conferred on individuals as such and is included, like the articles relating to other personal rights conferred on individuals, in part III of the Covenant and is cognizable under the Optional Protocol.[1]

3.2.   The enjoyment of the rights to which article 27 relates does not prejudice the sovereignty and territorial integrity of a State party. At the same time, one or other aspect of the rights of individuals protected under that article - for example, to enjoy a particular culture - may consist in a way of life which is closely associated with territory and use of its resources.[2] This may particularly be true of members of indigenous communities constituting a minority.

4.   The Covenant also distinguishes the rights protected under article 27 from the guarantees under articles 2(1) and 26. The entitlement, under article 2(1), to enjoy the rights under the Covenant without discrimination applies to all individuals within the territory or under the jurisdiction of the State whether or not those persons belong to a minority. In addition, there is a distinct

right provided under article 26 of equality before the law, equal protection of the law, and non-discrimination in respect of rights granted and obligations imposed by the States. It governs the exercise of all rights, whether protected under the Covenant or not, which the State party confers by law on individuals within its territory or under its jurisdiction, irrespective of whether they belong to the minorities specified in article 27 or not.[3] Some States parties who claim that they do not discriminate on grounds of ethnicity, language or religion wrongly contend, on that basis alone, that they have no minorities.

5.1. The terms used in article 27 indicate that the persons designed to be protected are those who belong to a group and who share in common a culture, a religion and/or a language. Those terms also indicate that the individuals designed to be protected need not be citizens of the State party. In this regard, the obligations deriving from article 2(1) are also relevant, since a State party is required under that article to ensure that the rights protected under the Covenant are available to all individuals within its territory and subject to its jurisdiction, except rights which are expressly made to apply to citizens, for example, political rights under article 25. A State party may not, therefore, restrict the rights under article 27 to its citizens alone.

5.2. Article 27 confers rights on persons belonging to minorities which "exist" in a State party. Given the nature and scope of the rights envisaged under the article, it is not relevant to determine the degree of permanence that the term "exist" connotes. Those rights simply are that individuals belonging to those minorities should not be denied the right, in community with members of their group, to enjoy their own culture, to practice their religion and speak their language. Just as they need not be nationals or citizens, they need not be permanent residents. Thus, migrant workers or even visitors in a State party constituting such minorities are entitled not to be denied the exercise of those rights. As any other individual in the territory of the State party, they would, also for this purpose, have the general rights, for example, to freedom of association, of assembly, and of expression. The existence of an ethnic, religious or linguistic minority in a given State party does not depend upon a decision by that State party but requires to be established by objective criteria.

5.3. The right of individuals belonging to a linguistic minority to use their language among themselves, in private or in public, is distinct from other language rights protected under the Covenant. In particular, it should be distinguished from the general right to freedom of expression protected under article 19. The latter right is available to all persons, irrespective of whether they belong to minorities or not. Further, the right protected under article 27 should be distinguished from the particular right which article 14(3)(f) of the Covenant confers on accused persons to interpretation where they cannot understand or speak the language used in the courts. Article 14(3)(f) does not, in any other circumstances, confer on accused persons the right to use or speak the language of their choice in court proceedings.[4]

6.1. Although article 27 is expressed in negative terms, that article, nevertheless, does recognize the existence of a "right" and requires that it shall not be denied. Consequently, a State party is under an obligation to ensure that the existence and the exercise of this right are protected against their denial or violation. Positive measures of protection are, therefore, required not only against the acts of the State party itself, whether through its legislative, judicial or administrative authorities, but also against the acts of other persons within the State party.

6.2. Although the rights protected under article 27 are individual rights, they depend in turn on the ability of the minority group to maintain its culture, language or religion. Accordingly, positive measures by States may also be necessary to protect the identity of a minority and the rights of its members to enjoy and develop their culture and language and to practice their religion, in community with the other members of the group. In this connection, it has to be observed that such positive measures must respect the provisions of articles 2(1) and 26 of the Covenant, both as regards the treatment between different minorities and the treatment between the persons belonging to them and the remaining part of the population. However, as long as those measures are aimed at correcting conditions which prevent or impair the enjoyment of the rights guaranteed under article 27, they may constitute a legitimate differentiation under the Covenant, provided that they are based on reasonable and objective criteria.

7. With regard to the exercise of the cultural rights protected under article 27, the Committee observes that culture manifests itself in many forms, including a particular way of life associated with the use of land resources, especially in the case of indigenous peoples. That right may include such traditional activities as fishing or hunting and the right to live in reserves protected by law.[5] The enjoyment of those rights may require positive legal measures of protection and measures to ensure the effective participation of members of minority communities in decisions which affect them.

8. The Committee observes that none of the rights protected under article 27 of the Covenant may be legitimately exercised in a manner or to an extent inconsistent with the other provisions of the Covenant.

9. The Committee concludes that article 27 relates to rights whose protection imposes specific obligations on States parties. The protection of these rights is directed towards ensuring the survival and continued development of the cultural, religious and social identity of the minorities concerned, thus enriching the fabric of society as a whole. Accordingly, the Committee observes that these rights must be protected as such and should not be confused with other personal rights conferred on one and all under the Covenant. States parties, therefore, have an obligation to ensure that the exercise of these rights is fully protected and they should indicate in their reports the measures they have adopted to this end.

Notes

1. See *Official Records of the General Assembly, Thirty-ninth Session, Supplement No. 40*, (A/39/40), annex VI, General Comment No. 12 (21) (article 1), also issued in document CCPR/C/21/Rev.1; ibid. *Forty-fifth Session, Supplement No. 40*, (A/45/40), vol. II, annex IX, Sect. A, communication No. 167/1984, (*Bernard Ominayak, Chief of the Lubicon Lake Band, v. Canada),* views adopted on 26 March 1990.
2. See ibid., *Forty-third Session, Supplement No. 40*, (A/43/40), annex VII, sect. G, communication No. 197/1985, (*Kitok v. Sweden),* views adopted on 27 July 1988.
3. See ibid., *Forty-second Session, Supplement No. 40*, (A/42/40), annex VIII, sect. D, communica-

tion No. 182/1984, (*F.H. Zwaan-de-Vries v. the Netherlands*), views adopted on 9 April 1987; ibid. sect. C, communication No. 180/1984 (*L.G.Danning v. the Netherlands*), views adopted on 9 April 1987.

4. See ibid., *Forty-fifth Session, Supplement No. 40*, (A/45/40), vol. II, annex X, sect. A, communication No. 220/1987, (*T.K. v. France*), decision of 8 November 1989; ibid. sect. B, communication No. 222/1987, (*M.K. v. France*), decision of 9 November 1989.

5. See Notes 1 and 2 above, communication No. 167/1984, (*Bernard Ominayak, Chief of the Lubicon Lake Band, v. Canada*),views adopted on 26 March 1990 and communication No. 197/1985, (*Kitok v. Sweden*), views adopted on 27 July 1998.

THE UNITED NATIONS DECLARATION ON THE ELIMINATION OF ALL FORMS OF INTOLERANCE AND DISCRIMINATION BASED ON RELIGION OR BELIEF

The General Assembly of the United Nations initiated the preparation of a draft declaration and a draft international convention on the elimination of all forms of religious intolerance by resolution 1781(XVII) of 7 December 1962. The 1981 declaration reprinted below is the culmination of a portion of that mandate. In 1967 the Commission on Human Rights adopted a preamble and twelve substantive articles of a draft convention. At its twenty-second session, also in 1967, the General Assembly was able to adopt the preamble and the first article of this draft. No substantial further action has been taken on the draft convention. The provisions adopted by the Commission on Human Rights, along with a number of draft procedural articles adopted by the Sub-Commission on Prevention of Discrimination and Protection of Minorities, are reprinted in Note by the Secretary-General, *Elimination of All Forms of Religious Intolerance*, U.N. Doc. A/7930 (27 July 1970) as well as in the 1967 *Yearbook of the United Nations* at 491-494.

In 1988 the Sub-Commission was asked "to examine ... the issues and factors which should be considered before any drafting of a further binding instrument on freedom of religion or belief takes place." In response to this request, see the Working Paper prepared by Theo van Boven on the usefulness of preparing a binding instrument on religious discrimination and intolerance, U.N. Doc. E/CN.4/Sub.2/1989/32.

United Nations Declaration on the Elimination of All Forms of Intolerance and Discrimination Based on Religion or Belief

Proclaimed by United Nations General Assembly Resolution 36/55 on 25 November 1981.

The General Assembly,

Considering that one of the basic principles of the Charter of the United Nations is that of the dignity and equality inherent in all human beings, and that all Member States have pledged themselves to take joint and separate action in co-operation with the Organization to promote and encourage universal respect for and observance of human rights and fundamental freedoms for all, without distinction as to race, sex, language or religion,

Considering that the Universal Declaration of Human Rights and the International Covenants on Human Rights proclaim the principles of non-discrimination and equality before the law and the right to freedom of thought, conscience, religion and belief,

Considering that the disregard and infringement of human rights and fundamental freedoms, in particular of the right to freedom of thought, conscience, religion or whatever belief, have brought, directly or indirectly, wars and great suffering to mankind, especially where they serve as a means of foreign interference in the internal affairs of other States and amount to kindling hatred between peoples and nations,

Considering that religion or belief, for anyone who professes either, is one of the fundamental elements in his conception of life and that freedom of religion or belief should be fully respected and guaranteed,

Considering that it is essential to promote understanding, tolerance and respect in matters relating to freedom of religion and belief and to ensure that the use of religion or belief for ends inconsistent with the Charter of the United Nations, other relevant instruments of the United Nations and the purposes and principles of the present Declaration is inadmissible,

Convinced that freedom of religion and belief should also contribute to the attainment of the goals of world peace, social justice and friendship among peoples and to the elimination of ideologies or practices of colonialism and racial discrimination,

Noting with satisfaction the adoption of several, and the coming into force of some, conventions, under the aegis of the United Nations and of the specialized agencies, for the elimination of various forms of discrimination,

Concerned by manifestations of intolerance and by the existence of discrimination in matters of religion or belief still in evidence in some areas of the world,

Resolved to adopt all necessary measures for the speedy elimination of such intolerance in all its forms and manifestations and to prevent and combat discrimination on the grounds of religion or belief,

102

Proclaims this Declaration on the Elimination of All Forms of Intolerance and of Discrimination Based on Religion or Belief:

Article 1

1. Everyone shall have the right to freedom of thought, conscience and religion. This right shall include freedom to have a religion or whatever belief of his choice, and freedom, either individually or in community with others and in public or private, to manifest his religion or belief in worship, observance, practice and teaching.

2. No one shall be subject to coercion which would impair his freedom to have a religion or belief of his choice.

3. Freedom to manifest one's religion or belief may be subject only to such limitations as are prescribed by law and are necessary to protect public safety, order, health or morals or the fundamental rights and freedoms of others.

Article 2

1. No one shall be subject to discrimination by any State, institution, group of persons or person on the grounds of religion or other beliefs.

2. For the purposes of the present Declaration, the expression "intolerance and discrimination based on religion or belief" means any distinction, exclusion, restriction or preference based on religion or belief and having as its purpose or as its effect nullification or impairment of the recognition, enjoyment or exercise of human rights and fundamental freedoms on an equal basis.

Article 3

Discrimination between human beings on the grounds of religion or belief constitutes an affront to human dignity and a disavowal of the principles of the Charter of the United Nations, and shall be condemned as a violation of the human rights and fundamental freedoms proclaimed in the Universal Declaration of Human Rights and enunciated in detail in the International Covenants on Human Rights, and as an obstacle to friendly and peaceful relations between nations.

Article 4

1. All States shall take effective measures to prevent and eliminate discrimination on the grounds of religion or belief in the recognition, exercise and enjoyment of human rights and fundamental freedoms in all fields of civil, economic, political, social and cultural life.

2. All States shall make all efforts to enact or rescind legislation where necessary to prohibit any such discrimination, and to take all appropriate measures to combat intolerance on the grounds of religion or other beliefs in this matter.

Article 5

1. The parents or, as the case may be, the legal guardians of the child have the right to organize the life within the family in accordance with their religion or belief and bearing in mind the moral education in which they believe the child should be brought up.

2. Every child shall enjoy the right to have access to education in the matter of religion or belief in accordance with the wishes of his parents or, as the case may be, legal guardians, and shall not be compelled to receive teaching on religion or belief against the wishes of his parents or legal guardians, the best interests of the child being the guiding principle.

3. The child shall be protected from any form of discrimination on the ground of religion or belief. He shall be brought up in a spirit of understanding, tolerance, friendship among peoples, peace and universal brotherhood, respect for freedom of religion or belief of others, and in full consciousness that his energy and talents

should be devoted to the service of his fellow men.

4. In the case of a child who is not under the care either of his parents or of legal guardians, due account shall be taken of their expressed wishes or of any other proof of their wishes in the matter of religion or belief, the best interests of the child being the guiding principle.

5. Practices of a religion or belief in which a child is brought up must not be injurious to his physical or mental health or to his full development, taking into account article 1, paragraph 3, of the present Declaration.

Article 6

In accordance with article 1 of the present Declaration, and subject to the provisions of article 1, paragraph 3, the right to freedom of thought, conscience, religion or belief shall include, *inter alia*, the following freedoms:

(a) To worship or assemble in connexion with a religion or belief, and to establish and maintain places for these purposes;

(b) To establish and maintain appropriate charitable or humanitarian institutions;

(c) To make, acquire and use to an adequate extent the necessary articles and materials related to the rites or customs of a religion or belief;

(d) To write, issue and disseminate relevant publications in these areas;

(e) To teach a religion or belief in places suitable for these purposes;

(f) To solicit and receive voluntary financial and other contributions from individuals and institutions;

(g) To train, appoint, elect or designate by succession appropriate leaders called for by the requirements and standards of any religion or belief;

(h) To observe days of rest and to celebrate holidays and ceremonies in accordance with the precepts of one's religion or belief;

(i) To establish and maintain communications with individuals and communities in matters of religion and belief at the national and international levels.

Article 7

The rights and freedoms set forth in the present Declaration shall be accorded in national legislation in such a manner that everyone shall be able to avail himself of such rights and freedoms in practice.

Article 8

Nothing in the present Declaration shall be construed as restricting or derogating from any right defined in the Universal Declaration of Human Rights and the International Covenants on Human Rights.

CONVENTION ON THE PREVENTION AND PUNISHMENT OF THE CRIME OF GENOCIDE

Adopted and Opened for Signature by United Nations General Assembly Resolution 260A (III) on 9 December 1948. Entered into Force 12 January 1951.

The Contracting Parties,

Having considered the declaration made by the General Assembly of the United Nations in its resolution 96 (I) dated 11 December 1946 that genocide is a crime under international law, contrary to the spirit and aims of the United Nations and condemned by the civilized world;

Recognizing that at all periods of history genocide has inflicted great losses on humanit; and

Being convinced that, in order to liberate mankind from such an odious scourge, international co-operation is required,

Hereby agree as hereinafter provided.

Article I

The Contracting Parties confirm that genocide, whether committed in time of peace or in time of war, is a crime under international law which they undertake to prevent and to punish.

Article II

In the present Convention, genocide means any of the following acts committed with intent to destroy, in whole or in part, a national, ethnical, racial or religious group, as such:

(a) Killing members of the group;

(b) Causing serious bodily or mental harm to members of the group;

(c) Deliberately inflicting on the group conditions of life calculated to bring about its physical destruction in whole or in part;

(d) Imposing measures intended to prevent births within the group;

(e) Forcibly transferring children of the group to another group.

Article III

The following acts shall be punishable:

(a) Genocide;

(b) Conspiracy to commit genocide;

(c) Direct and public incitement to commit genocide;

(d) Attempt to commit genocide;

(e) Complicity in genocide.

Article IV

Persons committing genocide or any of the other acts enumerated in article III shall be punished, whether they are constitutionally responsible rulers, public officials or private individuals.

Article V

The Contracting Parties undertake to enact, in accordance with their respective Constitutions the necessary legislation to give effect to the provisions of the present Convention and, in particular, to provide effective penalties for persons guilty of genocide or any of the other acts enumerated in article III.

Article VI

Persons charged with genocide or any of the other acts enumerated in article III shall be tried by a competent tribunal of the State in the territory of which the act was committed, or by such international penal tribunal as may have jurisdiction with respect to those Contracting Parties which shall have accepted its jurisdiction.

Article VII

Genocide and the other acts enumerated in article III shall not be considered as political crimes for the purpose of extradition.

The Contracting Parties pledge themselves in such cases to grant extradition in accordance with their laws and treaties in force.

Article VIII

Any Contracting Party may call upon the competent organs of the United Nations to take such action under the Charter of the United Nations as they consider appropriate for the prevention and suppression of acts of genocide or any of the other acts enumerated in article III.

Article IX

Disputes between the Contracting Parties relating to the interpretation, application or fulfilment of the present Convention, including those relating to the responsibility of a State for genocide or for any of the other acts enumerated in article III, shall be submitted to the International Court of Justice at the request of any of the parties to the dispute.

Article X

The present Convention, of which the Chinese, English, French, Russian and Spanish texts are equally authentic, shall bear the date of 9 December 1948.

Article XI

The present Convention shall be open until 31 December 1949 for signature on behalf of any Member of the United Nations and of any non-member State to which an invitation to sign has been addressed by the General Assembly.

The present Convention shall be ratified, and the instruments of ratification shall be deposited with the Secretary-General of the United Nations.

After 1 January 1950, the present Convention may be acceded to on behalf of any Member of the United Nations and of any nonmember State which has received an invitation as aforesaid.

Instruments of accession shall be deposited with the Secretary-General of the United Nations.

Article XII

Any Contracting Party may at any time, by notification addressed to the Secretary-General of the United Nations, extend the application of the present Convention to all or any of the territories for the conduct of whose foreign relations that Contracting Party is responsible.

Article XIII

On the day when the first twenty instruments of ratification or accession have been deposited, the Secretary-General shall draw up a *procès-verbal* and transmit a copy of it to each Member of the United Nations and to each of the non-member States contemplated in article XI.

The present Convention shall come into force on the ninetieth day following the date of deposit of the twentieth instrument of ratification or accession.

Any ratification or accession effected subsequent to the latter date shall become effective on the ninetieth day following the deposit of the instrument of ratification or accession.

Article XIV

The present Convention shall remain in effect for a period of ten years as from the date of its coming into force.

It shall thereafter remain in force for

successive periods of five years for such Contracting Parties as have not denounced it at least six months before the expiration of the current period.

Denunciation shall be effected by a written notification addressed to the Secretary-General of the United Nations.

Article XV

If, as a result of denunciations, the number of Parties to the present Convention should become less than sixteen, the Convention shall cease to be in force as from the date on which the last of these denunciations shall become effective.

Article XVI

A request for the revision of the present Convention may be made at any time by any Contracting Party by means of a notification in writing addressed to the Secretary-General.

The General Assembly shall decide upon the steps, if any, to be taken in respect of such request.

Article XVII

The Secretary-General of the United Nations shall notify all Members of the United Nations and the non-member States contemplated in article XI of the following:

(a) Signatures, ratifications and accessions received in accordance with article XI;

(b) Notifications received in accordance with article XII;

(c) The date upon which the present Convention comes into force in accordance with article XIII;

(d) Denunciations received in accordance with article XIV;

(e) The abrogation of the Convention in accordance with article XV;

(f) Notifications received in accordance with article XVI.

Article XVIII

The original of the present Convention shall be deposited in the archives of the United Nations.

A certified copy of the Convention shall be transmitted to all Members of the United Nations and to the non-member States contemplated in article XI.

Article XIX

The present Convention shall be registered by the Secretary-General of the United Nations on the date of its coming into force.

UNESCO CONVENTION AGAINST DISCRIMINATION
IN EDUCATION [SELECTIONS]

Adopted by the General Conference of the United Nations Educational, Scientific and
Cultural Organization on 14 December 1960.
Entered into Force 22 May 1962.

The General Conference of the United Nations Educational, Scientific and Cultural Organization, meeting in Paris from 14 November to 15 December 1960, at its eleventh session,

Recalling that the Universal Declaration of Human Rights asserts the principle of non-discrimination and proclaims that every person has the right to education,

Considering that discrimination in education is a violation of rights enunciated in that Declaration,

Considering that, under the terms of its Constitution, the United Nations Educational, Scientific and Cultural Organization has the purpose of instituting collaboration among the nations with a view to furthering for all universal respect for human rights and equality of educational opportunity,

Recognizing that, consequently, the United Nations Educational, Scientific and Cultural Organization, while respecting the diversity of national educational systems, has the duty not only to proscribe any form of discrimination in education but also to promote equality of opportunity and treatment for all in education,

Having before it proposals concerning the different aspects of discrimination in education, constituting item 17.1.4 of the agenda of the session,

Having decided at its tenth session that this question should be made the subject of an international convention as well as of recommendations to Member States,

Adopts this Convention on the fourteenth day of December 1960.

Article 1

1. For the purposes of this Convention, the term "discrimination" includes any distinction, exclusion, limitation or preference which, being based on race, colour, sex, language, religion, political or other opinion, national or social origin, economic condition or birth, has the purpose or effect of nullifying or impairing equality of treatment in education and in particular:

(a) Of depriving any person or group of persons of access to education of any type or at any level;

(b) Of limiting any person or group of persons to education of an inferior standard;

(c) Subject to the provisions of Article 2 of this Convention, of establishing or maintaining separate educational systems or institutions for persons or groups of persons; or

(d) Of inflicting on any person or group of persons conditions which are incompatible with the dignity of man.

2. For the purposes of this Convention, the term "education" refers to

all types and levels of education, and includes access to education, the standard and quality of education, and the conditions under which it is given.

Article 2

When permitted in a State, the following situations shall not be deemed to constitute discrimination, within the meaning of Article 1 of this Convention:

(a) The establishment or maintenance of separate educational systems or institutions for pupils of the two sexes, if these systems or institutions offer equivalent access to education, provide a teaching staff with qualifications of the same standard as well as school premises and equipment of the same quality, and afford the opportunity to take the same or equivalent courses of study;

(b) The establishment or maintenance, for religious or linguistic reasons, of separate educational systems or institutions offering an education which is in keeping with the wishes of the pupil's parents or legal guardians, if participation in such systems or attendance at such institutions is optional and if the education provided conforms to such standards as may be laid down or approved by the competent authorities, in particular for education of the same level;

(c) The establishment or maintenance of private educational institutions, if the object of the institutions is not to secure the exclusion of any group but to provide educational facilities in addition to those provided by the public authorities, if the institutions are conducted in accordance with that object, and if the education provided conforms with such standards as may be laid down or approved by the competent authorities, in particular for education of the same level.

Article 3

In order to eliminate and prevent dis-crimination within the meaning of this Convention, the States Parties thereto undertake:

(a) To abrogate any statutory provisions and any administrative instructions and to discontinue any administrative practices which involve discrimination in education;

(b) To ensure, by legislation where necessary, that there is no discrimination in the admission of pupils to educational institutions;

(c) Not to allow any differences of treatment by the public authorities between nationals, except on the basis of merit or need, in the matter of school fees and the grant of scholarships or other forms of assistance to pupils and necessary permits and facilities for the pursuit of studies in foreign countries;

(d) Not to allow, in any form of assistance granted by the public authorities to educational institutions, any restrictions or preference based solely on the ground that pupils belong to a particular group;

(e) To give foreign nationals resident within their territory the same access to education as that given to their own nationals.

Article 4

The States Parties to this Convention undertake furthermore to formulate, develop and apply a national policy which, by methods appropriate to the circumstances and to national usage, will tend to promote equality of opportunity and of treatment in the matter of education and in particular:

(a) To make primary education free and compulsory; make secondary education in its different forms generally available and accessible to all; make higher education equally accessible to all on the basis of individual capacity; assure compliance by all with the obligation to attend school prescribed by law;

(b)   To ensure that the standards of education are equivalent in all public education institutions of the same level, and that the conditions relating to the quality of education provided are also equivalent;

(c)   To encourage and intensify by appropriate methods the education of persons who have not received any primary education or who have not completed the entire primary education course and the continuation of their education on the basis of individual capacity;

(d)   To provide training for the teaching profession without discrimination.

Article 5

1.   The States Parties to this Convention agree that:

(a)   Education shall be directed to the full development of the human personality and to the strengthening of respect for human rights and fundamental freedoms; it shall promote understanding, tolerance and friendship among all nations, racial or religious groups, and shall further the activities of the United Nations for the maintenance of peace;

(b)   It is essential to respect the liberty of parents and, where applicable, of legal guardians, firstly to choose for their children institutions other than those maintained by the public authorities but conforming to such minimum educational standards as may be laid down or approved by the competent authorities and, secondly, to ensure in a manner consistent with the procedures followed in the State for the application of its legislation, the religious and moral education of the children in conformity with their own convictions; and no person or group of persons should be compelled to receive religious instruction inconsistent with his or their conviction;

(c)   It is essential to recognize the right of members of national minorities to carry on their own educational activities, including the maintenance of schools and, depending on the educational policy of each State, the use or the teaching of their own language, provided however:

(i)   That this right is not exercised in a manner which prevents the members of these minorities from understanding the culture and language of the community as a whole and from participating in its activities, or which prejudices national sovereignty;

(ii)   That the standard of education is not lower than the general standard laid down or approved by the competent authorities; and

(iii)   That attendance at such schools is optional.

2.   The States Parties to this Convention undertake to take all necessary measures to ensure the application of the principles enunciated in paragraph 1 of this article.

Article 6

In the application of this Convention, the States Parties to it undertake to pay the greatest attention to any recommendations hereafter adopted by the General Conference of the United Nations Educational, Scientific and Cultural Organization defining the measures to be taken against the different forms of discrimination in education and for the purpose of ensuring equality of opportunity and treatment in education.

Article 7

The States Parties to this Convention shall in their periodic reports submitted to the General Conference of the United Nations Educational, Scientific and Cultural Organization on dates and in a manner to be determined by it, give information on the legislative and administrative provisions which they have adopted and other action which they have taken for the application of this Convention, including that taken for the formulation and the development of the national policy defined in Article 4 as well as the results achieved and the obstacles encountered in the application of that policy.

Article 8

Any dispute which may arise between any two or more States Parties to this Convention concerning the interpretation or application of this Convention which is not settled by negotiations shall at the request of the parties to the dispute be referred, failing other means of settling the dispute, to the International Court of Justice for decision.

Article 9

Reservations to this Convention shall not be permitted.

Article 10

This Convention shall not have the effect of diminishing the rights which individuals or groups may enjoy by virtue of agreements concluded between two or more States, where such rights are not contrary to the letter or spirit of this Convention.

*   *   *

The States Parties to this Convention

*   *   *

Have agreed as follows:

PART I

Article 1

1. In this Convention, the term "racial discrimination" shall mean any distinction, exclusion, restriction or preference based on race, colour, descent, or national or ethnic origin which has the purpose or effect of nullifying or impairing the recognition, enjoyment or exercise, on an equal footing, of human rights and fundamental freedoms in the political, economic, social, cultural or any other field of public life.

2. This Convention shall not apply to distinctions, exclusions, restrictions or preferences made by a State Party to this Convention between citizens and non-citizens.

3. Nothing in this Convention may be interpreted as affecting in any way the legal provisions of States Parties concerning nationality, citizenship or naturalization, provided that such provisions do not discriminate against any particular nationality.

4. Special measures taken for the sole purpose of securing adequate advancement of certain racial or ethnic groups or individuals requiring such protection as may be necessary in order to ensure such groups or individuals equal enjoyment or exercise of human rights and fundamental freedoms shall not be deemed racial discrimination, provided, however, that such measures do not, as a consequence, lead to the maintenance of separate rights for different racial groups and that they shall not be continued after the objectives for which they were taken have been achieved.

Article 2

1. States Parties condemn racial discrimination and undertake to pursue by all appropriate means and without delay a policy of eliminating racial discrimination in all its forms and promoting understanding among all races, and, to this end:

(a) Each State Party undertakes to engage in no act or practice of racial discrimination against persons, groups of persons or institutions and to ensure that all public authorities and public institutions, national and local, shall act in conformity with this obligation;

(b) Each State Party undertakes not to sponsor, defend or support racial discrimination by any persons or organizations;

(c) Each State Party shall take effective measures to review governmental, national and local policies, and to amend, rescind or nullify any laws and regulations which have the effect of creating or perpetuating racial discrimination wherever it exists;

(d) Each State Party shall prohibit and bring to an end, by all appropriate means, including legislation as required by circumstances, racial discrimination by any persons, group or organization;

(e) Each State Party undertakes to encourage, where appropriate, integrationist multi-racial organizations and movements and other means of eliminating barriers between races, and to discourage anything which tends to strengthen racial division.

2. States Parties shall, when the circumstances so warrant, take, in the social, economic, cultural and other fields, special and concrete measures to ensure the adequate development and protection of certain racial groups or individuals belonging to them, for the purpose of guaranteeing them the full and equal enjoyment of human rights and fundamental freedoms. These measures shall in no case entail as a consequence the maintenance of unequal or separate rights for different racial groups after the objectives for which they were taken have been achieved.

Article 3

States Parties particularly condemn racial segregation and *apartheid* and undertake to prevent, prohibit and eradicate all practices of this nature in territories under their jurisdiction.

Article 4

States Parties condemn all propaganda and all organizations which are based on ideas or theories of superiority of one race or group of persons of one colour or ethnic origin, or which attempt to justify or promote racial hatred and discrimination in any form, and undertake to adopt immediate and positive measures designed to eradicate all incitement to, or acts of, such discrimination and, to this end, with due regard to the principles embodied in the Universal Declaration of Human Rights and the rights expressly set forth in article 5 of this Convention, *inter alia*:

(a) Shall declare an offence punishable by law all dissemination of ideas based on racial superiority or hatred, incitement to

racial discrimination, as well as all acts of violence or incitement to such acts against any race or group of persons of another colour or ethnic origin, and also the provision of any assistance to racist activities, including the financing thereof;

(b) Shall declare illegal and prohibit organizations, and also organized and all other propaganda activities, which promote and incite racial discrimination, and shall recognize participation in such organizations or activities as an offence punishable by law;

(c) Shall not permit public authorities or public institutions, national or local, to promote or incite racial discrimination.

Article 5

In compliance with the fundamental obligations laid down in article 2 of this Convention, States Parties undertake to prohibit and to eliminate racial discrimination in all its forms and to guarantee the right of everyone, without distinction as to race, colour, or national or ethnic origin, to equality before the law, notably in the enjoyment of the following rights:

(a) The right to equal treatment before the tribunals and all other organs administering justice;

(b) The right to security of person and protection by the State against violence or bodily harm, whether inflicted by government officials or by any individual, group or institution;

(c) Political rights, in particular the rights to participate in elections — to vote and to stand for election — on the basis of universal and equal suffrage, to take part in the Government as well as in the conduct of public affairs at any level and to have equal access to public service;

(d) Other civil rights, in particular:

(i) The right to freedom of movement and residence within the border of the State;

(ii) The right to leave any country,

including one's own, and to return to one's country;

(iii) The right to nationality;

(iv) The right to marriage and choice of spouse;

(v) The right to own property alone as well as in association with others;

(vi) The right to inherit;

(vii) The right to freedom of thought, conscience and religion;

(viii) The right to freedom of opinion and expression;

(ix) The right to freedom of peaceful assembly and association;

(e) Economic, social and cultural rights, in particular:

(i) The rights to work, to free choice of employment, to just and favourable conditions of work, to protection against unemployment, to equal pay for equal work, to just and favourable remuneration;

(ii) The right to form and join trade unions;

(iii) The right to housing;

(iv) The right to public health, medical care, social security and social services;

(v) The right to education and training;

(vi) The right to equal participation in cultural activities;

(f) The right of access to any place or service intended for use by the general public, such as transport, hotels, restaurants, cafes, theatres and parks.

Article 6

States Parties shall assure to everyone within their jurisdiction effective protection and remedies, through the competent national tribunals and other State institutions, against any acts of racial discrimination which violate his human rights and fundamental freedoms contrary to this Convention, as well as the right to seek from such tribunals just and adequate reparation or satisfaction for any damage suffered as a result of such discrimination.

Article 7

States Parties undertake to adopt immediate and effective measures, particularly in the fields of teaching, education, culture and information, with a view to combating prejudices which lead to racial discrimination and to promoting understanding, tolerance and friendship among nations and racial or ethnical groups, as well as to propagating the purposes and principles of the Charter of the United Nations, the Universal Declaration of Human Rights, the United Nations Declaration on the Elimination of All Forms of Racial Discrimination, and this Convention.

*   *   *

NOTE: THE COMMITTEE ON THE ELIMINATION OF RACIAL DISCRIMINATION

The Committee on the Elimination of Racial Discrimination (CERD) was established under the Convention to consider reports of states parties on the measures taken to give effect to the provisions of the Convention and, for those state parties that have agreed, to consider communications from individuals claiming violations of the Convention. CERD prepares annual reports for the United Nations General Assembly that include summaries of the consideration of the reports of states parties, decisions and general recommendations adopted by the Committee, and opinions of the Committee on individual communications. The reports are published as *Official Records of the General Assembly, Supplement No. 18.* The Convention contains the authoritative international law definition of discrimination, and its obligations are important in situations where there is little distinction between ethnicity and religion, especially in the case of minorities. In its consideration of reports of states parties, CERD has addressed a number of instances of restriction of the right to freedom of religion and discrimination of religious minorities.

CONVENTION ON THE ELIMINATION OF ALL FORMS OF DISCRIMINATION AGAINST WOMEN [SELECTIONS]

Adopted and Opened for Signature by United Nations General Assembly Resolution 34/180 on 18 December 1979.
Entered into Force 3 September 1981.

The States Parties to the present Convention,

* * *

Aware that a change in the traditional role of men as well as the role of women in society and in the family is needed to achieve full equality between men and women ... .

* * *

Have agreed on the following:

PART I

Article 1

For the purposes of the present Convention, the term "discrimination against women" shall mean any distinction, exclusion or restriction made on the basis of sex which has the effect or purpose of impairing or nullifying the recognition, enjoyment or exercise by women, irrespective of their marital status, on a basis of equality of men and women, of human rights and fundamental freedoms in the political, economic, social, cultural, civil or any other field.

Article 2

States Parties condemn discrimination against women in all its forms, agree to pursue by all appropriate means and without delay a policy of eliminating discrimination against women and, to this end, undertake:

(a)　To embody the principle of the equality of men and women in their national constitutions or other appropriate legislation if not yet incorporated therein and to ensure, through law and other appropriate means, the practical realization of this principle;

(b)　To adopt appropriate legislative and other measures, including sanctions where appropriate, prohibiting all discrimination against women;

(c)　To establish legal protection of the rights of women on an equal basis with men and to ensure through competent national tribunals and other public institutions the effective protection of women against any act of discrimination;

(d)　To refrain from engaging in any act or practice of discrimination against women and to ensure that public authorities and institutions shall act in conformity with this obligation;

(e)　To take all appropriate measures to eliminate discrimination against women by any person, organization or enterprise;

(f)　To take all appropriate measures, including legislation, to modify or abolish existing laws, regulations, customs and practices which constitute discrimination against women;

(g)　To repeal all national penal provisions which constitute discrimination against women.

Article 3

States Parties shall take in all fields, in particular in the political, social, economic and cultural fields, all appropriate measures, including legislation, to ensure the full development and advancement of women, for the purpose of guaranteeing them the exercise and enjoyment of human rights and fundamental freedoms on a basis of equality with men.

Article 4

1.   Adoption by States Parties of temporary special measures aimed at accelerating de facto equality between men and women shall not be considered discrimination as defined in the present Convention, but shall in no way entail as a consequence the maintenance of unequal or separate standards; these measures shall be discontinued when the objectives of equality of opportunity and treatment have been achieved.

2.   Adoption by States Parties of special measures, including those measures contained in the present Convention, aimed at protecting maternity shall not be considered discriminatory.

Article 5

States Parties shall take all appropriate measures:

(a)   To modify the social and cultural patterns of conduct of men and women, with a view to achieving the elimination of prejudices and customary and all other practices which are based on the idea of the inferiority or the superiority of either of the sexes or on stereotyped roles for men and women;

(b)   To ensure that family education includes a proper understanding of maternity as a social function and the recognition of the common responsibility of men and women in the upbringing and development of their children, it being understood that the interest of the children is the primordial consideration in all cases.

*   *   *

PART III

Article 10

States Parties shall take all appropriate measures to eliminate discrimination against women in order to ensure to them equal rights with men in the field of education and in particular to ensure, on a basis of equality of men and women:

(a)   The same conditions for career and vocational guidance, for access to studies and for the achievement of diplomas in educational establishments of all categories in rural as well as in urban areas; this equality shall be ensured in pre-school, general, technical, professional and higher technical education, as well as in all types of vocational training;

(b)   Access to the same curricula, the same examinations, teaching staff with qualifications of the same standard and school premises and equipment of the same quality;

(c)   The elimination of any stereotyped concept of the roles of men and women at all levels and in all forms of education by encouraging coeducation and other types of education which will help to achieve this aim and, in particular, by the revision of textbooks and school programmes and the adaptation of teaching methods;

(d)   The same opportunities to benefit from scholarships and other study grants;

(e)   The same opportunities for access to programmes of continuing education, including adult and functional literacy programmes, particularly those aimed at reducing, at the earliest possible time, any gap in education existing between men and women;

(f)   The reduction of female student drop-out rates and the organization of programmes for girls and women who have left school prematurely;

(g) The same opportunities to participate actively in sports and physical education;

(h) Access to specific educational information to help to ensure the health and well-being of families, including information and advice on family planning.

* * *

Article 13

States Parties shall take all appropriate measures to eliminate discrimination against women in other areas of economic and social life in order to ensure, on a basis of equality of men and women, the same rights, in particular:

(a) The right to family benefits;

(b) The right to bank loans, mortgages and other forms of financial credit;

(c) The right to participate in recreational activities, sports and all aspects of cultural life.

* * *

PART IV

Article 15

1. States Parties shall accord to women equality with men before the law.

2. States Parties shall accord to women, in civil matters, a legal capacity identical to that of men and the same opportunities to exercise that capacity. In particular, they shall give women equal rights to conclude contracts and to administer property and shall treat them equally in all stages of procedure in courts and tribunals.

3. States Parties agree that all contracts and all other private instruments of any kind with a legal effect which is directed at restricting the legal capacity of women shall be deemed null and void.

4. States Parties shall accord to men and women the same rights with regard to the law relating to the movement of persons and the freedom to choose their residence and domicile.

Article 16

1. States Parties shall take all appropriate measures to eliminate discrimination against women in all matters relating to marriage and family relations and in particular shall ensure, on a basis of equality of men and women:

(a) The same right to enter into marriage;

(b) The same right freely to choose a spouse and to enter into marriage only with their free and full consent;

(c) The same rights and responsibilities during marriage and at its dissolution;

(d) The same rights and responsibilities as parents, irrespective of their marital status, in matters relating to their children; in all cases the interests of the children shall be paramount;

(e) The same rights to decide freely and responsibly on the number and spacing of their children and to have access to the information, education and means to enable them to exercise these rights;

(f) The same rights and responsibilities with regard to guardianship, wardship, trusteeship and adoption of children, or similar institutions where these concepts exist in national legislation; in all cases the interests of the children shall be paramount;

(g) The same personal rights as husband and wife, including the right to choose a family name, a profession and an occupation;

(h) The same rights for both spouses in respect of the ownership, acquisition, management, administration, enjoyment and disposition of property, whether free of charge or for a valuable consideration.

2. The betrothal and the marriage of a child shall have no legal effect, and all necessary action, including legislation, shall be taken to specify a minimum age for marriage and to make the registration of marriages in an official registry compulsory.

* * *

NOTE: THE COMMITTEE ON THE ELIMINATION OF DISCRIMINATION AGAINST WOMEN

The Committee on the Elimination of Discrimination Against Women (CEDAW) was established under the Convention to consider reports of states parties on the measures taken to give effect to the provisions of the Convention. CEDAW prepares annual reports for the United Nations General Assembly that include the Committee's general recommendations and summaries of the consideration of the reports of states parties. The reports are published as *Official Records of the General Assembly, Supplement No. 38*. The obligations of the Convention are significant in situations where the rights of women, particularly the obligation to ensure the equal rights of women and men, may come into conflict with religious or customary beliefs and practices.

A number of states parties have made declarations or reservations to the Convention due to perceived conflicts with national laws implementing or based on religious law. For example, several Muslim states have made reservations to all or portions of Article 16 (marriage and family relations) with the objection that these provisions conflict with shari'a. Israel has made a similar reservation to safeguard the implementation of personal status law in the courts of its various religious communities. Other states, such as Brazil, Ireland, Malta, Korea and Thailand, have also submitted reservations. See Note by the Secretary-General, *Declarations, Reservations, Objections and Notifications of Withdrawal of Reservations Relating to the Convention on the Elimination of All Forms of Discrimination Against Women*. U.N. Doc. CEDAW/SP/1992/2 (1991).

CEDAW has issued several general recommendations touching on conflicts between the obligations of the Convention and traditional religious and cultural practices. General Recommendation 14 on Female Circumcision, U.N. Doc. A/45/38 at 80, calls on states parties to take the necessary affirmative measures to eradicate that practice. General Recommendation 19 on Violence Against Women, U.N. Doc. A/47/38 at 1, identifies traditional attitudes that perpetuate such violent and coercive practices as forced marriage, dowry deaths and female circumcision as contributing to discrimination against women. General Recommendation 21 on Equality in Marriage and Family Relations, U.N. Doc. A/49/38, contains important provisions on the relationship between personal status law (in many states based on traditional religious law) and the principle of equal rights of men and women in the decision to marry, the marriage itself, the dissolution of marriage and inheritance. The portion of General Recommendation 21 commenting on Article 16 of the Convention is reprinted below.

COMMITTEE ON THE ELIMINATION OF DISCRIMINATION AGAINST WOMEN: GENERAL RECOMMENDATION 21 ON EQUALITY IN MARRIAGE AND FAMILY RELATIONS

Adopted by the Committee on the Elimination of Discrimination Against Women at its Thirteenth Session in 1994.

U.N. Doc. A/49/38, reprinted in U.N. Doc. HRI/GEN/1/rev.1 at 90 (1994).

1.   The Convention on the Elimination of All Forms of Discrimination against Women (General Assembly resolution 34/180, annex) affirms the equality of human rights for women and men in society and in the family. The Convention has an important place among international treaties concerned with human rights.

2.   Other conventions and declarations also confer great significance on the family and woman's status within it. These include the Universal Declaration of Human Rights (General Assembly resolution 217/A (III), the International Covenant on Civil and Political Rights (resolution 2200 A (XXI), annex), the Convention on the Nationality of Married Women (resolution 1040 (XI), annex), the Convention on Consent to Marriage, Minimum Age for Marriage and Registration of Marriages (resolution 1763 A (XVII), annex) and the subsequent Recommendation thereon (resolution 2018 (XX)) and the Nairobi Forward-looking Strategies for the Advancement of Women.

3.   The Convention on the Elimination of All Forms of Discrimination against Women recalls the inalienable rights of women which are already embodied in the above-mentioned conventions and declarations, but it goes further by recognizing the importance of culture and tradition in shaping the thinking and behaviour of men and women and the significant part they play in restricting the exercise of basic rights by women.

Background

4.   The year 1994 has been designated by the General Assembly in its resolution 44/82 as the International Year of the Family. The Committee wishes to take the opportunity to stress the significance of compliance with women's basic rights within the family as one of the measures which will support and encourage the national celebrations that will take place.

5.   Having chosen in this way to mark the International Year of the Family, the Committee wishes to analyse three articles in the Convention that have special significance for the status of women in the family:

*   *   *

Article 16

1.   *States parties shall take all appropriate measures to eliminate discrimination against women in all matters relating to marriage and family relations and in particular shall ensure, on a basis of equality of men and women:*

(a)   The same right to enter into marriage;

(b)   The same right freely to choose a spouse and to enter into marriage only with their free and full consent;

(c)   The same rights and responsibilities during marriage and at its dissolution;

(d)   The same rights and responsibilities as parents, irrespective of their marital status, in matters relating to their children; in all cases the interests of the children shall be paramount;

(e)   The same rights to decide freely and responsibly on the number and spacing of their children and to have access to the information, education and means to enable them to exercise these rights;

(f)   The same rights and responsibilities with regard to guardianship, wardship, trusteeship and adoption of children, or similar institutions where these concepts exist in national legislation; in all cases the interests of the children shall be paramount;

(g)   The same personal rights as husband and wife, including the right to choose a family name, a profession and an occupation;

(h)   The same rights for both spouses in respect of the ownership, acquisition, management, administration, enjoyment and disposition of property, whether free of charge or for a valuable consideration.

2.   The betrothal and the marriage of a child shall have no legal effect, and all necessary action, including legislation, shall be taken to specify a minimum age for marriage and to make the registration of marriages in an official registry compulsory.

Comment

Public and private life

11.   Historically, human activity in public and private life has been viewed differently and regulated accordingly. In all societies women who have traditionally performed their roles in the private or domestic sphere have long had those activities treated as inferior.

12.   As such activities are invaluable for the survival of society, there can be no justification for applying different and discriminatory laws or customs to them. Reports of States parties disclose that there are still countries where *de jure* equality does not exist. Women are thereby prevented from having equal access to resources and from enjoying equality of status in the family and society. Even where *de jure* equality exists, all societies assign different roles, which are regarded as inferior, to women. In this way, principles of justice and equality contained in particular in article 16 and also in articles 2, 5 and 24 of the Convention are being violated.

Various forms of family

13.   The form and concept of the family can vary from State to State, and even between regions within a State. Whatever form it takes, and whatever the legal system, religion, custom or tradition within the country, the treatment of women in the family both at law and in private must accord with the principles of equality and justice for all people, as article 2 of the Convention requires.

Polygamous marriages

14.   States parties' reports also disclose that polygamy is practised in a number of countries. Polygamous marriage contravenes a woman's right to equality with men, and can have such serious emotional and financial consequences for her and her dependants that such marriages ought to be discouraged and prohibited. The Committee notes with concern that some States parties, whose constitutions guarantee equal rights,

permit polygamous marriage in accordance with personal or customary law. This violates the constitutional rights of women, and breaches the provisions of article 5 (a) of the Convention.

Article 16 (1) (a) and (b)

15. While most countries report that national constitutions and laws comply with the Convention, custom, tradition and failure to enforce these laws in reality contravene the Convention.

16. A woman's right to choose a spouse and enter freely into marriage is central to her life and to her dignity and equality as a human being. An examination of States parties' reports discloses that there are countries which, on the basis of custom, religious beliefs or the ethnic origins of particular groups of people, permit forced marriages or remarriages. Other countries allow a woman's marriage to be arranged for payment or preferment and in others women's poverty forces them to marry foreign nationals for financial security. Subject to reasonable restrictions based for example on a woman's youth or consanguinity with her partner, a woman's right to choose when, if, and whom she will marry must be protected and enforced at law.

Article 16 (1) (c)

17. An examination of States parties' reports discloses that many countries in their legal systems provide for the rights and responsibilities of married partners by relying on the application of common law principles, religious or customary law, rather than by complying with the principles contained in the Convention. These variations in law and practice relating to marriage have wide-ranging consequences for women, invariably restricting their rights to equal status and responsibility within marriage. Such limitations often result in the husband being accorded the status of head of household and primary decision-maker and therefore contravene the provisions of the Convention.

18. Moreover, generally a de facto union is not given legal protection at all. Women living in such relationships should have their equality of status with men both in family life and in the sharing of income and assets protected by law. Such women should share equal rights and responsibilities with men for the care and raising of dependent children or family members.

Article 16 (1) (d) and (f)

19. As provided in article 5 (b), most States recognize the shared responsibility of parents for the care, protection and maintenance of children. The principle that "the best interests of the child shall be the paramount consideration" has been included in the Convention on the Rights of the Child (General Assembly resolution 44/25, annex) and seems now to be universally accepted. However, in practice, some countries do not observe the principle of granting the parents of children equal status, particularly when they are not married. The children of such unions do not always enjoy the same status as those born in wedlock and, where the mothers are divorced or living apart, many fathers fail to share the responsibility of care, protection and maintenance of their children.

20. The shared rights and responsibilities enunciated in the Convention should be enforced at law and as appropriate through legal concepts of guardianship, wardship, trusteeship and adoption. States parties should ensure that by their laws both parents, regardless of their marital status and whether they live with their children or not, share equal rights and responsibilities for their children.

Article 16 (1) (e)

21.   The responsibilities that women have to bear and raise children affect their right of access to education, employment and other activities related to their personal development. They also impose inequitable burdens of work on women. The number and spacing of their children have a similar impact on women's lives and also affect their physical and mental health, as well as that of their children. For these reasons, women are entitled to decide on the number and spacing of their children.

22.   Some reports disclose coercive practices which have serious consequences for women, such as forced pregnancies, abortions or sterilization. Decisions to have children or not, while preferably made in consultation with spouse or partner, must not nevertheless be limited by spouse, parent, partner or Government. In order to make an informed decision about safe and reliable contraceptive measures, women must have information about contraceptive measures and their use, and guaranteed access to sex education and family planning services, as provided in article 10 (h) of the Convention.

23.   There is general agreement that where there are freely available appropriate measures for the voluntary regulation of fertility, the health, development and well-being of all members of the family improves. Moreover, such services improve the general quality of life and health of the population, and the voluntary regulation of population growth helps preserve the environment and achieve sustainable economic and social development.

Article 16 (1) (g)

24.   A stable family is one which is based on principles of equity, justice and individual fulfilment for each member. Each partner must therefore have the right to choose a profession or employment that is best suited to his or her abilities, qualifications and aspirations, as provided in article 11 (a) and (c) of the Convention. Moreover, each partner should have the right to choose his or her name, thereby preserving individuality and identity in the community and distinguishing that person from other members of society. When by law or custom a woman is obliged to change her name on marriage or at its dissolution, she is denied these rights.

Article 16 (1) (h)

25.   The rights provided in this article overlap with and complement those in article 15 (2) in which an obligation is placed on States to give women equal rights to enter into and conclude contracts and to administer property.

26.   Article 15 (1) guarantees women equality with men before the law. The right to own, manage, enjoy and dispose of property is central to a woman's right to enjoy financial independence, and in many countries will be critical to her ability to earn a livelihood and to provide adequate housing and nutrition for herself and for her family.

27.   In countries that are undergoing a programme of agrarian reform or redistribution of land among groups of different ethnic origins, the right of women, regardless of marital status, to share such redistributed land on equal terms with men should be carefully observed.

28.   In most countries, a significant proportion of the women are single or divorced and many have the sole responsibility to support a family. Any discrimination in the division of property that rests on the premise that the man alone is responsible for the support of the women and children of his family and that he can and will hon-

ourably discharge this responsibility is clearly unrealistic. Consequently, any law or custom that grants men a right to a greater share of property at the end of a marriage or de facto relationship, or on the death of a relative, is discriminatory and will have a serious impact on a woman's practical ability to divorce her husband, to support herself or her family and to live in dignity as an independent person.

29. All of these rights should be guaranteed regardless of a woman's marital status.

Marital property

30. There are countries that do not acknowledge that right of women to own an equal share of the property with the husband during a marriage or de facto relationship and when that marriage or relationship ends. Many countries recognize that right, but the practical ability of women to exercise it may be limited by legal precedent or custom.

31. Even when these legal rights are vested in women, and the courts enforce them, property owned by a woman during marriage or on divorce may be managed by a man. In many States, including those where there is a community-property regime, there is no legal requirement that a woman be consulted when property owned by the parties during marriage or de facto relationship is sold or otherwise disposed of. This limits the woman's ability to control disposition of the property or the income derived from it.

32. In some countries, on division of marital property, greater emphasis is placed on financial contributions to property acquired during a marriage, and other contributions, such as raising children, caring for elderly relatives and discharging household duties are diminished. Often, such contributions of a non-financial nature by the wife

enable the husband to earn an income and increase the assets. Financial and non-financial contributions should be accorded the same weight.

33. In many countries, property accumulated during a de facto relationship is not treated at law on the same basis as property acquired during marriage. Invariably, if the relationship ends, the woman receives a significantly lower share than her partner. Property laws and customs that discriminate in this way against married or unmarried women with or without children should be revoked and discouraged.

Inheritance

34. Reports of States parties should include comment on the legal or customary provisions relating to inheritance laws as they affect the status of women as provided in the Convention and in Economic and Social Council resolution 884D (XXXIV), in which the Council recommended that States ensure that men and women in the same degree of relationship to a deceased are entitled to equal shares in the estate and to equal rank in the order of succession. That provision has not been generally implemented.

35. There are many countries where the law and practice concerning inheritance and property result in serious discrimination against women. As a result of this uneven treatment, women may receive a smaller share of the husband's or father's property at his death than would widowers and sons. In some instances, women are granted limited and controlled rights and receive income only from the deceased's property. Often inheritance rights for widows do not reflect the principles of equal ownership of property acquired during marriage. Such provisions contravene the Convention and should be abolished.

Article 16 (2)

36. In the Vienna Declaration and Programme of Action adopted by the World Conference on Human Rights, held at Vienna from 14 to 25 June 1993, States are urged to repeal existing laws and regulations and to remove customs and practices which discriminate against and cause harm to the girl child.

Article 16 (2) and the provisions of the Convention on the Rights of the Child preclude States parties from permitting or giving validity to a marriage between persons who have not attained their majority. In the context of the Convention on the Rights of the Child, "a child means every human being below the age of 18 years unless, under the law applicable to the child, majority is attained earlier". Notwithstanding this definition, and bearing in mind the provisions of the Vienna Declaration, the Committee considers that the minimum age for marriage should be 18 years for both man and woman. When men and women marry, they assume important responsibilities. Consequently, marriage should not be permitted before they have attained full maturity and capacity to act. According to the World Health Organization, when minors, particularly girls, marry and have children, their health can be adversely affected and their education is impeded. As a result their economic autonomy is restricted.

37. This not only affects women personally but also limits the development of their skills and independence and reduces access to employment, thereby detrimentally affecting their families and communities.

38. Some countries provide for different ages for marriage for men and women. As such provisions assume incorrectly that women have a different rate of intellectual development from men, or that their stage of physical and intellectual development at marriage is immaterial, these provisions should be abolished. In other countries, the betrothal of girls or undertakings by family members on their behalf is permitted. Such measures contravene not only the Convention, but also a women's right freely to choose her partner.

39. Parties should also require the registration of all marriages whether contracted civilly or according to custom or religious law. The State can thereby ensure compliance with the Convention and establish equality between partners, a minimum age for marriage, prohibition of bigamy and polygamy and the protection of the rights of children.

Recommendations

Violence against women

40. In considering the place of women in family life, the Committee wishes to stress that the provisions of general recommendation 19 (eleventh session) concerning violence against women have great significance for women's abilities to enjoy rights and freedoms on an equal basis with men. States parties are urged to comply with that general recommendation to ensure that, in both public and family life, women will be free of the gender-based violence that so seriously impedes their rights and freedoms as individuals.

Reservations

41. The Committee has noted with alarm the number of States parties which have entered reservations to the whole or part of article 16, especially when a reservation has also been entered to article 2, claiming that compliance may conflict with a commonly held vision of the family based, *inter alia,* on cultural or religious beliefs or on the country's economic or political status.

42. Many of these countries hold a belief in the patriarchal structure of a family which places a father, husband or son in a favourable position. In some countries where fundamentalist or other extremist views or economic hardships have encouraged a return to old values and traditions, women's place in the family has deteriorated sharply. In others, where it has been recognized that a modern society depends for its economic advance and for the general good of the community on involving all adults equally, regardless of gender, these taboos and reactionary or extremist ideas have progressively been discouraged.

43. Consistent with articles 2, 3 and 24 in particular, the Committee requires that all States parties gradually progress to a stage where, by its resolute discouragement of notions of the inequality of women in the home, each country will withdraw its reservation, in particular to articles 9, 15 and 16 of the Convention.

44. States parties should resolutely discourage any notions of inequality of women and men which are affirmed by laws, or by religious or private law or by custom, and progress to the stage where reservations, particularly to article 16, will be withdrawn.

45. The Committee noted, on the basis of its examination of initial and subsequent periodic reports, that in some States parties to the Convention that had ratified or acceded without reservation, certain laws, especially those dealing with family, do not actually conform to the provisions of the Convention.

46. Their laws still contain many measures which discriminate against women based on norms, customs and socio-cultural prejudices. These States, because of their specific situation regarding these articles, make it difficult for the Committee to evaluate and understand the status of women.

47. The Committee, in particular on the basis of articles 1 and 2 of the Convention, requests that those States parties make the necessary efforts to examine the de facto situation relating to the issues and to introduce the required measures in their national legislations still containing provisions discriminatory to women.

Reports

48. Assisted by the comments in the present general recommendation, in their reports States parties should:

(a) Indicate the stage that has been reached in the country's progress to removal of all reservations to the Convention, in particular reservations to article 16;

(b) Set out whether their laws comply with the principles of articles 9, 15 and 16 and where, by reason of religious or private law or custom, compliance with the law or with the Convention is impeded.

Legislation

49. States parties should, where necessary to comply with the Convention, in particular in order to comply with articles 9, 15 and 16, enact and enforce legislation.

Encouraging compliance with the Convention

50. Assisted by the comments in the present general recommendation, and as required by articles 2, 3 and 24, States parties should introduce measures directed at encouraging full compliance with the principles of the Convention, particularly where religious or private law or custom conflict with those principles.

CONVENTION ON THE RIGHTS OF THE CHILD [SELECTIONS]

Adopted And Opened for Signature by United Nations General Assembly
Resolution 44/25 on 20 November 1989.
Entered into Force 2 September 1990.

PREAMBLE

The States Parties to the present Convention,

*   *   *

Taking due account of the importance of the traditions and cultural values of each people for the protection and harmonious development of the child,

*   *   *

Have agreed as follows:

PART I

Article 1

For the purposes of the present Convention a child means every human being below the age of 18 years unless, under the law applicable to the child, majority is attained earlier.

Article 2

1.   States Parties shall respect and ensure the rights set forth in the present Convention to each child within their jurisdiction without discrimination of any kind, irrespective of the child's or his or her parent's or legal guardian's race, colour, sex, language, religion, political or other opinion, national, ethnic or social origin, property, disability, birth or other status.

2.   States Parties shall take all appropriate measures to ensure that the child is protected against all forms of discrimination or punishment on the basis of the status, activities, expressed opinions, or beliefs of the child's parents, legal guardians, or family members.

Article 3

1.   In all actions concerning children, whether undertaken by public or private social welfare institutions, courts of law, administrative authorities or legislative bodies, the best interests of the child shall be a primary consideration.

2.   States Parties undertake to ensure the child such protection and care as is necessary for his or her well-being, taking into account the rights and duties of his or her parents, legal guardians, or other individuals legally responsible for him or her, and, to this end, shall take all appropriate legislative and administrative measures.

3.   States Parties shall ensure that the institutions, services and facilities responsible for the care or protection of children shall conform with the standards established by competent authorities, particularly in the areas of safety, health, in the number and suitability of their staff, as well as competent supervision.

Article 4

States Parties shall undertake all appropriate legislative, administrative, and other measures for the implementation of the rights recognized in the present Convention. With regard to economic, social and cultural rights, States Parties shall undertake such measures to the maximum extent of their available resources and, where needed, within the framework of international co-operation.

Article 5

States Parties shall respect the responsibilities, rights and duties of parents or, where applicable, the members of the extended family or community as provided for by local custom, legal guardians or other persons legally responsible for the child, to provide, in a manner consistent with the evolving capacities of the child, appropriate direction and guidance in the exercise by the child of the rights recognized in the present Convention.

*   *   *

Article 12

1.   States Parties shall assure to the child who is capable of forming his or her own views the right to express those views freely in all matters affecting the child, the views of the child being given due weight in accordance with the age and maturity of the child.

*   *   *

Article 13

1.   The child shall have the right to freedom of expression; this right shall include freedom to seek, receive and impart information and ideas of all kinds, regardless of frontiers, either orally, in writing or in print, in the form of art, or through any other media of the child's choice.

2.   The exercise of this right may be subject to certain restrictions, but these shall only be such as are provided by law and are necessary:

(a)   for respect of the rights or reputations of others; or

(b)   for the protection of national security or of public order (*ordre public*), or of public health or morals.

Article 14

1   States Parties shall respect the right of the child to freedom of thought, conscience and religion.

2.   State Parties shall respect the rights and duties of the parents and, when applicable, legal guardians, to provide direction to the child in the exercise of his or her right in a manner consistent with the evolving capacities of the child.

3.   Freedom to manifest one's religion or beliefs may be subject only to such limitations as are prescribed by law and are necessary to protect public safety, order, health, or morals, or the fundamental rights and freedoms of others.

Article 15

1.   States Parties recognise the rights of the child to freedom of association and to freedom of peaceful assembly.

2   No restrictions may be placed on the exercise of these rights other than those imposed in conformity with the law and which are necessary in a democratic society in the interests of national security or public safety, public order (*ordre public*), the protection of public health or morals or the protection of the rights and freedoms of others.

*   *   *

Article 17

States Parties recognize the important function performed by the mass media and shall ensure that the child has access to information and material from a diversity of national and international sources, especially those aimed at the promotion of his or her social, spiritual and moral well-being and physical and mental health.   To this end, States Parties shall:

(a)   Encourage the mass media to disseminate information and material of social and cultural benefit to the child and in accordance with the spirit of article 29;

(b)   Encourage international co-operation in the production, exchange and dissemination of such information and material from a diversity of cultural, national and international sources;

(c) Encourage the production and dissemination of children's books;

(d) Encourage the mass media to have particular regard to the linguistic needs of the child who belongs to a minority group or who is indigenous;

(e) Encourage the development of appropriate guidelines for the protection of the child from information and material injurious to his or her well-being, bearing in mind the provisions of articles 13 and 18 [ed. note: article 18 on parental responsibility].

*   *   *

Article 20

1. A child temporarily or permanently deprived of his or her family environment, or in whose own best interests cannot be allowed to remain in that environment, shall be entitled to special protection and assistance provided by the State.

2. States Parties shall in accordance with their national laws ensure alternative care for such a child.

3. Such care could include, *inter alia*, foster placement, *Kafala* of Islamic law, adoption or if necessary placement in suitable institutions for the care of children. When considering solutions, due regard shall be paid to the desirability of continuity in a child's upbringing and to the child's ethnic, religious, cultural and linguistic background.

*   *   *

Article 24

1. States Parties recognize the right of the child to the enjoyment of the highest attainable standard of health and to facilities for the treatment of illness and rehabilitation of health. States Parties shall strive to ensure that no child is deprived of his or her right of access to such health care services.

2. States Parties shall pursue full implementation of this right and, in particular, shall take appropriate measures:

(a) to diminish infant and child mortality;

(b) to ensure the provision of necessary medical assistance and health care to all children with emphasis on the development of primary health care;

(c) to combat disease and malnutrition, including within the framework of primary health care, through *inter alia* the application of readily available technology and through the provision of adequate nutritious foods and clean drinking-water, taking into consideration the dangers and risks of environmental pollution;

(d) to ensure appropriate pre-natal and post-natal health care for mothers;

(e) to ensure that all segments of society, in particular parents and children, are informed, have access to education and are supported in the use of basic knowledge of child health and nutrition, the advantages of breast-feeding, hygiene and environmental sanitation and the prevention of accidents;

(f) to develop preventive health care, guidance for parents and family planning education and services.

3. States Parties shall take all effective and appropriate measures with a view to abolishing traditional practices prejudicial to the health of children.

4. States Parties undertake to promote and encourage international co-operation with a view to achieving progressively the full realization of the right recognized in this article. In this regard, particular account shall be taken of the needs of developing countries.

*   *   *

Article 28

1. States Parties recognize the right of the child to education, and with a view to achieving this right progressively and on the basis of equal opportunity, they shall, in particular:

(a) make primary education compulsory and available free to all;

(b) encourage the development of different forms of secondary education, including general and vocational education, make them available and accessible to every child, and take appropriate measures such as the introduction of free education and offering financial assistance in case of need;

(c) make higher education accessible to all on the basis of capacity by every appropriate means;

(d) make educational and vocational information and guidance available and accessible to all children;

(e) take measures to encourage regular attendance at schools and the reduction of drop-out rates.

2. States Parties shall take all appropriate measures to ensure that school discipline is administered in a manner consistent with the child's human dignity and in conformity with the present Convention.

3. States Parties shall promote and encourage international co-operation in matters relating to education, in particular with a view to contributing to the elimination of ignorance and illiteracy throughout the world and facilitating access to scientific and technical knowledge and modern teaching methods. In this regard, particular account shall be taken of the needs of developing countries.

Article 29

1. States Parties agree that the education of the child shall be directed to:

(a) the development of the child's personality, talents and mental and physical abilities to their fullest potential;

(b) the development of respect for human rights and fundamental freedoms, and for the principles enshrined in the Charter of the United Nations;

(c) the development of respect for the child's parents, his or her own cultural identity, language and values, for the national values of the country in which the child is living, the country from which he or she may originate, and for civilizations different from his or her own;

(d) the preparation of the child for responsible life in a free society, in the spirit of understanding, peace, tolerance, equality of sexes, and friendship among all peoples, ethnic, national and religious groups and persons of indigenous origin;

(e) the development of respect for the natural environment.

2. No part of this article or article 28 shall be construed so as to interfere with the liberty of individuals and bodies to establish and direct educational institutions, subject always to the observance of the principles set forth in paragraph 1 of the present article and to the requirements that the education given in such institutions shall conform to such minimum standards as may be laid down by the State.

Article 30

In those States in which ethnic, religious or linguistic minorities or persons of indigenous origin exist, a child belonging to such a minority or who is indigenous shall not be denied the right, in community with other members of his or her group, to enjoy his or her own culture, to profess and practice his or her own religion, or to use his or her own language.

* * *

NOTE: THE COMMITTEE ON THE RIGHTS OF THE CHILD

The Committee on the Rights of the Child was established under the Convention to receive reports of states parties on the measures adopted to give effect to the rights recognized under the Convention, the progress made in securing the enjoyment of those rights and any factors or limitations affecting the degree of fulfillment of obligations under the Convention. The Committee prepares reports for the General Assembly periodically that include recommendations made by the Committee and summaries of the consideration of the reports of states parties. The reports are published as *Official Records of the General Assembly, Supplement No. 41*. The obligations of the Convention are important in situations concerning the role of religion in education and where the rights of the child and the religious rights of the parents may conflict.

DRAFT UNITED NATIONS DECLARATION ON THE RIGHTS OF INDIGENOUS PEOPLES [SELECTIONS]

Adopted by the U.N. Sub-Commission on the Prevention of Discrimination and Protection of Minorities by Resolution 1994/45 on 26 August 1994.

U.N. Docs. E/CN.4/1995/2; E/CN.4/Sub.2/1994/56.

Affirming that indigenous peoples are equal in dignity and rights to all other peoples, while recognizing the right of all peoples to be different, to consider themselves different, and to be respected as such,

Affirming also that all peoples contribute to the diversity and richness of civilizations and cultures, which constitute the common heritage of humankind,

Affirming further that all doctrines, policies and practices based on or advocating superiority of peoples or individuals on the basis of national origin, racial, religious, ethnic or cultural differences are racist, scientifically false, legally invalid, morally condemnable and socially unjust,

Reaffirming also that indigenous peoples, in the exercise of their rights, should be free from discrimination of any kind,

Concerned that indigenous peoples have been deprived of their human rights and fundamental freedoms, resulting, *inter alia*, in their colonization and dispossession of their lands, territories and resources, thus preventing them from exercising, in particular, their right to development in accordance with their own needs and interests,

Recognizing the urgent need to respect and promote the inherent rights and characteristics of indigenous peoples, especially their rights to their lands, territories and resources, which derive from their political, economic and social structures and from their cultures, spiritual traditions, histories and philosophies,

Welcoming the fact that indigenous peoples are organizing themselves for political, economic, social and cultural enhancement and in order to bring an end to all forms of discrimination and oppression wherever they occur,

Convinced that control by indigenous peoples over developments affecting them and their lands, territories and resources will enable them to maintain and strengthen their institutions, cultures and traditions, and to promote their development in accordance with their aspirations and needs,

Recognizing also that respect for indigenous knowledge, cultures and traditional practices contributes to sustainable and equitable development and proper management of the environment,

*   *   *

Solemnly proclaims the following United Nations Declaration on the Rights of Indigenous Peoples:

PART I

Article 1

Indigenous peoples have the right to the full and effective enjoyment of all human rights and fundamental freedoms recognized in the Charter of the United Nations, the Universal Declaration of Human Rights and international human rights law.

Article 2
Indigenous individuals and peoples are free and equal to all other individuals and peoples in dignity and rights, and have the right to be free from any kind of adverse discrimination, in particular that based on their indigenous origin or identity.

Article 3
Indigenous peoples have the right of self-determination. By virtue of that right they freely determine their political status and freely pursue their economic, social and cultural development.

Article 4
Indigenous peoples have the right to maintain and strengthen their distinct political, economic, social and cultural characteristics, as well as their legal systems, while retaining their rights to participate fully, if they so choose, in the political, economic, social and cultural life of the State.

*   *   *

PART II

*   *   *

Article 7
Indigenous peoples have the collective and individual right not to be subjected to ethnocide and cultural genocide, including prevention of and redress for:

(a) Any action which has the aim or effect of depriving them of their integrity as distinct peoples, or of their cultural values or ethnic identities;

(b) Any action which has the aim or effect of dispossessing them of their lands, territories or resources;

(c) Any form of population transfer which has the aim or effect of violating or undermining any of their rights;

(d) Any form of assimilation or integration by other cultures or ways of life imposed on them by legislative, administrative or other measures;

(e) Any form of propaganda directed against them.

Article 8
Indigenous peoples have the collective and individual right to maintain and develop their distinct identities and characteristics, including the right to identify themselves as indigenous and to be recognized as such.

Article 9
Indigenous peoples and individuals have the right to belong to an indigenous community or nation, in accordance with the traditions and customs of the community or nation concerned. No disadvantage of any kind may arise from the exercise of such a right.

*   *   *

PART III

Article 12
Indigenous peoples have the right to practise and revitalize their cultural traditions and customs. This includes the right to maintain, protect and develop the past, present and future manifestations of their cultures, such as archaeological and historical sites, artifacts, designs, ceremonies, technologies and visual and performing arts and literature, as well as the right to the restitution of cultural, intellectual, religious and spiritual property taken without their free and informed consent or in violation of their laws, traditions and customs.

Article 13

Indigenous peoples have the right to manifest, practise, develop and teach their spiritual and religious traditions, customs and ceremonies; the right to maintain, protect, and have access in privacy to their religious and cultural sites; the right to the use and control of ceremonial objects; and the right to the repatriation of human remains.

States shall take effective measures, in conjunction with the indigenous peoples concerned, to ensure that indigenous sacred places, including burial sites, be preserved, respected and protected.

Article 14

Indigenous peoples have the right to revitalize, use, develop and transmit to future generations their histories, languages, oral traditions, philosophies, writing systems and literatures, and to designate and retain their own names for communities, places and persons.

States shall take effective measures, whenever any right of indigenous peoples may be threatened, to ensure this right is protected and also to ensure that they can understand and be understood in political, legal and administrative proceedings, where necessary through the provision of interpretation or by other appropriate means.

PART IV

Article 15

Indigenous children have the right to all levels and forms of education of the State. All indigenous peoples also have this right and the right to establish and control their educational systems and institutions providing education in their own languages, in a manner appropriate to their cultural methods of teaching and learning.

Indigenous children living outside their communities have the right to be provided access to education in their own culture and language.

States shall take effective measures to provide appropriate resources for these purposes.

Article 16

Indigenous peoples have the right to have the dignity and diversity of their cultures, traditions, histories and aspirations appropriately reflected in all forms of education and public information.

States shall take effective measures, in consultation with the indigenous peoples concerned, to eliminate prejudice and discrimination and to promote tolerance, understanding and good relations among indigenous peoples and all segments of society.

*　　*　　*

PART VI

Article 25

Indigenous peoples have the right to maintain and strengthen their distinctive spiritual and material relationship with the lands, territories, waters and coastal seas and other resources which they have traditionally owned or otherwise occupied or used, and to uphold their responsibilities to future generations in this regard.

Article 26

Indigenous peoples have the right to own, develop, control and use the lands and territories, including the total environment of the lands, air, waters, coastal seas, sea-ice, flora and fauna and other resources which they have traditionally owned or otherwise occupied or used. This includes the right to the full recognition of their laws, traditions and customs, land-tenure systems and institutions for the development and management of resources, and the right to effective measures by States to prevent any interference with, alienation of or encroachment upon these rights.

Article 27

Indigenous peoples have the right to the restitution of the lands, territories and resources which they have traditionally owned or otherwise occupied or used, and which have been confiscated, occupied, used or damaged without their free and informed consent. Where this is not possible, they have the right to just and fair compensation. Unless otherwise freely agreed upon by the peoples concerned, compensation shall take the form of lands, territories and resources equal in quality, size and legal status.

Article 28

Indigenous peoples have the right to the conservation, restoration and protection of the total environment and the productive capacity of their lands, territories and resources, as well as to assistance for this purpose from States and through international co-operation. Military activities shall not take place in the lands and territories of indigenous peoples, unless otherwise freely agreed upon by the peoples concerned.

States shall take effective measures to ensure that no storage or disposal of hazardous materials shall take place in the lands and territories of indigenous peoples.

States shall also take effective measures to ensure, as needed, that programmes for monitoring, maintaining and restoring the health of indigenous peoples, as developed and implemented by the peoples affected by such materials, are duly implemented.

Article 29

Indigenous peoples are entitled to the recognition of the full ownership, control and protection of their cultural and intellectual property.

They have the right to special measures to control, develop and protect their sciences, technologies and cultural manifestations, including human and other genetic resources, seeds, medicines, knowledge of the properties of fauna and flora, oral traditions, literatures, designs and visual and performing arts.

Article 30

Indigenous peoples have the right to determine and develop priorities and strategies for the development or use of their lands, territories and other resources, including the right to require that States obtain their free and informed consent prior to the approval of any project affecting their lands, territories and other resources, particularly in connection with the development, utilization or exploitation of mineral, water or other resources. Pursuant to agreement with the indigenous peoples concerned, just and fair compensation shall be provided for any such activities and measures taken to mitigate adverse environmental, economic, social, cultural or spiritual impact.

PART VII

Article 31

Indigenous peoples, as a specific form of exercising their right to self-determination, have the right to autonomy or self-government in matters relating to their internal and local affairs, including culture, religion, education, information, media, health, housing, employment, social welfare, economic activities, land and resources management, environment and entry by non-members, as well as ways and means for financing these autonomous functions.

Article 32

Indigenous peoples have the collective right to determine their own citizenship in accordance with their customs and traditions. Indigenous citizenship does not impair the right of indigenous individuals to obtain citizenship of the States in which they live.

Indigenous peoples have the right to determine the structures and to select the membership of their institutions in accordance with their own procedures.

Article 33
Indigenous peoples have the right to promote, develop and maintain their institutional structures and their distinctive juridical customs, traditions, procedures and practices, in accordance with internationally recognized human rights standards.

Article 34
Indigenous peoples have the collective right to determine the responsibilities of individuals to their communities.

Article 35
Indigenous peoples, in particular those divided by international borders, have the right to maintain and develop contacts, relations and co-operation, including activities for spiritual, cultural, political, economic and social purposes, with other peoples across borders.

States shall take effective measures to ensure the exercise and implementation of this right.

Article 36
Indigenous peoples have the right to the recognition, observance and enforcement of treaties, agreements and other constructive arrangements concluded with States or their successors, according to their original spirit and intent, and to have States honour and respect such treaties, agreements and other constructive arrangements. Conflicts and disputes which cannot otherwise be settled should be submitted to competent international bodies agreed to by all parties concerned.

PART VIII

Article 37
States shall take effective and appropriate measures, in consultation with the indigenous peoples concerned, to give full effect to the provisions of this Declaration. The rights recognized herein shall be adopted and included in national legislation in such a manner that indigenous peoples can avail themselves of such rights in practice.

*   *   *

PART IX

*   *   *

Article 43
All the rights and freedoms recognized herein are equally guaranteed to male and female indigenous individuals.

*   *   *

NOTE: THE RIGHTS OF INDIGENOUS PEOPLES

The Draft Declaration on the Rights of Indigenous Peoples is the result of over a decade of work by the United Nations Working Group on Indigenous Populations (WGIP), established by the Economic and Social Council in 1982. The mandate of the WGIP includes (1) the development of international standards for the recognition and protection of the rights of indigenous peoples and (2) an annual examination of the status of human rights of indigenous peoples throughout the world. The WGIP makes annual reports on their work to the Sub-Commission on Prevention of Discrimination and Protection of Minorities. In connection with rights related to religion or belief, the draft declaration reflects the unique nature of indigenous religions and the significant history of contact between indigenous peoples and missionary groups. It declares such far-reaching rights as the right to protection against — and redress for — acts of ethnocide or cultural genocide (article 7) and the right to maintain the distinctive spiritual relationship of indigenous peoples with their lands and surrounding natural environment (article 25). The draft declaration was submitted to the Commission on Human Rights in 1995. The Commission has established a working group to consider and elaborate on the draft declaration.

Two international conventions on indigenous peoples have been concluded under the auspices of the International Labour Organization (ILO): ILO Convention No. 169 Concerning Indigenous and Tribal Peoples in Independent Countries (1989), which generally superseded ILO Convention No. 107 Concerning the Protection and Integration of Indigenous and other Tribal and Semi-Tribal Populations in Independent Countries (1957). A major study on the conditions of indigenous peoples, including efforts at assimilation, religious conversion and suppression of religious practices was prepared for the Sub-Commission on Prevention of Discrimination and Protection of Minorities by Special Rapporteur José F. Martínez Cobo, *Study of the Problem of Discrimination Against Indigenous Populations*, U.N. Doc. E/CN.4/Sub.2/1986/7 and Add. 1-4.

REGIONAL HUMAN RIGHTS CONVENTIONS

Rights related to religion and belief are protected in the general human rights conventions adopted by three major regional international organizations: the Organization of African Unity, the Organization of American States and the Council of Europe. The language of the regional conventions regarding these rights follows closely, although is not necessarily identical to, the Universal Declaration of Human Rights or the International Covenant on Civil and Political Rights. Reprinted below are the relevant provisions of The African Charter on Human and Peoples' Rights, the American Convention on Human Rights and the European Convention for the Protection of Human Rights and Fundamental Freedoms and its Protocols. Each of these conventions established human rights commissions that examine reports from states parties and consider communications from individuals claiming violations of protected rights. The American and European Conventions both established special human rights courts. Rights related to religion or belief have been implicated in a number of reports or cases in the regional human rights systems.

EUROPEAN CONVENTION FOR THE PROTECTION OF HUMAN RIGHTS AND FUNDAMENTAL FREEDOMS [SELECTIONS] AND THE FIRST PROTOCOL [SELECTIONS]

Opened for Signature by the Council of Europe on 4 November 1950.
Entered into Force 3 September 1953.

The Governments signatory hereto, being Members of the Council of Europe,

Considering the Universal Declaration of Human Rights proclaimed by the General Assembly of the United Nations on 10th December 1948;

Considering that this declaration aims at securing the universal and effective recognition and observance of the rights therein declared;

Considering that the aim of the Council of Europe is the achievement of greater unity between its Members and that one of the methods by which that aim is to be pursued is the maintenance and further realisation of Human Rights and Fundamental Freedoms;

Reaffirming their profound belief in those fundamental freedoms which are the foundation of justice and peace in the world and are best maintained on the one hand by an effective political democracy and on the other by a common understanding and observance of the Human Rights upon which they depend;

Being resolved, as the governments of European countries which are like-minded and have a common heritage of political traditions, ideals, freedom and the rule of law to take the first steps for the collective enforcement of certain of the rights stated in the Universal Declaration,

Have agreed as follows:

Article 1

The High Contracting Parties shall secure to everyone within their jurisdiction the rights and freedoms defined in Section I of this Convention.

Section I

* * *

Article 8

1. Everyone has the right to respect for his private and family life, his home and his correspondence.
2. There shall be no interference by a public authority with the exercise of this right except such as is in accordance with the law and is necessary in a democratic society in the interests of national security, public safety or the economic well-being of the country, for the prevention of disorder or crime, for the protection of health or morals, or for the protection of the rights and freedoms of others.

Article 9

1. Everyone has the right to freedom of thought, conscience and religion; this right includes freedom to change his religion or belief and freedom, either alone or in community with others and in public or private, to manifest his religion or belief, in

worship, teaching, practice and observance.

2. Freedom to manifest one's religion or beliefs shall be subject only to such limitations as are prescribed by law and are necessary in a democratic society in the interests of public safety, for the protection of public order, health or morals, or for the protection of the rights and freedoms of others.

Article 10

1. Everyone has the right to freedom of expression. This right shall include freedom to hold opinions and to receive and impart information and ideas without interference by public authority and regardless of frontiers. This Article shall not prevent States from requiring the licensing of broadcasting, television or cinema enterprises.

2. The exercise of these freedoms, since it carries with it duties and responsibilities, may be subject to such formalities, conditions, restrictions or penalties as are prescribed by law and are necessary in a democratic society, in the interests of national security, territorial integrity or public safety, for the prevention of disorder or crime, for the protection of health or morals, for the protection of the reputation or rights of others, for preventing the disclosure of information received in confidence, or for maintaining the authority and impartiality of the judiciary.

Article 11

1. Everyone has the right to freedom of peaceful assembly and to freedom of association with others, including the right to form and to join trade unions for the protection of his interests.

2. No restrictions shall be placed on the exercise of these rights other than such as are prescribed by law and are necessary in a democratic society in the interests of national security or public safety, for the prevention of disorder or crime, for the pro-

tection of health or morals or for the protection of the rights and freedoms of others. This Article shall not prevent the imposition of lawful restrictions on the exercise of these rights by members of the armed forces, of the police or of the administration of the state.

Article 12

Men and women of marriageable age have the right to marry and to found a family, according to the national laws governing the exercise of this right.

Article 13

Everyone whose rights and freedoms as set forth in this Convention are violated shall have an effective remedy before a national authority notwithstanding that the violation has been committed by persons acting in an official capacity.

Article 14

The enjoyment of the rights and freedoms set forth in this Convention shall be secured without discrimination on any ground such as sex, race, colour, language, religion, political or other opinion, national or social origin, association with a national minority, property, birth or other status.

Article 15

1. In time of war or other public emergency threatening the life of the nation any High Contracting Party may take measures derogating from its obligations under this Convention to the extent strictly required by the exigencies of the situation, provided that such measures are not inconsistent with its other obligations under international law.

2. No derogation from Article 2, except in respect of deaths resulting from lawful acts of war, or from Articles 3, 4 (paragraph 1) and 7 shall be made under this provision.

3. Any High Contracting Party availing itself of this right of derogation shall keep the Secretary-General of the Council of Europe fully informed of the measures which it has taken and the reasons therefor. It shall also inform the Secretary-General of the Council of Europe when such measures have ceased to operate and the provisions of the Convention are again being fully executed.

Article 16

Nothing in Articles 10, 11 and 14 shall be regarded as preventing the High Contracting Parties from imposing restrictions on the political activity of aliens.

Article 17

Nothing in this Convention may be interpreted as implying for any State, group or person any right to engage in any activity or perform any act aimed at the destruction of any of the rights and freedoms set forth herein or at their limitation to a greater extent than is provided for in the Convention.

Article 18

The restrictions permitted under this Convention to the said rights and freedoms shall not be applied for any purpose other than those for which they have been prescribed.

* * *

FIRST PROTOCOL TO THE CONVENTION FOR THE PROTECTION OF HUMAN RIGHTS AND FUNDAMENTAL FREEDOMS

The governments signatory hereto, being members of the Council of Europe,

Being resolved to take steps to ensure the collective enforcement of certain rights and freedoms other than those already included in Section I of the Convention for the Protection of Human Rights and Fundamental Freedoms signed at Rome on 4th November, 1950 (hereinafter referred to as 'the Convention'),

Have agreed as follows:

* * *

Article 2

No person shall be denied the right to education. In the exercise of any functions which it assumes in relation to education and to teaching, the State shall respect the right of parents to ensure such education and teaching in conformity with their own religious and philosophical convictions.

* * *

PREAMBLE

The American States signatory to the present Convention,

Reaffirming their intention to consolidate in this hemisphere, within the framework of democratic institutions, a system of personal liberty and social justice based on respect for the essential rights of man;

Recognizing that the essential rights of man are not derived from one's being a national of a certain state, but are based upon attributes of the human personality, and that they therefore justify international protection in the form of a convention reinforcing or complementing the protection provided by the domestic law of the American states;

Considering that these principles have been set forth in the Charter of the Organization of American States, in the American Declaration of the Rights and Duties of Man, and in the Universal Declaration of Human Rights, and that they have been reaffirmed and refined in other international instruments, worldwide as well as regional in scope;

Reiterating that, in accordance with the Universal Declaration of Human Rights, the ideal of free men enjoying freedom from fear and want can be achieved only if conditions are created whereby everyone may enjoy his economic, social, and cultural rights, as well as his civil and political rights; and

Considering that the Third Special Inter-American Conference (Buenos Aires, 1967) approved the incorporation into the Charter of the Organization itself broader standards with respect to economic, social, and educational rights and resolved that an Inter-American convention on human rights should determine the structure, competence, and procedure of the organs responsible for these matters,

Have agreed upon the following:

PART I. STATE OBLIGATIONS AND RIGHTS PROTECTED

CHAPTER I - GENERAL OBLIGATIONS

Article 1
Obligation to Respect Rights

1. The States Parties to this Convention undertake to respect the rights and freedoms recognized herein and to ensure to all persons subject to their jurisdiction the free and full exercise of those rights and freedoms, without any discrimination for reasons of race, color, sex, language, religion, political or other opinion, national or social origin, economic status, birth, or any other social condition.

2. For the purposes of this Convention, "person" means every human being.

Article 2
Domestic Legal Effects

Where the exercise of any of the rights or freedoms referred to in Article 1 is not already ensured by legislative or other provisions, the States Parties undertake to adopt, in accordance with their constitutional processes and the provisions of this Convention, such legislative or other measures as may be necessary to give effect to those rights or freedoms.

CHAPTER II - CIVIL AND POLITICAL RIGHTS

*   *   *

Article 11
Right to Privacy

1. Everyone has the right to have his honor respected and his dignity recognized.
2. No one may be the object of arbitrary or abusive interference with his private life, his family, his home, or his correspondence, or of unlawful attacks on his honor or reputation.
3. Everyone has the right to the protection of the law against such interference or attacks.

Article 12
Freedom of Conscience and Religion

1. Everyone has the right to freedom of conscience and of religion. This right includes freedom to maintain or to change one's religion or beliefs, and freedom to profess or disseminate one's religion or beliefs, either individually or together with others, in public or in private.
2. No one shall be subject to restrictions that might impair his freedom to maintain or to change his religion or beliefs.
3. Freedom to manifest one's religion and beliefs may be subject only to the limitations prescribed by law that are necessary to protect public safety, order, health, or morals, or the rights or freedoms of others.
4. Parents or guardians, as the case may be, have the right to provide for the religious and moral education of their children or wards that is in accord with their own convictions.

Article 13
Freedom of Thought and Expression

1. Everyone has the right to freedom of thought and expression. This right includes freedom to seek, receive, and impart information and ideas of all kinds, regardless of frontiers, either orally, in writing, in print, in the form of art, or through any other medium of one's choice.
2. The exercise of the right provided for in the foregoing paragraph shall not be subject to prior censorship but shall be subject to subsequent imposition of liability, which shall be expressly established by law to the extent necessary to ensure:
   (a) respect for the rights or reputations of others; or
   (b) the protection of national security, public order, or public health or morals.
3. The right of expression may not be restricted by indirect methods or means, such as the abuse of government or private controls over newsprint, radio broadcasting frequencies, or equipment used in the dissemination of information, or by any other means tending to impede the communication and circulation of ideas and opinions.
4. Notwithstanding the provisions of paragraph 2 above, public entertainments may be subject by law to prior censorship for the sole purpose of regulating access to them for the moral protection of childhood and adolescence.
5. Any propaganda for war and any advocacy of national, racial, or religious

hatred that constitute incitements to lawless violence or to any other similar illegal action against any person or group of persons on any grounds including those of race, color, religion, language, or national origin shall be considered as offenses punishable by law.

Article 14
Right of Reply

1.   Anyone injured by inaccurate or offensive statements or ideas disseminated to the public in general by a legally regulated medium of communication has the right to reply or to make a correction using the same communications outlet, under such conditions as the law may establish.

2.   The correction or reply shall not in any case remit other legal liabilities that may have been incurred.

3.   For the effective protection of honor and reputation, every publisher, and every newspaper, motion picture, radio, and television company, shall have a person responsible who is not protected by immunities or special privileges.

Article 15
Right of Assembly

The right of peaceful assembly, without arms, is recognized. No restrictions may be placed on the exercise of this right other than those imposed in conformity with the law and necessary in a democratic society in the interest of national security, public safety or public order, or to protect public health or morals or the rights or freedoms of others.

Article 16
Freedom of Association

1.   Everyone has the right to associate freely for ideological, religious, political, economic, labor, social, cultural, sports, or other purposes.

2.   The exercise of this right shall be subject only to such restrictions established by law as may be necessary in a democratic society, in the interest of national security, public safety or public order, or to protect public health or morals or the rights and freedoms of others.

3.   The provisions of this article do not bar the imposition of legal restrictions, including even deprivation of the exercise of the right of association, on members of the armed forces and the police.

Article 17
Rights of the Family

1.   The family is the natural and fundamental group unit of society and is entitled to protection by society and the state.

2.   The right of men and women of marriageable age to marry and to raise a family shall be recognized, if they meet the conditions required by domestic laws, insofar as such conditions do not affect the principle of nondiscrimination established in this Convention.

3.   No marriage shall be entered into without the free and full consent of the intending spouses.

4.   The States Parties shall take appropriate steps to ensure the equality of rights and the adequate balancing of responsibilities of the spouses as to marriage, during marriage, and in the event of its dissolution. In case of dissolution, provision shall be made for the necessary protection of any children solely on the basis of their own best interests.

5.   The law shall recognize equal rights for children born out of wedlock and those born in wedlock.

*   *   *

Article 24
Right to Equal Protection

All persons are equal before the law. Consequently, they are entitled, without discrimination, to equal protection of the law.

*   *   *

CHAPTER IV - SUSPENSION OF GUARANTEES, INTERPRETATION, AND APPLICATION

Article 27
Suspension of Guarantees

1. In time of war, public danger, or other emergency that threatens the independence or security of a State Party, it may take measures derogating from its obligations under the present Convention to the extent and for the period of time strictly required by the exigencies of the situation, provided that such measures are not inconsistent with its other obligations under international law and do not involve discrimination on the ground of race, color, sex, language, religion, or social origin.

2. The foregoing provision does not authorize any suspension of the following articles: Article 3 (Right to Juridical Personality), Article 4 (Right to Life), Article 5 (Right to Humane Treatment), Article 6 (Freedom from Slavery), Article 9 (Freedom from Ex Post Facto Laws), Article 12 (Freedom of Conscience and Religion), Article 17 (Rights of the Family), Article 18 (Right to a Name), Article 19 (Rights of the Child), Article 20 (Right to Nationality), and Article 23 (Right to Participate in Government), or of the judicial guarantees essential for the protection of such rights.

3. Any State Party availing itself of the right of suspension shall immediately inform the other States Parties, through the Secretary General of the Organization of American States, of the provisions the application of which it has suspended, the reasons that gave rise to the suspension, and the date set for the termination of such suspension.

*   *   *

Article 30
Scope of Restrictions

The restrictions that, pursuant to this Convention, may be placed on the enjoyment or exercise of the rights or freedoms recognized herein may not be applied except in accordance with laws enacted for reasons of general interest and in accordance with the purpose for which such restrictions have been established.

*   *   *

CHAPTER V. PERSONAL RESPONSIBILITIES

Article 32
Relationship Between Duties and Rights

1. Every person has responsibilities to his family, his community, and mankind.

2. The rights of each person are limited by the rights of others, by the security of all, and by the just demands of the general welfare, in a democratic society.

*   *   *

THE AFRICAN CHARTER ON HUMAN AND PEOPLES' RIGHTS [SELECTIONS]

Adopted by the Organization of African Unity on 17 June 1981.
Entered into Force 21 October 1986.

PREAMBLE

The African States members of the Organization of African Unity, parties to the present convention entitled "African Charter on Human and Peoples' Rights",

Recalling Decision 115 (XVI) of the Assembly of Heads of State and Government at its Sixteenth Ordinary Session held in Monrovia, Liberia, from 17 to 20 July 1979 on the preparation of a "preliminary draft on an African Charter on Human and Peoples' Rights providing *inter alia* for the establishment of bodies to promote and protect human and peoples' rights";

Considering the Charter of the Organization of African Unity, which stipulates that "freedom, equality, justice and dignity are essential objectives for the achievement of the legitimate aspirations of the African peoples";

Reaffirming the pledge they solemnly made in Article 2 of the said Charter to eradicate all forms of colonialism from Africa, to coordinate and intensify their cooperation and efforts to achieve a better life for the peoples of Africa and to promote international cooperation having due regard to the Charter of the United Nations and the Universal Declaration of Human Rights;

Taking into consideration the virtues of their historical tradition and the values of African civilization which should inspire and characterize their reflection on the concept of human and peoples' rights;

Recognizing on the one hand, that fundamental human rights stem from the attributes of human beings, which justifies their national and international protection and on the other hand that the reality and respect of peoples' rights should necessarily guarantee human rights;

Considering that the enjoyment of rights and freedoms also implies the performance of duties on the part of everyone;

Convinced that it is henceforth essential to pay a particular attention to the right to development and that civil and political rights cannot be dissociated from economic, social and cultural rights in their conception as well as universality and that the satisfaction of economic, social and cultural rights is a guarantee for the enjoyment of civil and political rights;

Conscious of their duty to achieve the total liberation of Africa, the peoples of which are still struggling for their dignity and genuine independence, and undertaking to eliminate colonialism, neo-colonialism, apartheid, zionism and to dismantle aggressive foreign military bases and all forms of discrimination, particularly those based on race, ethnic group, color, sex, language, religion or political opinions;

Reaffirming their adherence to the principles of human and peoples' rights and freedoms contained in the declarations, conventions and other instruments adopted by the Organization of African Unity, the

Movement of Non-Aligned Countries and the United Nations;

Firmly convinced of their duty to promote and protect human and peoples' rights and freedoms taking into account the importance traditionally attached to these rights and freedoms in Africa;

Have agreed as follows:

PART I

RIGHTS AND DUTIES

Chapter 1. Human and Peoples' Rights

Article 1
The Member States of the Organization of African Unity parties to the present Charter shall recognize the rights, duties and freedoms enshrined in this Charter and shall undertake to adopt legislative or other measures to give effect to them.

Article 2
Every individual shall be entitled to the enjoyment of the rights and freedoms recognized and guaranteed in the present Charter without distinction of any kind such as race, ethnic group, colour, sex, language, religion, political or any other opinion, national and social origin, fortune, birth or other status.

Article 3
1. Every individual shall be equal before the law.
2. Every individual shall be entitled to equal protection of the law.

* * *

Article 8
Freedom of conscience, the profession and free practice of religion shall be guaranteed. No one may, subject to law and order,

be submitted to measures restricting the exercise of these freedoms.

Article 9
1. Every individual shall have the right to receive information.
2. Every individual shall have the right to express and disseminate his opinions within the law.

Article 10
1. Every individual shall have the right to free association provided that he abides by the law.
2. Subject to the obligation of solidarity provided for in Article 29 no one may be compelled to join an association.

Article 11
Every individual shall have the right to assemble freely with others. The exercise of this right shall be subject only to necessary restrictions provided for by law in particular those enacted in the interest of national security, the safety, health, ethics and rights and freedoms of others.

* * *

Article 17
1. Every individual shall have the right to education.
2. Every individual may freely take part in the cultural life of his community.
3. The promotion and protection of morals and traditional values recognized by the community shall be the duty of the State.

Article 18
1. The family shall be the natural unit and basis of society. It shall be protected by the State which shall take care of its physical health and morals.
2. The State shall have the duty to

assist the family which is the custodian of morals and traditional values recognized by the community.

3.   The State shall ensure the elimination of every discrimination against women and also ensure the protection of the rights of the woman and the child as stipulated in international declarations and conventions.

4.   The aged and the disabled shall also have the right to special measures of protection in keeping with their physical or moral needs.

Article 19

All peoples shall be equal; they shall enjoy the same respect and shall have the same rights. Nothing shall justify the domination of a people by another.

Article 20

1.   All peoples shall have right to existence. They shall have the unquestionable and inalienable right to self-determination. They shall freely determine their political status and shall pursue their economic and social development according to the policy they have freely chosen.

2.   Colonized or oppressed peoples shall have the right to free themselves from the bonds of domination by resorting to any means recognized by the international community.

3.   All peoples shall have the right to the assistance of the States parties to the present Charter in their liberation struggle against foreign domination, be it political, economic or cultural.

*   *   *

Article 22

1. All peoples shall have the right to their economic, social and cultural development with due regard to their freedom and identi-ty and in the equal enjoyment of the common heritage of mankind.

2.   States shall have the duty, individually or collectively, to ensure the exercise of the right to development.

*   *   *

Chapter II. Duties

Article 27

1.   Every individual shall have duties towards his family and society, the State and other legally recognized communities and the international community.

2.   The rights and freedoms of each individual shall be exercised with due regard to the rights of others, collective security, morality and common interest.

Article 28

Every individual shall have the duty to respect and consider his fellow beings without discrimination, and to maintain relations aimed at promoting, safeguarding and reinforcing mutual respect and tolerance.

Article 29

The individual shall also have the duty:

1.   To preserve the harmonious development of the family and to work for the cohesion and respect of the family; to respect his parents at all times, to maintain them in case of need;

2.   To serve his national community by placing his physical and intellectual abilities at its service;

3.   Not to compromise the security of the State whose national or resident he is;

4.   To preserve and strengthen social and national solidarity, particularly when the latter is threatened;

5.   To preserve and strengthen the national independence and the territorial integrity of his country and to contribute to its defence in accordance with the law;

6. To work to the best of his abilities and competence, and to pay taxes imposed by law in the interest of the society;

7. To preserve and strengthen positive African cultural values in his relations with other members of the society, in the spirit of tolerance, dialogue and consultation and, in general, to contribute to the promotion of the moral well-being of society;

8. To contribute to the best of his abilities, at all times and at all levels, to the promotion and achievement of African unity.

* * *

DOCUMENTS OF THE CONFERENCE ON SECURITY AND COOPERATION IN EUROPE

The Conference on Security and Co-operation in Europe (CSCE) was established in July 1973 by thirty-five nations from Western and Eastern Europe, the Union of Soviet Socialist Republics, the United States and Canada. At its initial conference in 1975, the CSCE adopted the Final Act, 1(a), known as the Helsinki Final Act. This document was primarily designed to address issues of peace and security, including the formal acceptance of post-World War II territorial arrangements in Eastern Europe. However, Principle VII of the Helsinki Final Act's ten "Principles Guiding Relations Between Participating States" requires states to respect human rights and fundamental freedoms. As with all subsequent CSCE agreements, the Helsinki Final Act is not a treaty in the sense that it creates binding legal obligations between states under international law, but is a political document that states have nevertheless agreed to uphold.

Provisions addressing rights related to religion and belief are contained in a variety of CSCE documents. The major provisions concerning religious freedom, non-discrimination on the basis of religion and the protection against advocacy of hatred and intolerance are reprinted in this section. Extensive provisions concerning the rights of national (including religious) minorities are reprinted in the section below on minority rights. Organizationally, questions of human rights are addressed under the rubric of the "human dimension" of the CSCE. The human dimension encompasses a wide range of issues in addition to human rights, including democracy and elections, the rule of law, and the protection of national minorities.

The Concluding Document of the Vienna Meeting of the CSCE — adopted in 1989 — elaborates a number of specific principles relating to the freedom to profess and practice religion or belief (principles 16-17). The Document of the Copenhagen Meeting of the Conference on the Human Dimension — adopted in 1990 — contains detailed provisions regarding (1) government action to condemn and control xenophobia, anti-Semitism and discrimination or persecution on religious or ideological grounds (reprinted in this section) and (2) the rights of national minorities (reprinted below in the section on minority rights).

Since 1990, the CSCE has undergone a period of reorganization and is now a permanent institution, renamed the Organization for Security and Co-operation in Europe (OSCE). Two recent developments are relevant to the protection of rights related to religion or belief. First, the Office for Democratic Institutions and Human Rights was established primarily to monitor democratic elections in participating states, but has been given a limited role in monitoring human rights as well. Second, the High Commissioner for National Minorities was established in order to identify as early as possible conflict situations involving national minorities and make recommendations to the state(s) involved and appropriate OSCE bodies. These recommendations can include general suggestions on the protection of minority rights.

CONFERENCE ON SECURITY COOPERATION IN EUROPE: FINAL ACT, 1(A) [SELECTIONS]

Adopted by the Conference on Security and Cooperation in Europe on 1 August 1975.

The Conference on Security and Co-operation in Europe, which opened at Helsinki on 3 July 1973 and continued at Geneva from 18 September 1973 to 21 July 1975, was concluded at Helsinki on 1 August 1975 by the High Representatives of Austria, Belgium, Bulgaria, Canada, Cyprus, Czechoslovakia, Denmark, Finland, France, the German Democratic Republic, the Federal Republic of Germany, Greece, the Holy See, Hungary, Iceland, Ireland, Italy, Liechtenstein, Luxembourg, Malta, Monaco, the Netherlands, Norway, Poland, Portugal, Romania, San Marino, Spain, Sweden, Switzerland, Turkey, the Union of Soviet Socialist Republics, the United Kingdom, the United States of America and Yugoslavia.

*　*　*

The High Representatives of the participating States have solemnly adopted the following:

Questions relating to Security in Europe

The States participating in the Conference on Security and Co-operation in Europe,

*　*　*

Recognizing the close link between peace and security in Europe and in the world as a whole and conscious of the need for each of them to make its contribution to the strengthening of world peace and securi-ty and to the promotion of fundamental rights, economic and social progress and well-being for all peoples;

Have adopted the following:

I.

(a) Declaration on Principles Guiding Relations Between Participating States

The participating States,

Reaffirming their commitment to peace, security and justice and the continuing development of friendly relations and co-operation;

Recognizing that this commitment, which reflects the interest and aspirations of peoples, constitutes for each participating State a present and future responsibility, heightened by experience of the past;

Reaffirming, in conformity with their membership in the United Nations and in accordance with the purposes and principles of the United Nations, their full and active support for the United Nations and for the enhancement of its role and effectiveness in strengthening international peace, security and justice, and in promoting the solution of international problems, as well as the development of friendly relations and co-operation among States;

Expressing their common adherence to the principles which are set forth below and are in conformity with the Charter of the United Nations, as well as their common will to act, in the application of these principles, in conformity with the purposes and principles of the Charter of the United Nations;

Declare their determination to respect and put into practice, each of them in its relations with all other participating States, irrespective of their political, economic or social systems as well as of their size, geographical location or level of economic development, the following principles, which all are of primary significance, guiding their mutual relations:

* * *

VII. Respect for human rights and fundamental freedoms, including the freedom of thought, conscience, religion or belief

The participating States will respect human rights and fundamental freedoms, including the freedom of thought, conscience, religion or belief, for all without distinction as to race, sex, language or religion.

They will promote and encourage the effective exercise of civil, political, economic, social, cultural and other rights and freedoms all of which derive from the inherent dignity of the human person and are essential for his free and full development.

Within this framework the participating States will recognize and respect the freedom of the individual to profess and practise, alone or in community with others,

religion or belief acting in accordance with the dictates of his own conscience.

The participating States on whose territory national minorities exist will respect the right of persons belonging to such minorities to equality before the law, will afford them the full opportunity for the actual enjoyment of human rights and fundamental freedoms and will, in this manner, protect their legitimate interests in this sphere.

The participating States recognize the universal significance of human rights and fundamental freedoms, respect for which is an essential factor for the peace, justice and well-being necessary to ensure the development of friendly relations and co-operation among themselves as among all States.

They will constantly respect these rights and freedoms in their mutual relations and will endeavour jointly and separately, including in co-operation with the United Nations, to promote universal and effective respect for them.

They confirm the right of the individual to know and act upon his rights and duties in this field.

In the field of human rights and fundamental freedoms, the participating States will act in conformity with the purposes and principles of the Charter of the United Nations and with the Universal Declaration of Human Rights. They will also fulfill their obligations as set forth in the international declarations and agreements in this field, including inter alia the International Covenants on Human Rights, by which they may be bound.

CONCLUDING DOCUMENT OF THE VIENNA MEETING OF REPRESENTATIVES OF THE PARTICIPATING STATES OF THE CONFERENCE ON SECURITY AND COOPERATION IN EUROPE [SELECTIONS]

Adopted in Vienna on 17 January 1989.

The representatives of the participating States of the Conference on Security and Co-operation in Europe (CSCE), Austria, Belgium, Bulgaria, Canada, Cyprus, Czechoslovakia, Denmark, Finland, France, the German Democratic Republic, the Federal Republic of Germany, Greece, the Holy See, Hungary, Iceland, Ireland, Italy, Liechtenstein, Luxembourg, Malta, Monaco, the Netherlands, Norway, Poland, Portugal, Romania, San Marino, Spain, Sweden, Switzerland, Turkey, the Union of Soviet Socialist Republics, the United Kingdom, the United States of America and Yugoslavia met in Vienna from 4 November 1986 to 17 January 1989 in accordance with the provisions of the Final Act relating to the Follow-Up to the conference, as well as on the basis of the other relevant CSCE documents.

*   *   *

The representatives of the participating States examined all the proposals submitted to the Meeting and agreed on the following:

*   *   *

PRINCIPLES

*   *   *

11. They confirm that they will respect human rights and fundamental free-doms, including the freedom of thought, conscience, religion or belief, for all without distinction as to race, sex, language or religion. They also confirm the universal significance of human rights and fundamental freedoms, respect for which is an essential factor for the peace, justice and security necessary to ensure the development of friendly relations and co-operation among themselves, as among all States.

12. They express their determination to guarantee the effective exercise of human rights and fundamental freedoms, all of which derive from the inherent dignity of the human person and are essential for his free and full development. They recognize that civil, political, economic, social, cultural and other rights and freedoms are all of paramount importance and must be fully realized by all appropriate means.

13. In this context they will

13a. develop their laws, regulations and policies in the field of civil, political, economic, social, cultural and other human rights and fundamental freedoms and put them into practice in order to guarantee the effective exercise of these rights and freedoms;

13b. consider acceding to the International Covenant on Civil and Political Rights, the International Covenant on Economic, Social and Cultural Rights, the

Optional Protocol to the Covenant on Civil and Political Rights and other relevant international instruments, if they have not yet done so;

13c. publish and disseminate the text of the Final Act, of the Madrid Concluding Document, and of the present Document as well as those of any relevant international instruments in the field of human rights, in order to ensure the availability of these documents in their entirety, to make them known as widely as possible and to render them accessible to all individuals in their countries, in particular through public library systems;

13d. ensure effectively the right of the individual to know and act upon his rights and duties in this field, and to that end publish and make accessible all laws, regulations and procedures relating to human rights and fundamental freedoms;

13e. respect the right of their citizens to contribute actively, individually or in association with others, to the promotion and protection of human rights and fundamental freedoms;

13f. encourage in schools and other educational institutions consideration of the promotion and protection of human rights and fundamental freedoms;

13g. ensure human rights and fundamental freedoms to everyone within their territory and subject to their jurisdiction, without distinction of any kind such as race, colour, sex, language, religion, political or other opinion, national or social origin, property, birth or other status;

13h. ensure that no individual exercising, expressing the intention to exercise or seeking to exercise these rights and freedoms, or any member of his family, will as a consequence be discriminated against in any manner;

13i. ensure that effective remedies as well as full information about them are available to those who claim that their human rights and fundamental freedoms have been violated; they will, *inter alia*, effectively apply the following remedies:

the right of the individual to appeal to executive, legislative, judicial or administrative organs;

the right to a fair and public hearing within a reasonable time before an independent and impartial tribunal, including the right to present legal arguments and to be represented by legal counsel of one's choice;

the right to be promptly and officially informed of the decision taken on any appeal, including the legal grounds on which this decision was based. This information will be provided as a rule in writing and, in any event, in a way that will enable the individual to make effective use of further available remedies.

* * *

16. In order to ensure the freedom of the individual to profess and practice religion or belief the participating States will, *inter alia*,

16a. take effective measures to prevent and eliminate discrimination against individuals or communities, on the grounds of religion or belief in the recognition, exercise and enjoyment of human rights and fundamental freedoms in all fields of civil, political, economic, social and cultural life, and ensure the effective equality between believers and non-believers;

16b. foster a climate of mutual tolerance and respect between believers of different communities as well as between believers and non-believers;

16c. grant upon their request to communities of believers, practising or prepared to practise their faith within the constitutional framework of their states, recognition of the status provided for them in their respective countries;

16d. respect the right of religious communities to

--establish and maintain freely accessible places of worship or assembly,

--organize themselves according to their own hierarchical and institutional structure,

--select, appoint and replace their personnel in accordance with their respective requirements and standards as well as with any freely accepted arrangement between them and their State,

--solicit and receive voluntary financial and other contributions;

16e. engage in consultations with religious faiths, institutions and organizations in order to achieve a better understanding of the requirements of religious freedom;

16f. respect the right of everyone to give and receive religious education in the language of his choice, individually or in association with others;

16g. in this context respect, *inter alia*, the liberty of parents to ensure the religious and moral education of their children in conformity with their own convictions;

16h. allow the training of religious personnel in appropriate institutions;

16i. respect the right of individual believers and communities of believers to acquire, possess, and use sacred books, religious publications in the language of their choice and other articles and materials related to the practice of religion or belief;

16j. allow religious faiths, institutions and organizations to produce and import and disseminate religious publications and materials;

16k. favorably consider the interest of religious communities in participating in public dialogue, *inter alia*, through mass media;

17. The participating States recognize that the exercise of the above-mentioned rights relating to the freedom of religion or belief may be subject only to such limitations as are provided by law and consistent with their obligations under international law and with their international commitments. They will ensure in their laws and regulations and in their application the full and effective implementation of the freedom of thought, conscience, religion or belief;

18. The participating States will exert sustained efforts to implement the provisions of the Final Act and of the Madrid Concluding Document pertaining to national minorities. They will take all the necessary legislative, administrative, judicial and other measures and apply the relevant international instruments by which they may be bound, to ensure the protection of human rights and fundamental freedoms of persons belonging to national minorities within their territory. They will refrain from any discrimination against such persons and contribute to the realization of their legitimate interests and aspirations in the field of human rights and fundamental freedoms.

19. They will protect and create conditions for the promotion of the ethnic, cultural, linguistic and religious identity of national minorities on their territory. They will respect the free exercise of rights by persons belonging to such minorities and ensure their full equality with others.

DOCUMENT OF THE COPENHAGEN MEETING OF THE CONFERENCE ON THE HUMAN DIMENSION OF THE CSCE [SELECTIONS]

Adopted in Copenhagen on 29 June 1990.

The representatives of the participating States of the Conference on Security and Co-operation in Europe (CSCE), Austria, Belgium, Bulgaria, Canada, Cyprus, Czechoslovakia, Denmark, Finland, France, the German Democratic Republic, the Federal Republic of Germany, Greece, the Holy See, Hungary, Iceland, Ireland, Italy, Liechtenstein, Luxembourg, Malta, Monaco, the Netherlands, Norway, Poland, Portugal, Romania, San Marino, Spain, Sweden, Switzerland, Turkey, the Union of Soviet Socialist Republics, the United Kingdom, the United States of America and Yugoslavia, met in Copenhagen from 5 to 29 June 1990, in accordance with the provisions relating to the Conference on the Human Dimension of the CSCE contained in the Concluding Document of the Vienna Follow-up Meeting of the CSCE.

*   *   *

In order to strengthen respect for, and enjoyment of, human rights and fundamental freedoms, to develop human contacts and to resolve issues of a related humanitarian character, the participating States agree on the following:

I

*   *   *

(5) They solemnly declare that among those elements of justice which are essential to the full expression of the inherent dignity and of the equal and inalienable rights of all human beings are the following:

*   *   *

(5.9) all persons are equal before the law and are entitled without any discrimination to the equal protection of the law. In this respect, the law will prohibit any discrimination and guarantee to all persons equal and effective protection against discrimination on any ground;

*   *   *

II

(9) The participating States reaffirm that

(9.1) everyone will have the right to freedom of expression including the right to communication. This right will include freedom to hold opinions and to receive and impart information and ideas without interference by public authority and regardless of frontiers. The exercise of this right may be subject only to such restrictions as are prescribed by law and are consistent with international standards. In particular, no limitation will be imposed on access to, and use of, means of reproducing documents of any kind, while respecting, however, rights relating to intellectual property, including copyright;

(9.2) everyone will have the right of

peaceful assembly and demonstration. Any restrictions which may be placed on the exercise of these rights will be prescribed by law and consistent with international standards;

(9.3) the right of association will be guaranteed. The right to form and -- subject to the general right of a trade union to determine its own membership -- freely to join a trade union will be guaranteed. These rights will exclude any prior control. Freedom of association for workers, including the freedom to strike, will be guaranteed, subject to limitations prescribed by law and consistent with international standards;

(9.4) everyone will have the right to freedom of thought, conscience and religion. This right includes freedom to change one's religion or belief and freedom to manifest one's religion or belief, either alone or in community with others, in public or in private, through worship, teaching, practice and observance. The exercise of these rights may be subject only to such restrictions as are prescribed by law and are consistent with international standards;

*   *   *

(18) The participating States

(18.1) note that the United Nations Commission on Human Rights has recognized the right of everyone to have conscientious objections to military service;

(18.2) note recent measures taken by a number of participating States to permit exemption from compulsory military service on the basis of conscientious objections;

(18.3) note the activities of several non-governmental organizations on the question of conscientious objections to compulsory military service;

(18.4) agree to consider introducing, where this has not yet been done, various forms of alternative service, which are compatible with the reasons for conscientious objection, such forms of alternative service being in principle of a non-combatant or civilian nature, in the public interest and of a non-punitive nature;

(18.5) will make available to the public information on this issue;

(18.6) will keep under consideration, within the framework of the Conference on the Human Dimension, the relevant questions related to the exemption from compulsory military service, where it exists, of individuals on the basis of conscientious objections to armed service, and will exchange information on these questions.

*   *   *

(24) The participating States will ensure that the exercise of all the human rights and fundamental freedoms set out above will not be subject to any restrictions except those which are provided by law and are consistent with their obligations under international law, in particular the International Covenant on Civil and Political Rights, and with their international commitments, in particular the Universal Declaration of Human Rights. These restrictions have the character of exceptions. The participating States will ensure that these restrictions are not abused and are not applied in an arbitrary manner, but in such a way that the effective exercise of these rights is ensured.

Any restriction on rights and freedoms must, in a democratic society, relate to one of the objectives of the applicable law and be strictly proportionate to the aim of that law.

(25) The participating States confirm that any derogations from obligations relating to human rights and fundamental freedoms during a state of public emergency must remain strictly within the limits provided for by international law, in particular

the relevant international instruments by which they are bound, especially with respect to rights from which there can be no derogation. They also reaffirm that

(25.1) measures derogating from such obligations must be taken in strict conformity with the procedural requirements laid down in those instruments;

(25.2) the imposition of a state of public emergency must be proclaimed officially, publicly, and in accordance with the provisions laid down by law;

(25.3) measures derogating from obligations will be limited to the extent strictly required by the exigencies of the situation;

(25.4) such measures will not discriminate solely on the grounds of race, colour, sex, language, religion, social origin or of belonging to a minority.

* * *

IV

* * *

(40) The participating States clearly and unequivocally condemn totalitarianism, racial and ethnic hatred, anti-Semitism, xenophobia and discrimination against anyone as well as persecution on religious and ideological grounds. In this context, they also recognize the particular problems of Roma (gypsies).

They declare their firm intention to intensify the efforts to combat these phenomena in all their forms and therefore will

(40.1) take effective measures, including the adoption, in conformity with their constitutional systems and their international obligations, of such laws as may be necessary, to provide protection against any acts that constitute incitement to violence against persons or groups based on national, racial, ethnic or religious discrimination, hostility or hatred, including anti-Semitism;

(40.2) commit themselves to take appropriate and proportionate measures to protect persons or groups who may be subject to threats or acts of discrimination, hostility or violence as a result of their racial, ethnic, cultural, linguistic or religious identity, and to protect their property;

(40.3) take effective measures, in conformity with their constitutional systems, at the national, regional and local levels to promote understanding and tolerance, particularly in the fields of education, culture and information;

(40.4) endeavour to ensure that the objectives of education include special attention to the problem of racial prejudice and hatred and to the development of respect for different civilizations and cultures;

(40.5) recognize the right of the individual to effective remedies and endeavour to recognize, in conformity with national legislation, the right of interested persons and groups to initiate and support complaints against acts of discrimination, including racist and xenophobic acts;

(40.6) consider adhering, if they have not yet done so, to the international instruments which address the problem of discrimination and ensure full compliance with the obligations therein, including those relating to the submission of periodic reports;

(40.7) consider, also, accepting those international mechanisms which allow States and individuals to bring communications relating to discrimination before international bodies.

PART III

Documents on the Rights of Religious Minorities

DECLARATION ON THE RIGHTS OF PERSONS BELONGING TO NATIONAL OR ETHNIC, RELIGIOUS AND LINGUISTIC MINORITIES

Adopted and Proclaimed by United Nations General Assembly Resolution 47/135 on 18 December 1992.

The General Assembly,

Reaffirming that one of the basic aims of the United Nations, as proclaimed in the Charter, is to promote and encourage respect for human rights and for fundamental freedoms for all, without distinction as to race, sex, language or religion,

Reaffirming faith in fundamental human rights, in the dignity and worth of the human person, in the equal rights of men and women and of nations large and small,

Desiring to promote the realization of the principles contained in the Charter, the Universal Declaration of Human Rights, the Convention on the Prevention and Punishment of the Crime of Genocide, the International Convention on the Elimination of All Forms of Racial Discrimination, the International Covenant on Civil and Political Rights, the International Covenant on Economic, Social and Cultural Rights, the Declaration on the Elimination of All Forms of Intolerance and of Discrimination Based on Religion or Belief, and the Convention on the Rights of the Child, as well as other relevant international instruments that have been adopted at the universal or regional level and those concluded between individual States Members of the United Nations,

Inspired by the provisions of article 27 of the International Covenant on Civil and Political Rights concerning the rights of persons belonging to ethnic, religious or linguistic minorities,

Considering that the promotion and protection of the rights of persons belonging to national or ethnic, religious and linguistic minorities contribute to the political and social stability of States in which they live,

Emphasizing that the constant promotion and realization of the rights of persons belonging to national or ethnic, religious and linguistic minorities, as an integral part of the development of society as a whole and within a democratic framework based on the rule of law, would contribute to the strengthening of friendship and co-operation among peoples and States,

Considering that the United Nations has an important role to play regarding the protection of minorities,

Bearing in mind the work done so far within the United Nations system, in particular by the Commission on Human Rights, the Subcommission on Prevention of Discrimination and Protection of Minorities and the bodies established pursuant to the International Covenants on Human Rights and other relevant international human rights instruments in promoting and protecting the rights of persons belonging to national or ethnic, religious and linguistic minorities,

Taking into account the important work which is done by intergovernmental and non-governmental organizations in protecting minorities and in promoting and protecting the rights of persons belonging to national or ethnic, religious and linguistic minorities,

Recognizing the need to ensure even more effective implementation of international human rights instruments with regard to the rights of persons belonging to national or ethnic, religious and linguistic minorities,

Proclaims this Declaration on the Rights of Persons Belonging to National or Ethnic, Religious and Linguistic Minorities:

Article 1

1.   States shall protect the existence and the national or ethnic, cultural, religious and linguistic identity of minorities within their respective territories and shall encourage conditions for the promotion of that identity.

2.   States shall adopt appropriate legislative and other measures to achieve those ends.

Article 2

1.   Persons belonging to national or ethnic, religious and linguistic minorities (hereinafter referred to as persons belonging to minorities) have the right to enjoy their own culture, to profess and practise their own religion, and to use their own language, in private and in public, freely and without interference or any form of discrimination.

2.   Persons belonging to minorities have the right to participate effectively in cultural, religious, social, economic and public life.

3.   Persons belonging to minorities have the right to participate effectively in decisions on the national and, where appropriate, regional level concerning the minori-

ty to which they belong or the regions in which they live, in a manner not incompatible with national legislation.

4.   Persons belonging to minorities have the right to establish and maintain their own associations.

5.   Persons belonging to minorities have the right to establish and maintain, without any discrimination, free and peaceful contacts with other members of their group and with persons belonging to other minorities, as well as contacts across frontiers with citizens of other States to whom they are related by national or ethnic, religious or linguistic ties.

Article 3

1.   Persons belonging to minorities may exercise their rights, including those set forth in the present Declaration, individually as well as in community with other members of their group, without any discrimination.

2.   No disadvantage shall result for any person belonging to a minority as the consequence of the exercise or non-exercise of the rights set forth in the present Declaration.

Article 4

1.   States shall take measures where required to ensure that persons belonging to minorities may exercise fully and effectively all their human rights and fundamental freedoms without any discrimination and in full equality before the law.

2.   States shall take measures to create favourable conditions to enable persons belonging to minorities to express their characteristics and to develop their culture, language, religion, traditions and customs, except where specific practices are in violation of national law and contrary to international standards.

3.   States should take appropriate measures so that, wherever possible, persons belonging to minorities may have adequate

opportunities to learn their mother tongue or to have instruction in their mother tongue.

4. States should, where appropriate, take measures in the field of education, in order to encourage knowledge of the history, traditions, language and culture of the minorities existing within their territory. Persons belonging to minorities should have adequate opportunities to gain knowledge of the society as a whole.

5. States should consider appropriate measures so that persons belonging to minorities may participate fully in the economic progress and development in their country.

Article 5

1. National policies and programmes shall be planned and implemented with due regard for the legitimate interests of persons belonging to minorities.

2. Programmes of co-operation and assistance among States should be planned and implemented with due regard for the legitimate interests of persons belonging to minorities.

Article 6

States should cooperate on questions relating to persons belonging to minorities, *inter alia*, exchanging information and experiences, in order to promote mutual understanding and confidence.

Article 7

States should cooperate in order to promote respect for the rights set forth in the present Declaration.

Article 8

1. Nothing in the present Declaration shall prevent the fulfilment of international obligations of States in relation to persons belonging to minorities. In particular, States shall fulfil in good faith the obligations and commitments they have assumed under international treaties and agreements to which they are parties.

2. The exercise of the rights set forth in the present Declaration shall not prejudice the enjoyment by all persons of universally recognized human rights and fundamental freedoms.

3. Measures taken by States to ensure the effective enjoyment of the rights set forth in the present Declaration shall not *prima facie* be considered contrary to the principle of equality contained in the Universal Declaration of Human Rights.

4. Nothing in the present Declaration may be construed as permitting any activity contrary to the purposes and principles of the United Nations, including sovereign equality, territorial integrity and political independence of States.

Article 9

The specialized agencies and other organizations of the United Nations system shall contribute to the full realization of the rights and principles set forth in the present Declaration, within their respective fields of competence.

COUNCIL OF EUROPE: FRAMEWORK CONVENTION FOR THE PROTECTION OF NATIONAL MINORITIES

Opened for Signature by the Council of Europe
on 1 February 1995.
European Treaty Series No. 157.

The member States of the Council of Europe and the other States, signatories to the present framework Convention,

Considering that the aim of the Council of Europe is to achieve greater unity between its members for the purpose of safeguarding and realising the ideals and principles which are their common heritage;

Considering that one of the methods by which that aim is to be pursued is the maintenance and further realisation of human rights and fundamental freedoms;

Wishing to follow-up the Declaration of the Heads of State and Government of the member States of the Council of Europe adopted in Vienna on 9 October 1993;

Being resolved to protect within their respective territories the existence of national minorities;

Considering that the upheavals of European history have shown that the protection of national minorities is essential to stability, democratic security and peace in this continent;

Considering that a pluralist and genuinely democratic society should not only respect the ethnic, cultural, linguistic and religious identity of each person belonging to a national minority, but also create appropriate conditions enabling them to express, preserve and develop this identity;

Considering that the creation of a climate of tolerance and dialogue is necessary to enable cultural diversity to be a source and a factor, not of division, but of enrichment for each society;

Considering that the realisation of a tolerant and prosperous Europe does not depend solely on co-operation between States but also requires transfrontier co-operation between local and regional authorities without prejudice to the constitution and territorial integrity of each State;

Having regard to the Convention for the Protection of Human Rights and Fundamental Freedoms and the Protocols thereto;

Having regard to the commitments concerning the protection of national minorities in United Nations conventions and declarations and in the documents of the Conference on Security and Co-operation in Europe, particularly the Copenhagen Document of 29 June 1990;

Being resolved to define the principles to be respected and the obligations which flow from them, in order to ensure, in the member States and such other States as may become Parties to the present instrument, the effective protection of national minorities and of the rights and freedoms of persons belonging to those minorities, within the rule of law, respecting the territorial integrity and national sovereignty of states;

Being determined to implement the principles set out in this framework Convention through national legislation and appropriate governmental policies,

Have agreed as follows:

SECTION I

Article 1

The protection of national minorities and of the rights and freedoms of persons belonging to those minorities forms an integral part of the international protection of human rights, and as such falls within the scope of international co-operation.

Article 2

The provisions of this framework Convention shall be applied in good faith, in a spirit of understanding and tolerance and in conformity with the principles of good neighbourliness, friendly relations and co-operation between States.

Article 3

1. Every person belonging to a national minority shall have the right freely to choose to be treated or not to be treated as such and no disadvantage shall result from this choice or from the exercise of the rights which are connected to that choice.

2. Persons belonging to national minorities may exercise the rights and enjoy the freedoms flowing from the principles enshrined in the present framework Convention individually as well as in community with others.

SECTION II

Article 4

1. The Parties undertake to guarantee to persons belonging to national minorities the right of equality before the law and of equal protection of the law. In this respect, any discrimination based on belonging to a national minority shall be prohibited.

2. The Parties undertake to adopt, where necessary, adequate measures in order to promote, in all areas of economic, social, political and cultural life, full and effective equality between persons belonging to a national minority and those belonging to the majority. In this respect, they shall take due account of the specific conditions of the persons belonging to national minorities.

3. The measures adopted in accordance with paragraph 2 shall not be considered to be an act of discrimination.

Article 5

1. The Parties undertake to promote the conditions necessary for persons belonging to national minorities to maintain and develop their culture, and to preserve the essential elements of their identity, namely their religion, language, traditions and cultural heritage.

2. Without prejudice to measures taken in pursuance of their general integration policy, the Parties shall refrain from policies or practices aimed at assimilation of persons belonging to national minorities against their will and shall protect these persons from any action aimed at such assimilation.

Article 6

1. The Parties shall encourage a spirit of tolerance and intercultural dialogue and take effective measures to promote mutual respect and understanding and co-operation among all persons living on their territory, irrespective of those persons' ethnic, cultural, linguistic or religious identity, in particular in the fields of education, culture and the media.

2. The Parties undertake to take appropriate measures to protect persons who may be subject to threats or acts of discrim-

ination, hostility or violence as a result of their ethnic, cultural, linguistic or religious identity.

Article 7

The Parties shall ensure respect for the right of every person belonging to a national minority to freedom of peaceful assembly, freedom of association, freedom of expression, and freedom of thought, conscience and religion.

Article 8

The Parties undertake to recognise that every person belonging to a national minority has the right to manifest his or her religion or belief and to establish religious institutions, organisations and associations.

Article 9

1. The Parties undertake to recognise that the right to freedom of expression of every person belonging to a national minority includes freedom to hold opinions and to receive and impart information and ideas in the minority language, without interference by public authorities and regardless of frontiers. The Parties shall ensure, within the framework of their legal systems, that persons belonging to a national minority are not discriminated against in their access to the media.

2. Paragraph 1 shall not prevent Parties from requiring the licensing, without discrimination and based on objective criteria, of sound radio and television broadcasting, or cinema enterprises.

3. The Parties shall not hinder the creation and the use of printed media by persons belonging to national minorities. In the legal framework of sound radio and television broadcasting, they shall ensure, as far as possible, and taking into account the provisions of paragraph 1, that persons belonging to national minorities are granted the possibility of creating and using their own media.

4. In the framework of their legal systems, the Parties shall adopt adequate measures in order to facilitate access to the media for persons belonging to national minorities and in order to promote tolerance and permit cultural pluralism.

Article 10

1. The Parties undertake to recognise that every person belonging to a national minority has the right to use freely and without interference his or her minority language, in private and in public, orally and in writing.

2. In areas inhabited by persons belonging to national minorities traditionally or in substantial numbers, if those persons so request and where such a request corresponds to a real need, the Parties shall endeavour to ensure, as far as possible, the conditions which would make it possible to use the minority language in relations between those persons and the administrative authorities.

3. The Parties undertake to guarantee the right of every person belonging to a national minority to be informed promptly, in a language which he or she understands, of the reasons for his or her arrest, and of the nature and cause of any accusation against him or her, and to defend himself or herself in this language, if necessary with the free assistance of an interpreter.

Article 11

1. The Parties undertake to recognise that every person belonging to a national minority has the right to use his or her surname (patronym) and first names in the minority language and the right to official recognition of them, according to modalities provided for in their legal system.

2. The Parties undertake to recognise that every person belonging to a national minority has the right to display in his or

her minority language signs, inscriptions and other information of a private nature visible to the public.

3.   In areas traditionally inhabited by substantial numbers of persons belonging to a national minority, the Parties shall endeavour, in the framework of their legal system, including, where appropriate, agreements with other States, and taking into account their specific conditions, to display traditional local names, street names and other topographical indications intended for the public also in the minority language when there is a sufficient demand for such indications.

Article 12

1.   The Parties shall, where appropriate, take measures in the fields of education and research to foster knowledge of the culture, history, language and religion of their national minorities and of the majority.

2.   In this context the Parties shall *inter alia* provide adequate opportunities for teacher training and access to textbooks, and facilitate contacts among students and teachers of different communities.

3.   The Parties undertake to promote equal opportunities for access to education at all levels for persons belonging to national minorities.

Article 13

1.   Within the framework of their education systems, the Parties shall recognise that persons belonging to a national minority have the right to set up and to manage their own private educational and training establishments.

2.   The exercise of this right shall not entail any financial obligation for the Parties.

Article 14

1.   The Parties undertake to recognise that every person belonging to a nation-al minority has the right to learn his or her minority language.

2.   In areas inhabited by persons belonging to national minorities traditionally or in substantial numbers, if there is sufficient demand, the Parties shall endeavour to ensure, as far as possible and within the framework of their education systems, that persons belonging to those minorities have adequate opportunities for being taught the minority language or for receiving instruction in this language.

3.   Paragraph 2 of this article shall be implemented without prejudice to the learning of the official language or the teaching in this language.

Article 15

The Parties shall create the conditions necessary for the effective participation of persons belonging to national minorities in cultural, social and economic life and in public affairs, in particular those affecting them.

Article 16

The Parties shall refrain from measures which alter the proportions of the population in areas inhabited by persons belonging to national minorities and are aimed at restricting the rights and freedoms flowing from the principles enshrined in the present framework Convention.

Article 17

1.   The Parties undertake not to interfere with the right of persons belonging to national minorities to establish and maintain free and peaceful contacts across frontiers with persons lawfully staying in other States, in particular those with whom they share an ethnic, cultural, linguistic or religious identity, or a common cultural heritage.

2.   The Parties undertake not to interfere with the right of persons belonging

to national minorities to participate in the activities of non-governmental organisations, both at the national and international levels.

Article 18

1.   The Parties shall endeavour to conclude, where necessary, bilateral and multilateral agreements with other States, in particular neighbouring States, in order to ensure the protection of persons belonging to the national minorities concerned.

2.   Where relevant, the Parties shall take measures to encourage transfrontier co-operation.

Article 19

The Parties undertake to respect and implement the principles enshrined in the present framework Convention making, where necessary, only those limitations, restrictions or derogations which are provided for in international legal instruments, in particular the Convention for the Protection of Human Rights and Fundamental Freedoms, in so far as they are relevant to the rights and freedoms flowing from the said principles.

SECTION III

Article 20

In the exercise of the rights and freedoms flowing from the principles enshrined in the present framework Convention, any person belonging to a national minority shall respect the national legislation and the rights of others, in particular those of persons belonging to the majority or to other national minorities.

Article 21

Nothing in the present framework Convention shall be interpreted as implying any right to engage in any activity or perform any act contrary to the fundamental

principles of international law and in particular of the sovereign equality, territorial integrity and political independence of States.

Article 22

Nothing in the present framework Convention shall be construed as limiting or derogating from any of the human rights and fundamental freedoms which may be ensured under the laws of any Contracting Party or under any other agreement to which it is a Party.

Article 23

The rights and freedoms flowing from the principles enshrined in the present framework Convention, in so far as they are the subject of a corresponding provision in the Convention for the Protection of Human Rights and Fundamental Freedoms or in the Protocols thereto, shall be understood so as to conform to the latter provisions.

SECTION IV

Article 24

1.   The Committee of Ministers of the Council of Europe shall monitor the implementation of this framework Convention by the Contracting Parties.

2.   The Parties which are not members of the Council of Europe shall participate in the implementation mechanism, according to modalities to be determined.

Article 25

1.   Within a period of one year following the entry into force of this framework Convention in respect of a Contracting Party, the latter shall transmit to the Secretary-General of the Council of Europe full information on the legislative and other measures taken to give effect to the principles set out in this framework Convention.

2.   Thereafter, each Party shall

transmit to the Secretary-General on a periodical basis and whenever the Committee of Ministers so requests any further information of relevance to the implementation of this framework Convention.

3.   The Secretary-General shall forward to the Committee of Ministers the information transmitted under the terms of this Article.

Article 26

1.   In evaluating the adequacy of the measures taken by the Parties to give effect to the principles set out in this framework Convention the Committee of Ministers shall be assisted by an advisory committee, the members of which shall have recognised expertise in the field of the protection of national minorities.

2.   The composition of this advisory committee and its procedure shall be determined by the Committee of Ministers within a period of one year following the entry into force of this framework Convention.

SECTION V

Article 27

This framework Convention shall be open for signature by the member States of the Council of Europe. Up until the date when the Convention enters into force, it shall also be open for signature by any other State so invited by the Committee of Ministers. It is subject to ratification, acceptance or approval. Instruments of ratification, acceptance or approval shall be deposited with the Secretary-General of the Council of Europe.

Article 28

1.   This framework Convention shall enter into force on the first day of the month following the expiration of a period of three months after the date on which twelve member States of the Council of Europe have expressed their consent to be bound by the Convention in accordance with the provisions of Article 27.

2.   In respect of any member State which subsequently expresses its consent to be bound by it, the framework Convention shall enter into force on the first day of the month following the expiration of a period of three months after the date of the deposit of the instrument of ratification, acceptance or approval.

Article 29

1.   After the entry into force of this framework Convention and after consulting the Contracting States, the Committee of Ministers of the Council of Europe may invite to accede to the Convention, by a decision taken by the majority provided for in Article 20.d of the Statute of the Council of Europe, any non-member State of the Council of Europe which, invited to sign in accordance with the provisions of Article 27, has not yet done so, and any other non-member State.

2.   In respect of any acceding State, the framework Convention shall enter into force on the first day of the month following the expiration of a period of three months after the date of the deposit of the instrument of accession with the Secretary-General of the Council of Europe.

Article 30

1.   Any State may at the time of signature or when depositing its instrument of ratification, acceptance, approval or accession, specify the territory or territories for whose international relations it is responsible to which this framework Convention shall apply.

2.   Any State may at any later date, by a declaration addressed to the Secretary-General of the Council of Europe, extend the

application of this framework Convention to any other territory specified in the declaration. In respect of such territory the framework Convention shall enter into force on the first day of the month following the expiration of a period of three months after the date of receipt of such declaration by the Secretary-General.

3. Any declaration made under the two preceding paragraphs may, in respect of any territory specified in such declaration, be withdrawn by a notification addressed to the Secretary-General. The withdrawal shall become effective on the first day of the month following the expiration of a period of three months after the date of receipt of such notification by the Secretary-General.

Article 31

1. Any Party may at any time denounce this framework Convention by means of a notification addressed to the Secretary-General of the Council of Europe.

2. Such denunciation shall become effective on the first day of the month following the expiration of a period of six months after the date of receipt of the notification by the Secretary General.

Article 32

The Secretary General of the Council of Europe shall notify the member States of the Council, other signatory States and any State which has acceded to this framework Convention, of:

a. any signature;

b. the deposit of any instrument of ratification, acceptance, approval or accession;

c. any date of entry into force of this framework Convention in accordance with Articles 28, 29 and 30;

d. any other act, notification or communication relating to this framework Convention.

In witness whereof the undersigned, being duly authorised thereto, have signed this framework Convention.

Done at Strasbourg, this 1st day of February 1995, in English and French, both texts being equally authentic, in a single copy which shall be deposited in the archives of the Council of Europe. The Secretary-General of the Council of Europe shall transmit certified copies to each member State of the Council of Europe and to any State invited to sign or accede to this framework Convention.

DOCUMENT OF THE COPENHAGEN MEETING OF THE CONFERENCE ON THE HUMAN DIMENSION OF THE CSCE [SELECTIONS]

Adopted in Copenhagen on 29 June 1990.

The representatives of the participating States of the Conference on Security and Co-operation in Europe (CSCE), Austria, Belgium, Bulgaria, Canada, Cyprus, Czechoslovakia, Denmark, Finland, France, the German Democratic Republic, the Federal Republic of Germany, Greece, the Holy See, Hungary, Iceland, Ireland, Italy, Liechtenstein, Luxembourg, Malta, Monaco, the Netherlands, Norway, Poland, Portugal, Romania, San Marino, Spain, Sweden, Switzerland, Turkey, the Union of Soviet Socialist Republics, the United Kingdom, the United States of America and Yugoslavia, met in Copenhagen from 5 to 29 June 1990, in accordance with the provisions relating to the Conference on the Human Dimension of the CSCE contained in the Concluding Document of the Vienna Follow-up Meeting of the CSCE.

*   *   *

In order to strengthen respect for, and enjoyment of, human rights and fundamental freedoms, to develop human contacts and to resolve issues of a related humanitarian character, the participating States agree on the following:

*   *   *

IV

(30) The participating States recognize that the questions relating to national minorities can only be satisfactorily

resolved in a democratic political framework based on the rule of law, with a functioning independent judiciary. This framework guarantees full respect for human rights and fundamental freedoms, equal rights and status for all citizens, the free expression of all their legitimate interests and aspirations, political pluralism, social tolerance and the implementation of legal rules that place effective restraints on the abuse of governmental power.

They also recognize the important role of non-governmental organizations, including political parties, trade unions, human rights organizations and religious groups, in the promotion of tolerance, cultural diversity and the resolution of questions relating to national minorities.

They further reaffirm that respect for the rights of persons belonging to national minorities as part of universally recognized human rights is an essential factor for peace, justice, stability and democracy in the participating States.

(31) Persons belonging to national minorities have the right to exercise fully and effectively their human rights and fundamental freedoms without any discrimination and in full equality before the law.

The participating States will adopt, where necessary, special measures for the purpose of ensuring to persons belonging to national minorities full equality with the other citizens in the exercise and enjoyment of human rights and fundamental freedoms.

(32) To belong to a national minority is a matter of a person's individual choice and no disadvantage may arise from the exercise of such choice.

Persons belonging to national minorities have the right freely to express, preserve and develop their ethnic, cultural, linguistic or religious identity and to maintain and develop their culture in all its aspects, free of any attempts at assimilation against their will. In particular, they have the right

(32.1) to use freely their mother tongue in private as well as in public;

(32.2) to establish and maintain their own educational, cultural and religious institutions, organizations or associations, which can seek voluntary financial and other contributions as well as public assistance, in conformity with national legislation;

(32.3) to profess and practise their religion, including the acquisition, possession and use of religious materials, and to conduct religious educational activities in their mother tongue;

(32.4) to establish and maintain unimpeded contacts among themselves within their country as well as contacts across frontiers with citizens of other States with whom they share a common ethnic or national origin, cultural heritage or religious beliefs;

(32.5) to disseminate, have access to and exchange information in their mother tongue;

(32.6) to establish and maintain organizations or associations within their country and to participate in international non-governmental organizations.

Persons belonging to national minorities can exercise and enjoy their rights individually as well as in community with other members of their group. No disadvantage may arise for a person belonging to a national minority on account of the exercise or non-exercise of any such rights.

(33) The participating States will protect the ethnic, cultural, linguistic and religious identity of national minorities on their territory and create conditions for the promotion of that identity. They will take the necessary measures to that effect after due consultations, including contacts with organizations or associations of such minorities, in accordance with the decision-making procedures of each State.

Any such measures will be in conformity with the principles of equality and non-discrimination with respect to the other citizens of the participating State concerned.

(34) The participating States will endeavour to ensure that persons belonging to national minorities, notwithstanding the need to learn the official language or languages of the State concerned, have adequate opportunities for instruction of their mother tongue or in their mother tongue, as well as, wherever possible and necessary, for its use before public authorities, in conformity with applicable national legislation.

In the context of the teaching of history and culture in educational establishments, they will also take account of the history and culture of national minorities.

(35) The participating States will respect the right of persons belonging to national minorities to effective participation in public affairs, including participation in the affairs relating to the protection and promotion of the identity of such minorities.

The participating States note the efforts undertaken to protect and create conditions for the promotion of the ethnic, cultural, linguistic and religious identity of certain national minorities by establishing, as one of the possible means to achieve these aims, appropriate local or autonomous administrations corresponding to the specific historical and territorial circumstances of such minorities and in accordance with the policies of the State concerned.

(36) The participating States recognize the particular importance of increasing constructive co-operation among themselves on questions relating to national minorities. Such co-operation seeks to promote mutual understanding and confidence, friendly and good-neighbourly relations, international peace, security and justice.

Every participating State will promote a climate of mutual respect, understanding, co-operation and solidarity among all persons living on its territory, without distinction as to ethnic or national origin or religion, and will encourage the solution of problems through dialogue based on the principles of the rule of law.

(37) None of these commitments may be interpreted as implying any right to engage in any activity or perform any action in contravention of the purposes and principles of the Charter of the United Nations, other obligations under international law or the provisions of the Final Act, including the principle of territorial integrity of States.

(38) The participating States, in their efforts to protect and promote the rights of persons belonging to national minorities, will fully respect their undertakings under existing human rights conventions and other relevant international instruments and consider adhering to the relevant conventions, if they have not yet done so, including those providing for a right of complaint by individuals.

(39) The participating States will co-operate closely in the competent international organizations to which they belong, including the United Nations and, as appropriate, the Council of Europe, bearing in mind their on-going work with respect to questions relating to national minorities.

They will consider convening a meeting of experts for a thorough discussion of the issue of national minorities.

The representatives of Albania, Austria, Belgium, Bulgaria, Canada, Cyprus, the Czech and Slovak Federal Republic, Denmark, Finland, France, Germany, Greece, the Holy See, Hungary, Iceland, Ireland, Italy, Liechtenstein, Luxembourg, Malta, Monaco, the Netherlands-European Community, Norway, Poland, Portugal, Romania, San Marino, Spain, Sweden, Switzerland, Turkey, the Union of Soviet Socialist Republics, the United Kingdom, the United States of America and Yugoslavia met in Geneva from 1 to 19 July 1991 in accordance with the relevant provisions of the Charter of Paris for a New Europe.

An opening address to the Meeting was delivered by H.E. René Felber, Federal Councilor, Head of the Federal Department of Foreign Affairs of Switzerland, on behalf of the host country. Opening statements were made by H.E. Catharina Dales, Minister of the Interior of the Netherlands on behalf of the Netherlands-European Community, and by Heads of Delegation of the participating States. Contributions to the Meeting were made by Ms. Catherine Lalumière, Secretary-General of the Council of Europe, and Mr. Jan Martenson, Head of the United Nations Centre for Human Rights in Geneva. The Secretary of State of the host country, Mr. Klaus Jacobi, delivered a closing address to the Meeting.

In accordance with the relevant provisions of the Charter of Paris, the representatives of the participating States had a thorough discussion on the issues of national minorities and of the rights of persons belonging to them that reflected the diversity of situations and of the legal, historical, political and economic backgrounds. They had an exchange of views on practical experience with national minorities, in particular on national legislation, democratic institutions, international instruments and other possible forms of co-operation. Views were expressed on the implementation of the relevant CSCE commitments, and the representatives of the participating States also considered the scope for the improvement of relevant standards. They also considered new measures aimed at improving the implementation of the aforementioned commitments.

A number of proposals were submitted for consideration by the Meeting and, following their deliberations, the representatives of the participating States adopted this Report.

The text of the Report of the Geneva Meeting of Experts on National Minorities will be published in each participating State, which will disseminate it and make it known as widely as possible.

The representatives of the participating States note that the Council will take into account the summing up of the Meeting, in accordance with the Charter of Paris for a New Europe.

I.

Recognizing that their [sic] observance and full exercise of human rights and fundamental freedoms, including those of persons belonging to national minorities, are the foundation of the New Europe,

Reaffirming their deep conviction that friendly relations among their peoples, as well as peace, justice, stability and democracy, require that the ethnic, cultural, linguistic and religious identity of national minorities be protected, and conditions for the promotion of that identity be created,

Convinced that, in States with national minorities, democracy requires that all persons, including those belonging to national minorities, enjoy full and effective equality of rights and fundamental freedoms and benefit from the rule of law and democratic institutions,

Aware of the diversity of situations and constitutional systems in their countries, and therefore recognizing that various approaches to the implementation of CSCE commitments regarding national minorities are appropriate,

Mindful of the importance of exerting efforts to address national minorities issues, particularly in areas where democratic institutions are being consolidated and questions relating to national minorities are of special concern,

Aware that national minorities form an integral part of the society of the States in which they live and that they are a factor of enrichment of each respective State and society,

Confirming the need to respect and implement fully and fairly their undertakings in the field of human rights and fundamental freedoms as set forth in the international instruments by which they may be bound,

Reaffirming their strong determination to respect and apply, to their full extent, all their commitments relating to national minorities and persons belonging to them in the Helsinki Final Act, the Madrid Concluding Document and the Vienna Concluding Document, the Document of the Copenhagen Meeting of the Conference on the Human Dimension of the CSCE, the Document of the Cracow Symposium on the Cultural Heritage as well as the Charter of Paris for a New Europe, the participating States present below the summary of their conclusions.

The representatives of the participating States took as the fundamental basis of their work the commitments undertaken by them with respect to national minorities as contained in the relevant adopted CSCE documents, in particular those in the Charter of Paris for a New Europe and the Document of the Copenhagen Meeting of the Conference on the Human Dimension of the CSCE, which they fully reaffirmed.

II.

The participating States stress the continued importance of a thorough review of implementation of their CSCE commitments relating to persons belonging to national minorities.

They emphasize that human rights and fundamental freedoms are the basis for the protection and promotion of rights of persons belonging to national minorities. They further recognize that questions relating to national minorities can only be satisfactorily resolved in a democratic political framework based on the rule of law, with a functioning independent judiciary. This framework guarantees full respect for human rights and fundamental freedoms, equal rights and status for all citizens, including persons belonging to national minorities, the free expression of all their legitimate interests and aspirations, political pluralism, social tolerance and the implementation of legal rules that place effective restraints on the abuse of governmental power.

Issues concerning national minorities, as well as compliance with international obligations and commitments concerning the rights of persons belonging to them, are matters of legitimate international concern and consequently do not constitute exclusively an internal affair of the respective State.

They note that not all ethnic, cultural, linguistic or religious differences necessarily lead to the creation of national minorities.

III.

Respecting the right of persons belonging to national minorities to effective participation in public affairs, the participating States consider that when issues relating to the situation of national minorities are discussed within their countries, they themselves should have the effective opportunity to be involved, in accordance with the decision-making procedures of each State. They further consider that appropriate democratic participation of persons belonging to national minorities or their representatives in decision-making or consultative bodies constitutes an important element of effective participation in public affairs.

They consider that special efforts must be made to resolve specific problems in a constructive manner and through dialogue by means of negotiations and consultations with a view to improving the situation of persons belonging to national minorities. They recognize that the promotion of dialogue between States, and between States and persons belonging to national minorities, will be most successful when there is a free flow of information and ideas between all parties. They encourage unilateral, bilateral and multilateral efforts by governments to explore avenues for enhancing the effectiveness of their implementation of CSCE commitments relating to national minorities.

The participating States further consider that respect for human rights and fundamental freedoms must be accorded on a non-discriminatory basis throughout society. In areas inhabited mainly by persons belonging to a national minority, the human rights and fundamental freedoms of persons belonging to that minority, of persons belonging to the majority population of the respective State, and of persons belonging to other national minorities residing in these areas will be equally protected.

They reconfirm that persons belonging to national minorities have the right freely to express, preserve and develop their ethnic, cultural, linguistic or religious identity and to maintain and develop their culture in all its aspects, free of any attempts at assimilation against their will.

They will permit the competent authorities to inform the Office for Free Elections of all scheduled public elections on their territories, including those held below national level. The participating States will consider favourably, to the extent permitted by law, the presence of observers at elections held below the national level, including in areas inhabited by national minorities, and will endeavour to facilitate their access.

IV.

The participating States will create conditions for persons belonging to national minorities to have equal opportunity to be effectively involved in the public life, economic activities, and building of their societies.

In accordance with paragraph 31 of the Copenhagen Document, the participating States will take the necessary measures to prevent discrimination against individuals, particularly in respect of employment, housing and education, on the grounds of belonging or not belonging to a national minority. In that context, they will make provision, if they have not yet done so, for effective recourse to redress for individuals who have experienced discriminatory treatment on the grounds of their belonging or not belonging to a national minority, including by making available to individual victims of discrimination a broad array of administrative and judicial remedies.

The participating States are convinced that the preservation of the values and of the cultural heritage of national minorities requires the involvement of persons belonging to such minorities and that tolerance and respect for different cultures are of paramount importance in this regard. Accordingly, they confirm the importance of refraining from hindering the production of cultural materials concerning national minorities, including by persons belonging to them.

The participating States affirm that persons belonging to a national minority will enjoy the same rights and have the same duties of citizenship as the rest of the population.

The participating States reconfirm the importance of adopting, where necessary, special measures for the purpose of ensuring to persons belonging to national minorities full equality with the other citizens in the exercise and enjoyment of human rights and fundamental freedoms. They further recall the need to take the necessary measures to protect the ethnic, cultural, linguistic and religious identity of national minorities on their territory and create conditions for the promotion of that identity; any such measures will be in conformity with the principles of equality and non-discrimination with respect to the other citizens of the participating State concerned.

They recognize that such measures, which take into account, *inter alia*, historical and territorial circumstances of national minorities, are particularly important in areas where democratic institutions are being consolidated and national minorities issues are of special concern.

Aware of the diversity and varying constitutional systems among them, which make no single approach necessarily generally applicable, the participating States note with interest that positive results have been obtained by some of them in an appropriate democratic manner by, *inter alia*:

--advisory and decision-making bodies in which minorities are represented, in particular with regard to education, culture and religion;
--elected bodies and assemblies of national minority affairs;
--local and autonomous administration, as well as autonomy on a territorial basis, including the existence of consultative, legislative and executive bodies chosen through free and periodic elections;
--self-administration by a national minority of aspects concerning its

identity in situations where autonomy on a territorial basis does not apply;

--decentralized or local forms of government;

--bilateral and multilateral agreements and other arrangements regarding national minorities;

--for persons belonging to national minorities, provision of adequate types and levels of education in their mother tongue with due regard to the number, geographical settlement patterns and cultural traditions of national minorities;

--funding the teaching of minority languages to the general public, as well as the inclusion of minority languages in teacher-training institutions, in particular in regions inhabited by persons belonging to national minorities;

--in cases where instruction in a particular subject is not provided in their territory in the minority language at all levels, taking the necessary measures to find means of recognizing diplomas issued abroad for a course of study completed in that language;

--creation of government research agencies to review legislation and disseminate information related to equal rights and non-discrimination;

--provision of financial and technical assistance to persons belonging to national minorities who so wish to exercise their right to establish and maintain their own educational, cultural and religious institutions, organizations and associations;

--governmental assistance for addressing local difficulties relating to discriminatory practices (e.g. a citizens relations service);

--encouragement of grassroots community relations efforts between minority communities, between majority and minority communities, and between neighbouring communities sharing borders, aimed at helping to prevent local tensions from arising and address conflicts peacefully should they arise; and

--encouragement of the establishment of permanent mixed commissions, either inter-State or regional, to facilitate continuing dialogue between the border regions concerned.

The participating States are of the view that these or other approaches, individually or in combination, could be helpful in improving the situation of national minorities on their territories.

V.

The participating States respect the right of persons belonging to national minorities to exercise and enjoy their rights alone or in community with others, to establish and maintain organizations and associations within their country, and to participate in international non-governmental organizations.

The participating States reaffirm, and will not hinder the exercise of, the right of persons belonging to national minorities to establish and maintain their own educational, cultural and religious institutions, organizations and associations.

In this regard, they recognize the major and vital role that individuals, non-governmental organizations, and religious and other groups play in fostering cross-cultural understanding and improving relations at all levels of society, as well as across international frontiers.

They believe that the first-hand observations and experience of such organizations, groups, and individuals can be of great value in promoting the implementation of CSCE commitments relating to persons belonging to national minorities. They therefore will encourage and not hinder the work of such organizations, groups and individuals and welcome their contributions in this area.

VI.

The participating States, concerned by the proliferation of acts of racial, ethnic and religious hatred, anti-Semitism, xenophobia and discrimination, stress their determination to condemn, on a continuing basis, such acts against anyone.

In this context, they reaffirm their recognition of the particular problems of Roma (gypsies). They are ready to undertake effective measures in order to achieve full equality of opportunity between persons belonging to Roma ordinarily resident in their State and the rest of the resident population. They will also encourage research and studies regarding Roma and the particular problems they face.

They will take effective measures to promote tolerance, understanding, equality of opportunity and good relations between individuals of different origins within their country.

Further, the participating States will take effective measures, including the adoption, in conformity with their constitutional law and their international obligations, if they have not already done so, of laws that would prohibit acts that constitute incitement to violence based on national, racial, ethnic or religious discrimination, hostility or hatred, including anti-Semitism, and policies to enforce such laws.

Moreover, in order to heighten public awareness of prejudice and hatred, to improve enforcement of laws against hate-related crime and otherwise to further efforts to address hatred and prejudice in society, they will make efforts to collect, publish on a regular basis, and make available to the public, data about crimes on their respective territories that are based on prejudice as to race, ethnic identity or religion, including the guidelines used for the collection of such data. These data should not contain any personal information.

They will consult and exchange views and information at the international level, including at future meetings of the CSCE, on crimes that manifest evidence of prejudice and hate.

VII.

Convinced that the protection of the rights of persons belonging to national minorities necessitates free flow of information and exchange of ideas, the participating States emphasize the importance of communication between persons belonging to national minorities without interference by public authorities and regardless of frontiers. The exercise of such rights may be subject only to such restrictions as are prescribed by law and are consistent with international standards. They reaffirm that no one belonging to a national minority, simply by virtue of belonging to such a minority, will be subject to penal or administrative sanctions for having had contacts within or outside his/her own country.

In access to the media, they will not discriminate against anyone based on ethnic, cultural, linguistic or religious grounds. They will make information available that will assist the electronic mass media in taking into account, in their programmes, the ethnic, cultural, linguistic and religious identity of national minorities.

They reaffirm that establishment and maintenance of unimpeded contacts among persons belonging to a national minority, as well as contacts across frontiers by persons belonging to a national minority with persons with whom they share a common ethnic or national origin, cultural heritage or religious belief, contributes to mutual understanding and promotes good-neighbourly relations.

They therefore encourage transfrontier co-operation arrangements on a national, regional and local level, *inter alia*, on local border crossings, the preservation of and visits to cultural and historical monuments and sites, tourism, the improvement of traffic, the economy, youth exchange, the protection of the environment and the establishment of regional commissions.

They will also encourage the creation of informal working arrangements (e.g. workshops, committees both within and between the participating States) where national minorities live, to discuss issues of, exchange experience on, and present proposals on, issues related to national minorities.

With a view to improving their information about the actual situation of national minorities, the participating States will, on a voluntary basis distribute, through the CSCE Secretariat, information to other participating States about the situation of national minorities in their respective territories, as well as statements of national policy in that respect.

The participating States will deposit with the CSCE Secretariat copies of the contributions made in the Plenary of the CSCE Meeting of Experts on National Minorities which they wish to be available to the public.

VIII.

The participating States welcome the positive contribution made by the representatives of the United Nations and the Council of Europe to the proceedings of the Geneva Meeting of Experts on National Minorities. They note that the work and activities of these organizations will be of continuing relevance to the CSCE's consideration of national minorities issues.

The participating States note that appropriate CSCE mechanisms may be of relevance in addressing questions relating to national minorities. Further, they recommend that the third Meeting of the Conference on the Human Dimension of the CSCE consider expanding the Human Dimension Mechanism. They will promote the involvement of individuals in the protection of their rights, including the rights of persons belonging to national minorities.

Finally, the representatives of the participating States request the Executive Secretary of the Meeting to transmit this Report to the third Meeting of the Conference on the Human Dimension of the CSCE.

The representatives of the participating States express their profound gratitude to the people and Government of Switzerland for the excellent organization of the Geneva Meeting and the warm hospitality extended to the delegations that participated in the Meeting.

PART IV

SELECTED GOVERNMENT AND RELIGIOUS DOCUMENTS ON RELIGIOUS FREEDOM

THE ORGANIZATION OF THE ISLAMIC CONFERENCE

The Organization of the Islamic Conference was formed in 1972 by the adoption of the Charter of the Islamic Conference, 914 U.N.T.S. 103, at the Third Islamic Conference of Foreign Ministers. According to the Charter, membership is open to "every Muslim state" and currently there are approximately 50 member states. Member states include those states where Islam is the official state religion as well as those states where Islam is not the state religion, but the majority of the population is Muslim. The purposes of the Islamic Conference include the promotion of Islamic solidarity, increased co-operation between member states and the support of Muslim peoples in non-member states throughout the world. The Conference holds regular meetings of foreign ministers of the member states and has held seven summit conferences of heads of state. The Conference has established a variety of specialized agencies in the fields of economic development, education, trade, technology, culture and information. In the field of law, the Conference has recently sought to establish an International Islamic Court of Justice and an Islamic Commission of International Law. These institutions, along with the Cairo Declaration on Human Rights in Islam, apparently reflect the desire to develop a distinctively Islamic conceptualization of international law.

THE CAIRO DECLARATION ON HUMAN RIGHTS IN ISLAM

Adopted and Issued at the Nineteenth Islamic Conference
of Foreign Ministers in Cairo
on 5 August 1990.

The Member States of the Organization of the Islamic Conference,

Reaffirming the civilizing and historical role of the Islamic Ummah which God made the best nation that has given mankind a universal and well-balanced civilization in which harmony is established between this life and the hereafter and knowledge is combined with faith; and the role that this Ummah should play to guide a humanity confused by competing trends and ideologies and to provide solutions to the chronic problems of this materialistic civilization.

Wishing to contribute to the efforts of mankind to assert human rights, to protect man from exploitation and persecution, and to affirm his freedom and right to a dignified life in accordance with the Islamic Shari'ah

Convinced that mankind which has reached an advanced stage in materialistic science is still, and shall remain, in dire need of faith to support its civilization and of a self-motivating force to guard its rights;

Believing that fundamental rights and universal freedoms in Islam are an integral part of the Islamic religion and that no one as a matter of principle has the right to suspend them in whole or in part or violate or ignore them in as much as they are binding divine commandments, which are contained in the Revealed Books of God and were sent through the last of His Prophets to complete the preceding divine messages thereby making their observance an act of worship and their neglect or violation an abominable sin,

and accordingly every person is individually responsible — and the Ummah collectively responsible — for their safeguard.

Proceeding from the above-mentioned principles,

Declare the following:

Article 1
(a)   All human beings form one family whose members are united by submission to God and descent from Adam. All men are equal in terms of basic human dignity and basic obligations and responsibilities, without any discrimination on the grounds of race, colour, language, sex, religious belief, political affiliation, social status or other considerations. True faith is the guarantee for enhancing such dignity along the path to human perfection.

(b)   All human beings are God's subjects, and the most loved by him are those who are most useful to the rest of His subjects, and no one has superiority over another except on the basis of piety and good deeds.

Article 2
(a)   Life is a God-given gift and the right to life is guaranteed to every human being. It is the duty of individuals, societies and states to protect this right from any violation, and it is prohibited to take away life except for a Shari'ah-prescribed reason.

(b)   It is forbidden to resort to such means as may result in the genocidal annihilation of mankind.

185

(c)   The preservation of human life throughout the term of time willed by God is a duty prescribed by Shari'ah.

(d)   Safety from bodily harm is a guaranteed right. It is the duty of the state to safeguard it, and it is prohibited to breach it without a Shari'ah-prescribed reason.

Article 3

(a)   In the event of the use of force and in case of armed conflict, it is not permissible to kill non-belligerents such as old men, women and children. The wounded and the sick shall have the right to medical treatment; and prisoners of war shall have the right to be fed, sheltered and clothed. It is prohibited to mutilate dead bodies. It is a duty to exchange prisoners of war and to arrange visits or reunions of the families separated by the circumstances of war.

(b)   It is prohibited to fell trees, to damage crops or livestock, and to destroy the enemy's civilian buildings and installations by shelling, blasting or any other means.

Article 4

Every human being is entitled to inviolability and the protection of his good name and honour during his life and after his death. The state and society shall protect his remains and burial place.

Article 5

(a)   The family is the foundation of society, and marriage is the basis of its formation. Men and women have the right to marriage, and no restrictions stemming from race, colour or nationality shall prevent them from enjoying this right.

(b)   Society and the State shall remove all obstacles to marriage and shall facilitate marital procedure. They shall ensure family protection and welfare.

Article 6

(a)   Woman is equal to man in human dignity, and has rights to enjoy as well as duties to perform; she has her own civil entity and financial independence, and the right to retain her name and lineage.

(b)   The husband is responsible for the support and welfare of the family.

Article 7

(a)   As of the moment of birth, every child has rights due from the parents, society and the state to be accorded proper nursing, education and material, hygienic and moral care. Both the fetus and the mother must be protected and accorded special care.

(b)   Parents and those in such like capacity have the right to choose the type of education they desire for their children, provided they take into consideration the interest and future of the children in accordance with ethical values and the principles of the Shari'ah.

(c)   Both parents are entitled to certain rights from their children, and relatives are entitled to rights from their kin, in accordance with the tenets of the Shari'ah.

Article 8

Every human being has the right to enjoy his legal capacity in terms of both obligation and commitment. Should this capacity be lost or impaired, he shall be represented by his guardian.

Article 9

(a)   The quest for knowledge is an obligation, and the provision of education is a duty for society and the State. The State shall ensure the availability of ways and means to acquire education and shall guarantee educational diversity in the interest of society so as to enable man to be acquainted with the religion of Islam and the facts of the Universe for the benefit of mankind.

(b) Every human being has the right to receive both religious and worldly education from the various institutions of education and guidance, including the family, the school, the university, the media, etc., and in such an integrated and balanced manner as to develop his personality, strengthen his faith in God and promote his respect for and defence of both rights and obligations.

Article 10

Islam is the religion of unspoiled nature. It is prohibited to exercise any form of compulsion on man or to exploit his poverty or ignorance in order to convert him to another religion or to atheism.

Article 11

(a) Human beings are born free, and no one has the right to enslave, humiliate, oppress or exploit them, and there can be no subjugation but to God the Most-High.

(b) Colonialism of all types being one of the most evil forms of enslavement is totally prohibited. Peoples suffering from colonialism have the full right to freedom and self-determination. It is the duty of all States and peoples to support the struggle of colonized peoples for the liquidation of all forms of colonialism and occupation, and all States and peoples have the right to preserve their independent identity and exercise control over their wealth and natural resources.

Article 12

Every man shall have the right, within the framework of Shari'ah, to free movement and to select his place of residence whether inside or outside his country and, if persecuted, is entitled to seek asylum in another country. The country of refuge shall ensure his protection until he reaches safety, unless asylum is motivated by an act which Shari'ah regards as a crime.

Article 13

Work is a right guaranteed by the State and Society for each person able to work. Everyone shall be free to choose the work that suits him best and which serves his interests and those of society. The employee shall have the right to safety and security as well as to all other social guarantees. He may neither be assigned work beyond his capacity nor be subjected to compulsion or exploited or harmed in any way. He shall be entitled — without any discrimination between males and females — to fair wages for his work without delay, as well as to the holidays, allowances and promotions which he deserves. For his part, he shall be required to be dedicated and meticulous in his work. Should workers and employers disagree on any matter, the State shall intervene to settle the dispute and have the grievances redressed, the rights confirmed and justice enforced without bias.

Article 14

Everyone shall have the right to legitimate gains without monopolization, deceit or harm to oneself or to others. Usury (riba) is absolutely prohibited.

Article 15

(a) Everyone shall have the right to own property acquired in a legitimate way, and shall be entitled to the rights of ownership, without prejudice to oneself, others or to society in general. Expropriation is not permissible except for the requirements of public interest and upon payment of immediate and fair compensation

(b) Confiscation and seizure of property is prohibited except for a necessity dictated by law.

Article 16

Everyone shall have the right to enjoy the fruits of his scientific, literary, artistic or technical production and the right to protect the moral and material interests stemming therefrom, provided that such production is not contrary to the principles of Shari'ah.

Article 17

(a)   Everyone shall have the right to live in a clean environment, away from vice and moral corruption, an environment that would foster his self-development; and it is incumbent upon the State and society in general to afford that right.

(b)   Everyone shall have the right to medical and social care, and to all public amenities provided by society and the State within the limits of their available resources.

(c)   The State shall ensure the right of the individual to a decent living which will enable him to meet all his requirements and those of his dependents, including food, clothing, housing, education, medical care and all other basic needs.

Article 18

(a)   Everyone shall have the right to live in security for himself, his religion, his dependents, his honour and his property.

(b)   Everyone shall have the right to privacy in the conduct of his private affairs, in his home, among his family, with regard to his property and his relationships. It is not permitted to spy on him, to place him under surveillance or to besmirch his good name. The State shall protect him from arbitrary interference.

(c)   A private residence is inviolable in all cases. It will not be entered without permission from its inhabitants or in any unlawful manner, nor shall it be demolished or confiscated and its dwellers evicted.

Article 19

(a)   All individuals are equal before the law, without distinction between the ruler and the ruled.

(b)   The right to resort to justice is guaranteed to everyone.

(c)   Liability is in essence personal.

(d)   There shall be no crime or punishment except as provided for in the Shari'ah.

(e)   A defendant is innocent until his guilt is proven in a fair trial in which he shall be given all the guarantees of defence.

Article 20

It is not permitted without legitimate reason to arrest an individual, or restrict his freedom, to exile or to punish him. It is not permitted to subject him to physical or psychological torture or to any form of humiliation, cruelty or indignity. Nor is it permitted to subject an individual to medical or scientific experimentation without his consent or at the risk of his health or of his life. Nor is it permitted to promulgate emergency laws that would provide executive authority for such actions.

Article 21

Taking hostages under any form or for any purpose is expressly forbidden.

Article 22

(a)   Everyone shall have the right to express his opinion freely in such manner as would not be contrary to the principles of the Shari'ah.

(b)   Everyone shall have the right to advocate what is right, and propagate what is good, and warn against what is wrong and evil according to the norms of Islamic Shari'ah.

(c)   Information is a vital necessity to society. It may not be exploited or misused in such a way as may violate sanctities and the dignity of Prophets, undermine moral and ethical values or disintegrate, corrupt or harm society or weaken its faith.

(d)   It is not permitted to arouse nationalistic or doctrinal hatred or to do anything that may be an incitement to any form of racial discrimination.

Article 23

(a) Authority is a trust; and abuse or malicious exploitation thereof is absolutely prohibited, so that fundamental human rights may be guaranteed.

(b) Everyone shall have the right to participate, directly or indirectly in the administration of his country's public affairs. He shall also have the right to assume public office in accordance with the provisions of Shari'ah.

Article 24

All the rights and freedoms stipulated in this Declaration are subject to the Islamic Shari'ah.

Article 25

The Islamic Shari'ah is the only source of reference for the explanation or clarification of any of the articles of this Declaration.

Cairo, 14 Muharram 1411H
5 August 1990

THE UNITED STATES OF AMERICA

Thomas Jefferson drafted a bill for religious freedom and introduced it into the legislature of Virginia in 1779. At that time Virginia had suspended state financial support for the formerly established Church of England, and a debate was growing over the proper level and scope of such support for all denominations, particularly with respect to the support of clergy. In 1784, A Bill Establishing A Provision for Teachers of the Christian Religion was introduced, providing for a property tax under which each taxpayer could designate the "society of Christians" to which their tax money would go, or in the alternative, allow the money to go into the public treasury for the construction of public schools. The money turned over to a denomination could only be used for the support of a "Minister or a Teacher of the Gospel."

It was in response to this bill that James Madison wrote his Memorial and Remonstrance Against Religious Assessments. The document was circulated anonymously during the summer legislative recess of 1785 in order to engage public support to defeat the bill in the following 1785-86 session. The bill was defeated during that session, and in the wake of its defeat, Madison secured the passage of Jefferson's religious freedom bill with only a few minor alterations. The Statute for Religious Freedom was passed on January 16, 1785, and is still the law of the state of Virginia.

The Supreme Court of the United States has, on a number of recent occasions, looked to these documents and the historical events surrounding them to help determine the scope of the religion clauses of the First Amendment to the United States Constitution: "Congress shall make no law respecting an establishment of religion, or prohibiting the free exercise thereof ...." James Madison was perhaps the most influential person in the drafting and passage of the First Amendment in 1789 as a member of the House of Representatives in the first United States Congress.

A BILL ESTABLISHING A PROVISION FOR TEACHERS OF THE CHRISTIAN RELIGION

1784

Whereas the general diffusion of Christian knowledge hath a natural tendency to correct the morals of men, restrain their vices, and preserve the peace of society; which cannot be effected without a competent provision for learned teachers, who may be thereby enabled to devote their time and attention to the duty of instructing such citizens, as from their circumstances and want of education, cannot otherwise attain such knowledge; and it is judged that such provision may be made by the Legislature, without counteracting the liberal principle heretofore adopted and intended to be preserved by abolishing all distinctions of pre-eminence amongst the different societies or communities of Christians;

Be it therefore enacted by the General Assembly, That for the support of Christian teachers, per centum on the amount, or in the pound on the sum payable for tax on the property within this Commonwealth, is hereby assessed, and shall be paid by every person chargeable with the said tax at the time the same shall become due; and the Sheriffs of the several Counties shall have power to levy and collect the same in the same manner and under the like restrictions and limitations, as are or may be prescribed by the laws for raising the Revenues of this State.

And be it enacted, That for every sum so paid, the Sheriff or Collector shall give a receipt, expressing therein to what society of Christians the person from whom he may receive the same shall direct the money to be paid, keeping a distinct account thereof in his books. The Sheriff of every County, shall, on or before the___ day of___ in every year, return to the Court, upon oath, two alphabetical lists of the payments to him made, distinguishing in columns opposite to the names of the persons who shall have paid the same, the society to which the money so paid was by them appropriated; and one column for the names where no appropriation shall be made. One of which lists, after being recorded in a book to be kept for that purpose, shall be filed by the Clerk in his office; the other shall by the Sheriff be fixed up in the Court-house, there to remain for the inspection of all concerned. And the Sheriff, after deducting five per centum for the collection, shall forthwith pay to such person or persons as shall be appointed to receive the same by the Vestry, Elders, or Directors, however denominated of each such society, the sum so stated to be due to that society ....

And be it further enacted, That the money to be raised by virtue of this Act, shall be by the Vestries, Elders, or Directors of each religious society, appropriated to a provision for a Minister or Teacher of the Gospel of their denomination, or the providing places of divine worship, and to none other use whatsoever; except in the denominations of Quakers and Menonists, who may receive what is collected from their members, and place it in their general fund, to be disposed of in a manner which they shall think best calculated to promote their particular mode of worship.

And be it enacted, That all sums which at the time of payment to the Sheriff or Collector may not be appropriated by the person paying the same, shall be accounted for with the Court in manner as by this Act is directed; and after deducting for his collection, the Sheriff shall pay the amount thereof (upon account certified by the Court to the Auditors of Public Accounts, and by them to the Treasurer) into the public Treasury, to be disposed of under the direction of the General Assembly, for the encouragement of seminaries of learning within the Counties whence such sums shall arise, and to no other use or purpose whatsoever.

THIS Act shall commence, and be in force, from and after the day of ___ in the year ___.

James Madison: Memorial and Remonstrance Against Religious Assessments to the Honorable General Assembly of the Commonwealth of Virginia

1785

We, the subscribers, citizens of the said Commonwealth, having taken into serious consideration, a Bill printed by order of the last Session of General Assembly, entitled "A Bill establishing a provision for Teachers of the Christian Religion," and conceiving that the same, if finally armed with the sanctions of a law, will be a dangerous abuse of power, are bound as faithful members of a free State, to remonstrate against it, and to declare the reasons by which we are determined. We remonstrate against the said Bill,

1. Because we hold it for a fundamental and undeniable truth, "that religion, or the duty which we owe to our Creator, and the manner of discharging it, can be directed only by reason and conviction, not by force or violence."[1] The Religion then of every man must be left to the conviction and conscience of every man; and it is the right of every man to exercise it as these may dictate. This right is in its nature an unalienable right. It is unalienable; because the opinions of men, depending only on the evidence contemplated by their own minds, cannot follow the dictates of other men: It is unalienable also; because what is here a right towards men, is a duty towards the Creator. It is the duty of every man to render to the Creator such homage, and such only, as he believes to be acceptable to him. This duty is predecent both in order of time and degree of obligation, to the claims of Civil Society. Before any man can be considered as a member of Civil Society, he must be considered as a subject of the Governor of the Universe: And if a member of Civil Society, who enters into any subordinate Association, must always do it with a reservation of his duty to the general authority; much more must every man who becomes a member of any particular Civil Society, do it with a saving of his allegiance to the Universal Sovereign. We maintain therefore that in matters of Religion, no man's right is abridged by the institution of Civil Society, and that Religion is wholly exempt from its cognizance. True it is, that no other rule exists, by which any question which may divide a Society, can be ultimately determined, but the will of the majority; but it is also true, that the majority may trespass on the rights of the minority.

2. Because if religion be exempt from the authority of the Society at large, still less can it be subject to that of the Legislative Body. The latter are but the creatures and vicegerents of the former. Their jurisdiction is both derivative and limited: it is limited with regard to the coordinate departments, more necessarily is it limited with regard to the constituents. The preservation of a free government requires not merely, that the metes and bounds which separate each department of power may be invariably maintained; but more especially, that neither of them be suffered to overleap

the great Barrier which defends the rights of the people. The Rulers who are guilty of such an encroachment, exceed the commission from which they derive their authority, and are Tyrants. The People who submit to it are governed by laws made neither by themselves, nor by an authority derived from them, and are slaves.

3. Because, it is proper to take alarm at the first experiment on our liberties. We hold this prudent jealousy to be the first duty of citizens, and one of [the] noblest characteristics of the late Revolution. The freemen of America did not wait till usurped power had strengthened itself by exercise, and entangled the question in precedents. They saw all the consequences in the principle, and they avoided the consequences by denying the principle. We revere this lesson too much, soon to forget it. Who does not see that the same authority which can establish Christianity, in exclusion of all other Religions, may establish with the same ease any particular sect of Christians, in exclusion of all other Sects? That the same authority which can force a citizen to contribute three pence only of his property for the support of any one establishment, may force him to conform to any other establishment in all cases whatsoever?

4. Because, the bill violates that equality which ought to be the basis of every law, and which is more indispensable, in proportion as the validity or expediency of any law is more liable to be impeached. If "all men are by nature equally free and independent,"[2] all men are to be considered as entering into Society on equal conditions; as relinquishing no more, and therefore retaining no less, one than another, of their natural rights. Above all are they to be considered as retaining an "equal title to the free exercise of Religion according to the dictates of conscience".[3] Whilst we assert for ourselves a freedom to embrace, to profess and to observe the Religion which we believe to be of divine origin, we cannot deny an equal freedom to those whose minds have not yet yielded to the evidence which has convinced us. If this freedom be abused, it is an offence against God, not against man: To God, therefore, not to men, must an account of it be rendered. As the Bill violates equality by subjecting some to peculiar burdens; so it violates the same principle, by granting to others peculiar exemptions. Are the Quakers and Menonists the only sects who think a compulsive support of their religions unnecessary and unwarrantable? Can their piety alone be intrusted with the care of public worship? Ought their Religions to be endowed above all others, with extraordinary privileges, by which proselytes may be enticed from all others? We think too favorably of the justice and good sense of these denominations, to believe that they either covet preeminencies over their fellow citizens, or that they will be seduced by them, from the common opposition to the measure.

5. Because the bill implies either that the Civil Magistrate is a competent Judge of Religious truth; or that he may employ Religion as an engine of Civil policy. The first is an arrogant pretension falsified by the contradictory opinions of Rulers in all ages, and throughout the world: The second an unhallowed perversion of the means of salvation.

6. Because the establishment proposed by the Bill is not requisite for the support of the Christian Religion. To say that it is, is a contradiction to the Christian Religion itself; for every page of it disavows a dependence on the powers of this world: it is a contradiction to fact; for it is known that this Religion both existed and flourished, not only without the support of human laws, but in spite of every opposition from them;

and not only during the period of miraculous aid, but long after it had been left to its own evidence, and the ordinary care of Providence: Nay, it is a contradiction in terms; for a Religion not invented by human policy, must have preexisted and been supported, before it was established by human policy. It is moreover to weaken in those who profess this Religion a pious confidence in its innate excellence, and the patronage of its Author; and to foster in those who still reject it, a suspicion that its friends are too conscious of its fallacies, to trust it to its own merits.

7.   Because experience witnesseth that ecclesiastical establishments, instead of maintaining the purity and efficacy of Religion, have had a contrary operation. During almost fifteen centuries, has the legal establishment of Christianity been on trial. What have been its fruits? More or less in all places, pride and indolence in the Clergy; ignorance and servility in the laity; in both, superstition, bigotry and persecution. Enquire of the Teachers of Christianity for the ages in which it appeared in its greatest lustre; those of every sect, point to the ages prior to its incorporation with Civil policy. Propose a restoration of this primitive state in which its Teachers depended on the voluntary rewards of their flocks; many of them predict its downfall. On which side ought their testimony to have greatest weight, when for or when against their interest?

8.   Because the establishment in question is not necessary for the support of Civil Government. If it be urged as necessary for the support of Civil Government only as it is a means of supporting Religion, and it be not necessary for the latter purpose, it cannot be necessary for the former. If Religion be not within [the] cognizance of Civil Government, how can its legal establishment be said to be necessary to civil

Government? What influence in fact have ecclesiastical establishments had on Civil Society? In some instances they have been seen to erect a spiritual tyranny on the ruins of Civil authority; in many instances they have been seen upholding the thrones of political tyranny; in no instance have they been seen the guardians of the liberties of the people. Rulers who wished to subvert the public liberty, may have found an established clergy convenient auxiliaries. A just government, instituted to secure & perpetuate it, needs them not. Such a government will be best supported by protecting every citizen in the enjoyment of his Religion with the same equal hand which protects his person and his property; by neither invading the equal rights by any Sect, nor suffering any Sect to invade those of another.

9.   Because the proposed establishment is a departure from that generous policy, which, offering an asylum to the persecuted and oppressed of every Nation and Religion, promised a lustre to our country, and an accession to the number of its citizens. What a melancholy mark is the Bill of sudden degeneracy? Instead of holding forth an asylum to the persecuted, it is itself a signal of persecution. It degrades from the equal rank of Citizens all those whose opinions in Religion do not bend to those of the Legislative authority. Distant as it may be, in its present form, from the Inquisition it differs from it only in degree. The one is the first step, the other the last in the career of intolerance. The magnanimous sufferer under this cruel scourge in foreign Regions, must view the Bill as a Beacon on our Coast, warning him to seek some other haven, where liberty and philanthropy in their due extent may offer a more certain repose from his troubles.

10.   Because, it will have a like tendency to banish our Citizens. The allure-

ments presented by other situations are every day thinning their number. To superadd a fresh motive to emigration, by revoking the liberty which they now enjoy, would be the same species of folly which has dishonoured and depopulated flourishing kingdoms.

11. Because, it will destroy that moderation and harmony which the forbearance of our laws to intermeddle with Religion, has produced amongst its several sects. Torrents of blood have been spilt in the old world, by vain attempts of the secular arm to extinguish Religious discord, by proscribing all difference in Religious opinions. Time has at length revealed the true remedy. Every relaxation of narrow and rigorous policy, wherever it has been tried, has been found to assuage the disease. The American Theatre has exhibited proofs, that equal and complete liberty, if it does not wholly eradicate it, sufficiently destroys its malignant influence on the health and prosperity of the State. If with the salutary effects of this system under our own eyes, we begin to contract the bonds of Religious freedom, we know no name that will too severely reproach our folly. At least let warning be taken at the first fruit of the threatened innovation. The very appearance of the Bill has transformed that "Christian forbearance,[4] love and charity," which of late mutually prevailed, into animosities and jealousies, which may not soon be appeased. What mischiefs may not be dreaded should this enemy to the public quiet be armed with the force of a law?

12. Because, the policy of the bill is adverse to the diffusion of the light of Christianity. The first wish of those who enjoy this precious gift, ought to be that it may be imparted to the whole race of mankind. Compare the number of those who have as yet received it with the number still remaining under the dominion of false Religions; and how small is the former! Does the policy of the Bill tend to lessen the disproportion? No; it at once discourages those who are strangers to the light of [revelation] from coming into the Region of it; and countenances, by example the nations who continue in darkness, in shutting out those who might convey it to them. Instead of leveling as far as possible, every obstacle to the victorious progress of truth, the Bill with an ignoble and unchristian timidity would circumscribe it, with a wall of defence, against the encroachments of error.

13. Because attempts to enforce by legal sanctions, acts obnoxious to so great a proportion of Citizens, tend to enervate the laws in general, and to slacken the bands of Society. If it be difficult to execute any law which is not generally deemed necessary or salutary, what must be the case where it is deemed invalid and dangerous? and what may be the effect of so striking an example of impotency in the Government, on its general authority?

14. Because a measure of such singular magnitude and delicacy ought not to be imposed, without the clearest evidence that it is called for by a majority of citizens: and no satisfactory method is yet proposed by which the voice of the majority in this case may be determined, or its influence secured. "The people of the respective counties are indeed requested to signify their opinion respecting the adoption of the Bill to the next Session of Assembly." But the representation must be made equal, before the voice either of the Representatives or of the Counties, will be that of the people. Our hope is that neither of the former will, after due consideration, espouse the dangerous principle of the Bill. Should the event disappoint us, it will still leave us in full confidence, that a fair appeal to the latter will reverse the sentence against our liberties.

15. Because, finally, "the equal right of every citizen to the free exercise of his Religion according to the dictates of conscience" is held by the same tenure with all our other rights. If we recur to its origin, it is equally the gift of nature; if we weigh its importance, it cannot be less dear to us; if we consult the Declaration of those rights which pertain to the good people of Virginia, as the "basis and foundation of Government,"[5] it is enumerated with equal solemnity, or rather studied emphasis. Either then, we must say, that the will of the Legislature is the only measure of their authority; and that in the plentitude of this authority, they may sweep away all our fundamental rights; or, that they are bound to leave this particular right untouched and sacred: Either we must say, that they may controul the freedom of the press, may abolish the trial by jury, may swallow up the Executive and Judiciary Powers of the State; nay that they may despoil us of our very right of suffrage, and erect themselves into an independent and hereditary assembly: or we must say, that they have no authority to enact into law the Bill under consideration. We the subscribers say, that the General Assembly of this Commonwealth have no such authority: And that no effort may be omitted on our part against so dangerous an usurpation, we oppose to it, this remonstrance; earnestly praying, as we are in duty bound, that the Supreme Lawgiver of the Universe, by illuminating those to whom it is addressed, may on the one hand, turn their councils from every act which would affront his holy prerogative, or violate the trust committed to them: and on the other, guide them into every measure which may be worthy of his [blessing, may re]dound to their own praise, and may establish more firmly the liberties, the prosperity, and the Happiness of the Commonwealth.

Notes

1. Decl. Rights, Article 16.
2. Decl. Rights, Article 1.
3. Article 16.
4. Article 16.
5. Decl. Rights - Title.

VIRGINIA STATUTE FOR RELIGIOUS FREEDOM

Adopted by the Virginia Legislature on 16 January 1785.
Codified at Virginia Statutes § 57-1.

Whereas, Almighty God hath created the mind free; that all attempts to influence it by temporal punishment, or burthens, or by civil incapacitations, tend only to beget habits of hypocrisy and meanness, and are a departure from the plan of the Holy Author of our religion, who, being Lord both of body and mind, yet chose not to propagate it by coercions on either, as was in his Almighty power to do; that the impious presumption of legislators and rulers, civil as well as ecclesiastical, who, being themselves but fallible and uninspired men, have assumed dominion over the faith of others, setting up their own opinions and modes of thinking as the only true and infallible, and as such endeavoring to impose them on others, have established and maintained false religions over the greatest part of the world, and through all time; that to compel a man to furnish contributions of money for the propagation of opinions which he disbelieves, is sinful and tyrannical, and even the forcing him to support this or that teacher of his own religious persuasion, is depriving him of the comfortable liberty of giving his contributions to the particular pastor whose morals he would make his pattern, and whose powers he feels most persuasive to righteousness, and is withdrawing from the ministry those temporary rewards which, proceeding from an approbation of their personal conduct, are an additional incitement to earnest and unremitting labors, for the instruction of mankind; that our civil rights have no dependence on our religious opinions any more than our opinions in physics or geometry; that therefore the proscribing any citizen as unworthy the public confidence by laying upon him an incapacity of being called to offices of trust and emolument, unless he profess or renounce this or that religious opinion, is depriving him injuriously of those privileges and advantages to which, in common with his fellow citizens, he has a natural right; that it tends only to corrupt the principles of that religion it is meant to encourage, by bribing, with a monopoly of worldly honors and emoluments, those who will externally profess and conform to it; that though, indeed, those are criminal who do not withstand such temptation, yet, neither are those innocent who lay the bait in their way; that to suffer the civil magistrate to intrude his powers into the field of opinion, and to restrain the profession or propagation of principles on supposition of their ill tendency, is a dangerous fallacy, which at once destroys all religious liberty, because he, being of course judge of that tendency, will make his opinions the rules of judgment, and approve or condemn the sentiments of others only as they shall square with or differ from his own; that it is time enough for the rightful purposes of civil government, for its officers to interfere, when principles break out into overt acts against peace and good order; and finally, that truth is great and will prevail, if left to herself; that she is the proper and sufficient antagonist to error, and has nothing to fear from the conflict, unless by human interposition disarmed of her natural weapons, free argument and debate; errors ceasing to be dangerous when it is permitted freely to contradict them:

Be it enacted by the General Assembly, That no man shall be compelled to frequent or support any religious worship, place or ministry whatsoever, nor shall be enforced, restrained, molested or burthened, in his body or goods, nor   shall otherwise suffer on account of his religious opinions or belief; but that all men shall be free to profess, and by argument to maintain, their opinions in matters of religion, and that the same shall in no wise diminish, enlarge or affect their civil capacities.

And though we well know that this Assembly, elected by the people for the ordinary purposes of legislation only, have no power to restrain the acts of succeeding assemblies constituted with powers equal to our own, and that, therefore, to declare this act to be irrevocable would be of no effect in law; yet we are free to declare, and do declare, that the rights hereby asserted are of the natural rights of mankind; and that if any act shall be hereafter passed to repeal the present, or to narrow its operation, such act will be an infringement of natural right.

THE PEOPLE'S REPUBLIC OF CHINA: DOCUMENT 19: THE BASIC VIEWPOINT ON THE RELIGIOUS QUESTION DURING OUR COUNTRY'S SOCIALIST PERIOD [SELECTIONS]

Issued by the Central Committee of the Chinese Communist Party
on 31 March 1982.
Translation reprinted with permission from Religion in China Today:
Policy and Practice 8-26, copyright ©1989 by Donald E. MacInnis
and published by Orbis Books.

I. Religion as a Historical Phenomenon

Religion is a historical phenomenon pertaining to a definite period in the development of human society. It has its own cycle of emergence, development, and demise. Religious faith and religious sentiment, along with religious ceremonies and organizations consonant with this faith and sentiment, are all products of the history of society. The earliest emergence of the religious mentality reflected the low level of production and the sense of awe toward natural phenomena of primitive peoples. With the evolution of class society, the most profound social roots of the existence and development of religion lay in the following factors: the helplessness of the people in the face of the blind forces alienating and controlling them in this kind of society; the fear and despair of the workers in the face of the enormous misery generated by the oppressive social system; and in the need of the oppressor classes to use religion as an opiate and as an important and vital means in its control of the masses. In Socialist society, the class root or the existence of religion was virtually lost following the elimination of the oppressive system and its oppressor class. However, because the people's consciousness lags behind social realities, old thinking and habits cannot be thoroughly wiped out in a short period. A long process

of struggle is required to achieve great increases in production strength, great abundance in material wealth, and a high level of Socialist democracy, along with high levels of development in education, culture, science, and technology. Since we cannot free ourselves from various hardships brought on by serious natural and man-made disasters within a short period of time; since class struggle continues to exist within certain limits; and given the complex international environment, the long-term influence of religion among a part of the people in a Socialist society cannot be avoided. Religion will eventually disappear from human history. But it will disappear naturally only through the long-term development of Socialism and Communism, when all objective requirements are met. All Party members must have a sober-minded recognition of the protracted nature of the religious question under Socialist conditions. Those who think that with the establishment of the Socialist system and with a certain degree of economic and cultural progress, religion will die out within a short period, are not being realistic. Those who expect to rely on administrative decrees or other coercive measures to wipe out religious thinking and practices with one blow are even further from the basic viewpoint Marxism takes toward the religious question. They are entirely wrong and will do no small harm.

II. The Religions of China

* * *

But in our appraisal of the religious question, we must reckon fully with its definite complex nature. To sum up, we may say that in old China, during the long feudal period and the more than one hundred years of semicolonial, semifeudal society, all religions were manipulated and controlled by the ruling classes, with extremely negative results. Within China, the Buddhist, Daoist, and Islamic leaderships were mainly controlled by the feudal landowners, feudal lords, and reactionary warlords, as well as the bureaucratic capitalistic class. The later foreign colonialist and imperialist forces mainly controlled the Roman Catholic and Protestant churches.

After Liberation there was a thorough transformation of the socioeconomic system and a major reform of the religious system, and so the status of religion in China has already undergone a fundamental change. The contradictions of the religious question now belong primarily to the category of contradictions among the people. The religious question, however, will continue to exist over a long period within certain limits, will continue to have a definite mass nature, to be entangled in many areas with the ethnic question, and to be affected by some class-struggle and complex international factors. This question, therefore, continues to be one of great significance which we cannot ignore. The question is this: can we handle this religious question properly as we work toward national stability and ethnic unity, as we develop our international relations while resisting the infiltration of hostile forces from abroad, and as we go on constructing a Socialist civilization with both material and spiritual values? This, then, demands that the Party committees on each level must adopt toward the religious question an attitude in accord with what Lenin said, "Be especially alert," "Be very strict," "Think things through thoroughly". To overestimate the seriousness or complexity of the question and so to panic, or to ignore the existence and complexity of the actual question and so let matters drift, would be equally wrong.

* * *

IV. The Party's Present Policy toward Religion

The basic policy the Party has adopted toward the religious question is that of respect for and protection of the freedom of religious belief. This is a long-term policy, one which must be continually carried out until that future time when religion will itself disappear. What do we mean by freedom of religious belief? We mean that every citizen has the freedom to believe in religion and also the freedom not to believe in religion. S/he has also the freedom to believe in this religion or that religion. Within a particular religion, s/he has the freedom to believe in this sect or that sect. A person who was previously a nonbeliever has the freedom to become a religious believer, and one who has been a religious believer has the freedom to become a nonbeliever. We Communists are atheists and must unremittingly propagate atheism. Yet at the same time we must understand that it will be fruitless and extremely harmful to use simple coercion in dealing with the people's ideological and spiritual questions — and this includes religious questions. We must further understand that at the present historical stage the difference that exists between the mass of believers and non-believers in matters of ideology and belief is relatively secondary. If we then one-sidedly emphasize this difference, even to the point of giving it primary importance — for example, by discriminating against and attacking the mass of religious believers, while neglecting and denying that the basic political and economic welfare of the mass of both religious believers and non-believers is the same — then we forget that the Party's basic task is to unite all the people (and this includes the broad mass of believers and non-believers alike) in order that all may strive to construct a modern, powerful Socialist state. To behave otherwise would only exacerbate the estrangement between the mass of believers and non-believers as well as incite and aggravate religious fanaticism, resulting in serious consequences for our Socialist enterprise. Our Party, therefore, bases its policy of freedom of religious belief on the theory formulated by Marxism-Leninism, and it is the only correct policy genuinely consonant with the people's welfare.

Naturally, in the process of implementing and carrying out this policy which emphasizes and guarantees the people's freedom to believe in religion, we must, at the same time, emphasize and guarantee the people's freedom not to believe in religion. These are two indispensable aspects of the same question. Any action which forces a nonbeliever to believe in religion is an infringement of freedom of religious belief, just as is any action which forces a believer not to believe. Both are grave errors and not to be tolerated. The guarantee of freedom of religious belief, far from being a hindrance, is a means of strengthening the Party's efforts to disseminate scientific education as well as to strengthen its propaganda against superstition. Furthermore, it should be emphasized that the crux of the policy of freedom of religious belief is to make the question of religious belief a private matter, one of individual free choice for citizens.

The political power in a Socialist state can in no way be used to promote any one religion, nor can it be used to forbid any one religion, as long as it is only a question of normal religious beliefs and practices. At the same time, religion will not be permitted to meddle in the administrative or juridical affairs of state, nor to intervene in the schools or public education. It will be absolutely forbidden to force anyone, particularly people under eighteen years of age, to become a member of a church, to become a Buddhist monk or nun, or to go to temples or monasteries to study Buddhist scripture. Religion will not be permitted to recover in any way those special feudal privileges which have been abolished or to return to an exploitative and oppressive religious system. Nor will religion be permitted to make use in any way of religious pretexts to oppose the Party's leadership or the Socialist system, or to destroy national or ethnic unity.

To sum up, the basic starting point and firm foundation for our handling of the religious question and for the implementation of our policy and freedom of religious belief lies in our desire to unite the mass of believers and non-believers and enable them to center all their will and strength on the common goal of building a modernized, powerful Socialist state. Any action or speech that deviates in the least from this basic line is completely erroneous, and must be firmly resisted and opposed by both Party and people.

*   *   *

VII. The Patriotic Religious Organizations

To give full play to the function of the patriotic religious organizations is to implement the Party's religious policy and is an important organizational guarantee for the normalization of religious activities. There are a total of eight national patriotic religious organizations, namely: the Chinese Buddhist Association, the Chinese Daoist Association, the Chinese Islamic Association, the Chinese Catholic Patriotic Association, the Chinese Catholic Religious Affairs Committee, the Chinese Catholic Bishops' Conference, the Chinese Protestant "Three Self" Patriotic Movement, and the China Christian Council. Besides these, there are a number of social groups and local organizations having a religious character. The basic task of these patriotic religious organizations is to assist the Party and the government to implement the policy of freedom of religious belief, to help the broad mass of religious believers and persons in religious circles to continually raise their patriotic and Socialist consciousness, to represent the lawful rights and interest of religious circles, to organize normal religious activities, and to manage religious affairs well. All patriotic religious organizations should follow the Party's and government's leadership. Party and government cadres in turn should become adept in supporting and helping religious organizations to solve their own problems.

* * *

IX. Communist Party Members and Religion; Relations with Religious Ethnic Minorities

The fact that our Party proclaims and implements a policy of freedom of religious belief does not, of course, mean that Communist Party members can freely believe in religion. The policy of freedom of religious belief is directed toward the citizens of our country; it is not applicable to Party members. Unlike the average citizen, the Party member belongs to a Marxist political party, and there can be no doubt at all that s/he must be an atheist and not a theist.

Our Party has clearly stated on many previous occasions: A Communist Party member cannot be a religious believer; s/he cannot take part in religious activities. Any member who persists in going against this proscription should be told to leave the Party.

* * *

X. Criminal and Counter-Revolutionary Activities under the Cover of Religion

The resolute protection of all normal religious activity suggests, at the same time, a determined crackdown on all criminal and anti-revolutionary activities which hide behind the facade of religion, which includes all superstitious practices which fall outside the scope of religion and are injurious to the national welfare as well as to the life and property of the people. All anti-revolutionary or other criminal elements who hide behind the facade of religion will be severely punished according to the law. Former professional religious, released upon completion of their term of imprisonment, who return to criminal activities will be punished again in accordance with the law. All banned reactionary secret societies, sorcerers, and witches, without exception, are forbidden to resume their activities. All those who spread fallacies to deceive and who cheat people of their money will, without exception, be severely punished according to the law. Party cadres who profit by these illegal activities will be dealt with all the more severely. Finally, all who make their living by phrenology, fortune telling, and geomancy should be educated, admonished, and helped to earn their living through their own labor and not to engage again in these superstitious practices which only deceive people. Should they not obey, then they should be dealt with according to the law.

In dealing according to the law with all

anti-revolutionary and other criminal elements who lurk within religious ranks, Party committees on each level and pertinent government departments must pay very close attention to cultivating public opinion. They should make use of irrefutable facts to fully expose the way in which these bad elements use religion to further their destructive activities. Furthermore, they should take care to clearly delineate the line dividing normal religious activities from criminal ones, pointing out that cracking down on criminal activities is in no way to attack, but is rather to protect, normal religious activities. Only then can we successfully win over, unite with, and educate the broad mass of religious believers and bring about the normalization of religious activities.

*   *   *

XII. The Role of the Party and State Organs in Handling the Religious Question

The central authorities of Party and State emphasize once again that all Party members must clearly understand that the Party's religious policy is not just a temporary expedient, but a decisive strategy based on the scientific theoretical foundation of Marxism-Leninism and Mao Zedong Thought, which takes as its goal the national unification of the people for the common task of building a powerful, modernized Socialist state. Under Socialism, the only correct fundamental way to solve the religious question lies precisely in safeguarding the freedom of religious belief. Only after the gradual development of the Socialist, economic, cultural, scientific, and technological enterprise and of a Socialist civiliza-

tion with its own material and spiritual values, will the type of society and level of awareness that gave rise to the existence of religion gradually disappear. Such a great enterprise naturally cannot be accomplished within a short period of time, nor even within one, two or three generations. Only after a long period of history, after many generations have passed, and after the combined struggle of the broad masses of both believers and non-believers will this come about. At that time, the Chinese people, on Chinese soil, will have thoroughly rid themselves of all impoverishment, ignorance, and spiritual emptiness, and will have become a highly developed civilization of material and spiritual values, able to takes [sic] its place in the front ranks of mankind in the glorious world. At that time, the vast majority of our citizens will be able to deal with the world and our fellowmen from a conscious scientific viewpoint, and no longer have any need for recourse to an illusory world of gods to seek spiritual solace. This is precisely what Marx and Engels have predicted — that there will be an age when people will have freed themselves from all alienating forces controlling the world and will have come to the stage when they will consciously plan and control the whole of social life. This is also what Comrade Mao Zedong meant when he said that the people, relying on themselves alone, will create a new age both for themselves and for the world. Only when we enter this new age will all that shows a religious face in the present world finally disappear. Therefore, each of us Party members from generation to generation, must put forth all our best efforts in the struggle to bring about this brilliant future.

THE BAPTIST WORLD ALLIANCE: MANIFESTO ON RELIGIOUS FREEDOM

Adopted at the Seventh Baptist World Congress in Copenhagen
on 3 August 1947.
Reprinted with permission of the Baptist World Alliance.

God, in His infinite wisdom, having created all men free, instilling in them qualities of independent judgment, calls upon us to-day, as Christian people, to maintain this God-given freedom not only for ourselves, but for all men everywhere. For it is our conviction that all liberties, both civic and religious, are bound together, and when one is violated all are endangered.

In order to enjoy the fruits of religious liberty we also must, at one and the same time, maintain our intellectual, political, and economic freedom.

Since the foundation of all our freedoms is the dignity of man created in the likeness of the eternal God, it is our first duty to extend the rights of conscience to all people, irrespective of their race, colour, sex, or religion (or lack of religion).

STANDING FIRM IN THE FAITH

We would honour our forefathers who fought valiantly for religious liberty in many lands. We rejoice with those our brethren who have resisted gloriously all attempts to subject the living Word of God to the will of totalitarian States or other outside pressures. We would that all, within our great worldwide fellowship, might have chosen this same course.

We would encourage all those, who must now continue to endure the persecution of secular powers, to stand firm in the faith, knowing that final victory must be on the side of the eternal God.

We appeal to Baptists everywhere to join hands, hearts, and minds with all others who are striving to make mankind free. Remembering our historic heritage of religious liberty, and those of our own number who have given their lives for this cause, some even onto death, we must always do much more than our ordinary share to help create a world which will be free of fear, free of want, and free of all kinds of slavery.

Moreover, we should actively support the efforts now being made by the United Nations to win the peace, believing that in its Preamble, its Charter, and its various organisations there is the possibility and the hope of a brotherhood of mankind in a commonwealth of nations.

RELATIONS OF CHURCH AND STATE

We believe that as loyal citizens we have specific duties to the State. But as Christians we must, when any conflict arises between the State and our religious convictions, place the will of God before the dictates and decrees of men.

No State, however great, is divine. Nor is any State Christian if, contrary to the spirit and Gospel of our Lord Jesus Christ, it denies and opposes in word and in deed the very will of God. It is Christian only when it becomes Christian in spirit and in truth. There can be no true religious liberty in a tyrannical State.

We would insist, moreover, that civil liberties must not be infringed upon because of a particular religious faith or Church affiliation.

Furthermore, we maintain that it is most difficult to have Establishment (or a State Church) and religious liberty at the same time. We believe that the Church should be separated from the State just as much as the State should be separated from the Church.

No Church should be given special privileges by the State, nor should any Church seek such. There must be equality among Christian people. They must not desire power or dominance one over the other.

PRACTICE WITHIN THE CHURCH

Just as the State does not have absolute power over the life and soul of the individual, neither does any ecclesiastical organisation, no matter how great or universal, have absolute authority over the life and soul of the individual.

Authority comes from God alone. Each man is his own priest: there is need of no other.

Democracy, freedom of conscience, the freedom to seek, to believe, and to find, applies as much *within* the Church itself as it does to any Government.

The Church, including every local, national, and international religious body or Council, must be the first to practise within and without its fold the great principle of liberty.

Let it never be said of Baptists that they are guilty of with-holding from others what they desire for themselves, namely, the right to follow the dictates of their own hearts.

CHARTER OF FREEDOM

Holding the principles of freedom dear, we therefore seek for all people everywhere, and in particular, all minority groups, the following freedoms:

Freedom to determine their own faith and creed;

Freedom of public and private worship, preaching and teaching;

Freedom from any opposition by the State to religious ceremonies and forms of worship;

Freedom to determine the nature of their own ecclesiastical government and the qualifications of their ministers and members, including the right of the individual to join the Church of his own choice, and the right to associate for corporate Christian action;

Freedom to control the education of their ministers, to give religious instruction to their youth, and to provide for the adequate development of their own religious life;

Freedom of Christian service, relief work, and missionary activity, both at home and abroad; and

Freedom to own and use such facilities and properties as will make possible the accomplishment of these ends.

These are our fundamental principles of liberty. Let us now, with the help of Almighty God, transform them into positive action through a worldwide crusade for freedom.

THE WORLD COUNCIL OF CHURCHES: DECLARATION ON RELIGIOUS LIBERTY

Adopted at the First Assembly of the World Council of Churches
in Amsterdam in August 1948.
Reprinted with permission, © The World Council of Churches.

An essential element in a good international order is freedom of religion. This is an implication of the Christian faith and of the world-wide nature of Christianity. Christians, therefore, view the question of religious freedom as an international problem. They are concerned that religious freedom be everywhere secured. In pleading for this freedom, they do not ask for any privilege to be granted to Christians that is denied to others. While the liberty with which Christ has set men free can neither be given nor destroyed by any Government, Christians, because of that inner freedom, are both jealous of its outward expression and solicitous that all men should have freedom in religious life. The nature and destiny of man by virtue of his creation, redemption and calling, and man's activities in family, state and culture establish limits beyond which the government cannot with impunity go. The rights which Christian discipleship demands are such as are good for all men, and no nation has ever suffered by reason of granting such liberties. Accordingly:

The rights of religious freedom herein declared shall be recognized and observed for all persons without distinctions as to race, colour, sex, language, or religion, and without imposition of disabilities by virtue of legal provision of administrative acts.

1.   Every person has the right to determine his own faith and creed.

The right to determine faith and creed involves both the process whereby a person adheres to a belief and the process whereby he changes his belief. It includes the right to receive instruction and education.

This right becomes meaningful when man has the opportunity of access to information. Religious, social and political institutions have the obligation to permit the mature individual to relate himself to sources of information in such a way as to allow personal religious decision and belief.

The right to determine one's belief is limited by the right of parents to decide sources of information to which their children shall have access. In the process of reaching decisions, everyone ought to take into account his higher self-interests and the implications of his beliefs for the well-being of his fellowmen.

2.   Every person has the right to express his religious beliefs in worship, teaching and practice, and to proclaim the implications of his beliefs for relationships in a social or political community.

The right of religious expression includes freedom of worship both public and private; freedom to place information at the disposal of others by processes of teaching, preaching and persuasion; and freedom to pursue such activities as are dictated by conscience. It also includes freedom to express implications of belief for society and its government.

This right requires freedom from arbitrary limitation of religious expression in all means of communication, including speech, press, radio, motion pictures and art. Social and political institutions should grant immunity from discrimination and from legal disability on grounds of expressed religious conviction, at least to the point where recognized community interests are adversely affected.

Freedom of religious expression is limited by the rights of parents to determine the religious point of view to which their children shall be exposed. It is further subject to such limitations, prescribed by law as are necessary to protect order and welfare, morals and the rights and freedoms of others. Each person must recognize the rights of others to express their beliefs and must have respect for authority at all times, even when conscience forces him to take issue with the people who are in authority or with the position they advocate.

3.   Every person has a right to associate with others and to organize with them for religious purposes.

This right includes freedom to form religious organizations, to seek membership in religious organizations, and to sever relationships with religious organizations.

It requires that the rights of association and organization guaranteed by a community to its members include the right of forming associations for religious purposes.

It is subject to the same limits imposed on all associations by non-discriminatory laws.

4.   Every religious organization, formed or maintained by action in accordance with the rights of individual persons, has the right to determine its policies and practices for the accomplishment of its chosen purposes.

The rights which are claimed for the individual in his exercise of religious liberty become the rights of the religious organization, including the right to determine its faith and creed; to engage in religious worship, both public and private; to teach, educate, preach and persuade; to express implications of belief for society and government. To these will be added certain corporate rights which derive from the rights of individual persons, such as the right: to determine the form of organization, its government and conditions of membership; to select and train its own officers, leaders and workers; to publish and circulate religious literature; to carry on service and missionary activities at home and abroad; to hold property and to collect funds; to co-operate and to unite with other religious bodies at home and in other lands, including freedom to invite or to send personnel beyond national frontiers and to give or to receive financial assistance; to use such facilities, open to all citizens or associations, as will make possible the accomplishment of religious ends.

In order that these rights may be realized in social experience, the state must grant to religious organizations and their members the same rights which it grants to other organizations, including the right of self-government, of public meeting, of speech, of press and publications, of holding property, of collecting funds, of travel, of ingress and egress, and generally of administering their own affairs.

The community has the right to require obedience to non-discriminatory laws passed in the interest of public order and well-being. In the exercise of its rights, a religious organization must respect the rights of other religious organizations and must safeguard the corporate and individual rights of the entire community.

THE CATHOLIC CHURCH AND THE SECOND VATICAN COUNCIL

In January 1959 Pope John XXIII convoked the Catholic Church's Twenty-first Ecumenical Council, the first since 1869-70. This council, called the Second Vatican Council or Vatican II, met in four sessions from 1962-65. John XXIII died in 1963 and the council was continued by Pope Paul VI. Sixteen documents were promulgated at the council, on such topics as changes to the liturgy, the constitution of the church, and the relationship of the church to the modern world, the ecumenical movement and other Christian churches. Of central importance to human rights related to religion or belief is the *Declaration on Religious Freedom* (Dignitatis Humanae). In this declaration the church recognizes that everyone has the right to freedom of religion regardless of their own religious belief and outlines the basis and scope of that right. The recognition of religious freedom by the church has contributed to significant changes in the relationship between religious institutions and the state in many of the states where Catholicism is the dominant religion. Another important Second Vatican Council document on rights related to religion and belief is the *Declaration on the Relationship of the Church to Non-Christian Religions* (Nostra Aetate). In this document the church repudiates persecution on the basis of religion, deplores anti-Semitism in all of its forms and rejects "any discrimination against men or harassment of them because of their race, color, condition of life or religion."

DECLARATION ON RELIGIOUS FREEDOM: DIGNITATIS HUMANAE

Adopted by the Second Vatican Council and
Proclaimed by His Holiness, Pope Paul VI
on 7 December 1965.

1. A sense of the dignity of the human person has been impressing itself more and more deeply on the consciousness of contemporary man,[1] and the demand is increasingly made that men should act on their own judgment, enjoying and making use of a responsible freedom, not driven by coercion but motivated by a sense of duty. The demand is likewise made that constitutional limits should be set to the powers of government, in order that there may be no encroachment on the rightful freedom of the person and of associations. This demand for freedom in human society chiefly regards the quest for the values proper to the human spirit. It regards, in the first place, the free exercise of religion in society. This Vatican Council takes careful note of these desires in the minds of men. It proposes to declare them to be greatly in accord with truth and justice. To this end, it searches into the sacred tradition and doctrine of the Church — the treasury out of which the Church continually brings forth new things that are in harmony with the things that are old.

First, the council professes its belief that God Himself has made known to mankind the way in which men are to serve Him, and thus be saved in Christ and come to blessedness. We believe that this one true religion subsists in the Catholic and Apostolic Church, to which the Lord Jesus committed the duty of spreading it abroad among all men. Thus He spoke to the Apostles: "Go, therefore, and make disciples of all nations, baptizing them in the name of the Father and of the Son and of the Holy Spirit, teaching them to observe all things whatsoever I have enjoined upon you" (Matt. 28: 19-20). On their part, all men are bound to seek the truth, especially in what concerns God and His Church, and to embrace the truth they come to know, and to hold fast to it.

This Vatican Council likewise professes its belief that it is upon the human conscience that these obligations fall and exert their binding force. The truth cannot impose itself except by virtue of its own truth, as it makes its entrance into the mind at once quietly and with power.

Religious freedom, in turn, which men demand as necessary to fulfill their duty to worship God, has to do with immunity from coercion in civil society. Therefore it leaves untouched traditional Catholic doctrine on the moral duty of men and societies toward the true religion and toward the one Church of Christ.

Over and above all this, the council intends to develop the doctrine of recent popes on the inviolable rights of the human person and the constitutional order of society.

2. This Vatican Council declares that the human person has a right to religious freedom. This freedom means that all men are to be immune from coercion on the part of individuals or of social groups and of any

human power, in such wise that no one is to be forced to act in a manner contrary to his own beliefs, whether privately or publicly, whether alone or in association with others, within due limits.

The council further declares that the right to religious freedom has its foundation in the very dignity of the human person as this dignity is known through the revealed word of God and by reason itself.[2] This right of the human person to religious freedom is to be recognized in the constitutional law whereby society is governed and thus it is to become a civil right.

It is in accordance with their dignity as persons — that is, beings endowed with reason and free will and therefore privileged to bear personal responsibility — that all men should be at once impelled by nature and also bound by a moral obligation to seek the truth, especially religious truth. They are also bound to adhere to the truth, once it is known, and to order their whole lives in accord with the demands of truth. However, men cannot discharge these obligations in a manner in keeping with their own nature unless they enjoy immunity from external coercion as well as psychological freedom. Therefore the right to religious freedom has its foundation not in the subjective disposition of the person, but in his very nature. In consequence, the right to this immunity continues to exist even in those who do not live up to their obligation of seeking the truth and adhering to it and the exercise of this right is not to be impeded, provided that just public order be observed.

3.   Further light is shed on the subject if one considers that the highest norm of human life is the divine law — eternal, objective and universal — whereby God orders, directs and governs the entire universe and all the ways of the human community by a plan conceived in wisdom and love. Man has been made by God to participate in this law, with the result that, under the gentle disposition of divine Providence, he can come to perceive ever more fully the truth that is unchanging. Wherefore every man has the duty, and therefore the right, to seek the truth in matters religious in order that he may with prudence form for himself right and true judgments of conscience, under use of all suitable means.

Truth, however, is to be sought after in a manner proper to the dignity of the human person and his social nature. The inquiry is to be free, carried on with the aid of teaching or instruction, communication and dialogue, in the course of which men explain to one another the truth they have discovered, or think they have discovered, in order thus to assist one another in the quest for truth.

Moreover, as the truth is discovered, it is by a personal assent that men are to adhere to it.

On his part, man perceives and acknowledges the imperatives of the divine law through the mediation of conscience. In all his activity a man is bound to follow his conscience in order that he may come to God, the end and purpose of life. It follows that he is not to be forced to act in a manner contrary to his conscience. Nor, on the other hand, is he to be restrained from acting in accordance with his conscience, especially in matters religious. The reason is that the exercise of religion, of its very nature, consists before all else in those internal, voluntary and free acts whereby man sets the course of his life directly toward God. No merely human power can either command or prohibit acts of this kind.[3] The social nature of man, however, itself requires that he should give external expression to his internal acts of religion: that he should share with others in matters religious; that he should profess his religion in community. Injury therefore is done to the human person and to the very order established by God for human life, if the free exercise of religion is denied in society, provided just public order is observed.

There is a further consideration. The religious acts whereby men, in private and in public and out of a sense of personal conviction, direct their lives to God transcend by their very nature the order of terrestrial and temporal affairs. Government therefore ought indeed to take account of the religious life of the citizenry and show it favor, since the function of government is to make provision for the common welfare. However, it would clearly transgress the limits set to its power, were it to presume to command or inhibit acts that are religious.

4.   The freedom or immunity from coercion in matters religious which is the endowment of persons as individuals is also to be recognized as their right when they act in community. Religious communities are a requirement of the social nature both of man and of religion itself.

Provided the just demands of public order are observed, religious communities rightfully claim freedom in order that they may govern themselves according to their own norms, honor the Supreme Being in public worship, assist their members in the practice of the religious life, strengthen them by instruction, and promote institutions in which they may join together for the purpose of ordering their own lives in accordance with their religious principles.

Religious communities also have the right not to be hindered, either by legal measures or by administrative action on the part of government, in the selection, training,

appointment, and transferal of their own ministers, in communicating with religious authorities and communities abroad, in erecting buildings for religious purposes, and in the acquisition and use of suitable funds or properties.

Religious communities also have the right not to be hindered in their public teaching and witness to their faith, whether by the spoken or by the written word. However, in spreading religious faith and in introducing religious practices everyone ought at all times to refrain from any manner of action which might seem to carry a hint of coercion or of a kind of persuasion that would be dishonorable or unworthy, especially when dealing with poor or uneducated people. Such a manner of action would have to be considered an abuse of one's right and a violation of the right of others.

In addition, it comes within the meaning of religious freedom that religious communities should not be prohibited from freely undertaking to show the special value of their doctrine in what concerns the organization of society and the inspiration of the whole of human activity. Finally, the social nature of man and the very nature of religion afford the foundation of the right of men freely to hold meetings and to establish educational, cultural, charitable and social organizations, under the impulse of their own religious sense.

5.   The family, since it is a society in its own original right, has the right freely to live its own domestic religious life under the guidance of parents. Parents, moreover, have the right to determine, in accordance with their own religious beliefs, the kind of religious education that their children are to receive. Government, in consequence, must acknowledge the right of parents to make a genuinely free choice of schools and of other

means of education, and the use of this freedom of choice is not to be made a reason for imposing unjust burdens on parents, whether directly or indirectly. Besides, the right of parents are violated, if their children are forced to attend lessons or instructions which are not in agreement with their religious beliefs, or if a single system of education, from which all religious formation is excluded, is imposed upon all.

6. Since the common welfare of society consists in the entirety of those conditions of social life under which men enjoy the possibility of achieving their own perfection in a certain fullness of measure and also with some relative ease, it chiefly consists in the protection of the rights, and in the performance of the duties, of the human person.[4] Therefore the care of the right to religious freedom devolves upon the whole citizenry, upon social groups, upon government, and upon the Church and other religious communities, in virtue of the duty of all toward the common welfare, and in the manner proper to each.

The protection and promotion of the inviolable rights of man ranks among the essential duties of government.[5] Therefore government is to assume the safeguard of the religious freedom of all its citizens, in an effective manner, by just laws and by other appropriate means.

Government is also to help create conditions favorable to the fostering of religious life, in order that the people may be truly enabled to exercise their religious rights and to fulfill their religious duties, and also in order that society itself may profit by the moral qualities of justice and peace which have their origin in men's faithfulness to God and to His holy will.[6]

If, in view of peculiar circumstances obtaining among peoples, special civil recognition is given to one religious community in the constitutional order of society, it is at the same time imperative that the right of all citizens and religious communities to religious freedom should be recognized and made effective in practice.

Finally, government is to see to it that equality of citizens before the law, which is itself an element of the common good, is never violated, whether openly or covertly, for religious reasons. Nor is there to be discrimination among citizens.

It follows that a wrong is done when government imposes upon its people, by force or fear or other means, the profession or repudiation of any religion, or when it hinders men from joining or leaving a religious community. All the more is it a violation of the will of God and of the sacred rights of the person and the family of nations when force is brought to bear in any way in order to destroy or repress religion, either in the whole of mankind or in a particular country or in a definite community.

7. The right to religious freedom is exercised in human society: hence its exercise is subject to certain regulatory norms. In the use of all freedoms the moral principle of personal and social responsibility is to be observed. In the exercise of their rights, individual men and social groups are bound by the moral law to have respect both for the rights of others and for their own duties toward others and for the common welfare of all. Men are to deal with their fellows in justice and civility.

Furthermore, society has the right to defend itself against possible abuses committed on the pretext of freedom of religion. It is the special duty of government to provide this protection. However, government is not to act in an arbitrary fashion or in an unfair spirit of partisanship. Its action is to be controlled by juridical norms which are in conformity with the objective moral order. These norms arise out of the need for the effective safeguard of the rights of all citizens and for the peaceful settlement of conflicts of rights, also out of the need for an adequate care of genuine public peace, which comes about when men live together in good order and in true justice, and finally out of the need for a proper guardianship of public morality.

These matters constitute the basic component of the common welfare: they are what is meant by public order. For the rest, the usages of society are to be the usages of freedom in their full range: that is, the freedom of man is to be respected as far as possible and is not to be curtailed except when and insofar as necessary.

8. Many pressures are brought to bear upon the men of our day, to the point where the danger arises lest they lose the possibility of acting on their own judgment. On the other hand, not a few can be found who seem inclined to use the name of freedom as the pretext for refusing to submit to authority and for making light of the duty of obedience. Wherefore this Vatican Council urges everyone, especially those who are charged with the task of educating others, to do their utmost to form men who, on the one hand, will respect the moral order and be obedient to lawful authority, and, on the other hand, will be lovers of true freedom — men, in other words, who will come to decisions on their own judgment and in the light of truth, govern their activities with a sense of responsibility, and strive after what is true and right, willing always to join with others in cooperative effort.

Religious freedom therefore ought to have this further purpose and aim, namely, that men may come to act with greater responsibility in fulfilling their duties in community life.

9. The declaration of this Vatican Council on the right of man to religious freedom has its foundation in the dignity of the person, whose exigencies have come to be more fully known to human reason through centuries of experience. What is more, this doctrine of freedom has roots in divine revelation, and for this reason Christians are bound to respect it all the more conscientiously. Revelation does not indeed affirm in so many words the right of man to immunity from external coercion in matters religious. It does, however, disclose the dignity of the human person in its full dimensions. It gives evidence of the respect which Christ showed toward the freedom with which man is to fulfill his duty of belief in the word of God and it gives us lessons in the spirit which disciples of such a Master ought to adopt and continually follow. Thus further light is cast upon the general principles upon which the doctrine of this declaration on religious freedom is based. In particular, religious freedom in society is entirely consonant with the freedom of the act of Christian faith.

10. It is one of the major tenets of Catholic doctrine that man's response to God in faith must be free: no one therefore is to be forced to embrace the Christian faith against his own will.[7] This doctrine is contained in the word of God and it was constantly proclaimed by the Fathers of the Church.[8] The act of faith is of its very nature a free act. Man, redeemed by Christ the Savior and through Christ Jesus called to be God's adopted son,[9] cannot give his adherence to God revealing Himself unless, under the drawing of the Father,[10] he offers to God the reasonable and free submission of faith. It is therefore completely in accord with the

nature of faith that in matters religious every manner of coercion on the part of men should be excluded. In consequence, the principle of religious freedom makes no small contribution to the creation of an environment in which men can without hindrance be invited to the Christian faith, embrace it of their own free will, and profess it effectively in their whole manner of life.

11. God calls men to serve Him in spirit and in truth, hence they are bound in conscience but they stand under no compulsion. God has regard for the dignity of the human person whom He Himself created and man is to be guided by his own judgment and he is to enjoy freedom. This truth appears at its height in Christ Jesus, in whom God manifested Himself and His ways with men. Christ is at once our Master and our Lord[11] and also meek and humble of heart.[12] In attracting and inviting His disciples He used patience.[13] He wrought miracles to illuminate His teaching and to establish its truth, but His intention was to rouse faith in His hearers and to confirm them in faith, not to exert coercion upon them.[14] He did indeed denounce the unbelief of some who listened to Him, but He left vengeance to God in expectation of the day of judgment.[15] When He sent His Apostles into the world, He said to them: "He who believes and is baptized will be saved. He who does not believe will be condemned" (Mark 16:16). But He Himself, noting that the cockle had been sown amid the wheat, gave orders that both should be allowed to grow until the harvest time, which will come at the end of the world.[16] He refused to be a political messiah, ruling by force:[17] He preferred to call Himself the Son of Man, who came "to serve and to give his life as a ransom for the many" (Mark 10:45). He showed Himself the perfect servant of God,[18] who "does not break the bruised reed nor extinguish the smoking flax" (Matt. 12:20).

He acknowledged the power of government and its rights, when He commanded that tribute be given to Caesar: but He gave clear warning that the higher rights of God are to be kept inviolate: "Render to Caesar the things that are Caesar's and to God the things that are God's" (Matt. 22:21). In the end, when He completed on the cross the work of redemption whereby He achieved salvation and true freedom for men, He brought His revelation to completion. For He bore witness to the truth,[19] but He refused to impose the truth by force on those who spoke against it. Not by force of blows does His will assert its claims.[20] It is established by witnessing to the truth and by hearing the truth, and it extends its dominion by the love whereby Christ, lifted up on the cross, draws all men to Himself.[21]

Taught by the word and example of Christ, the Apostles followed the same way. From the very origins of the Church the disciples of Christ strove to convert men to faith in Christ as the Lord; not, however, by the use of coercion or of devices unworthy of the Gospel, but by the power, above all, of the word of God.[22] Steadfastly they proclaimed to all the plan of God our Savior, "who wills that all men should be saved and come to the acknowledgment of the truth" (1 Tim. 2:4). At the same time, however, they showed respect for those of weaker stuff, even though they were in error, and thus they made it plain that "each one of us is to render to God an account of himself" (Romans 14:12),[23] and for that reason is bound to obey his conscience. Like Christ Himself, the Apostles were unceasingly bent upon bearing witness to the truth of God, and they showed the fullest measure of boldness in "speaking the word with confidence" (Acts 4:31)[24] before the people and their rulers. With a firm faith they held that the Gospel is indeed the power of God unto salvation for all who believe.[25] Therefore they rejected all "carnal weapons";[26] they followed the example of the gentleness and respectfulness of Christ and they preached the word of God in the full confidence that there was resident in this word itself a divine power able to destroy all the forces arrayed against God[27] and bring men to faith in Christ and to His service.[28] As the Master, so too the Apostles recognized legitimate civil authority. "For there is no power except from God", the Apostle teaches, and thereafter commands: "Let everyone be subject to higher authorities .... He who resists authority resists God's ordinance" (Romans 13:1-5).[29] At the same time, however, they did not hesitate to speak out against governing powers which set themselves in opposition to the holy will of God: "It is necessary to obey God rather than men" (Acts 5:29).[30] This is the way along which the martyrs and other faithful have walked through all ages and over all the earth.

12.   In faithfulness therefore to the truth of the Gospel, the Church is following the way of Christ and the apostles when she recognizes and gives support to the principle of religious freedom as befitting the dignity of man and as being in accord with divine revelation. Throughout the ages the Church has kept safe and handed on the doctrine received from the Master and from the apostles. In the life of the People of God, as it has made its pilgrim way through the vicissitudes of human history, there has at times appeared a way of acting that was hardly in accord with the spirit of the Gospel or even opposed to it. Nevertheless, the doctrine of the Church that no one is to be coerced into faith has always stood firm.

Thus the leaven of the Gospel has long been about its quiet work in the minds of men, and to it is due in great measure the fact that in the course of time men have come more widely to recognize their dignity as persons, and the conviction has grown stronger that the person in society is to be kept free from all manner of coercion in matters religious.

13.   Among the things that concern the good of the Church and indeed the welfare of society here on earth — things therefore that are always and everywhere to be kept secure and defended against all injury — this certainly is preeminent, namely, that the Church should enjoy that full measure of freedom which her care for the salvation of men requires.[31] This is a sacred freedom, because the only-begotten Son endowed with it the Church which He purchased with His blood. Indeed it is so much the property of the Church that to act against it is to act against the will of God. The freedom of the Church is the fundamental principle in what concerns the relations between the Church and governments and the whole civil order.

In human society and in the face of government the Church claims freedom for herself in her character as a spiritual authority, established by Christ the Lord, upon which there rests, by divine mandate, the duty of going out into the whole world and preaching the Gospel to every creature.[32] The Church also claims freedom for herself in her character as a society of man who have the right to live in society in accordance with the precepts of the Christian faith.[33]

In turn, where the principle of religious freedom is not only proclaimed in words or simply incorporated in law but also given sincere and practical application, there the Church succeeds in achieving a stable situation of right as well as of fact and the independence which is necessary for the fulfillment of her divine mission.

This independence is precisely what the authorities of the Church claim in society.[34] At the same time, the Christian faithful, in common with all other men, possess the civil right not to be hindered in leading their lives in accordance with their consciences. Therefore, a harmony exists between the freedom of the Church and the religious freedom which is to be recognized as the right of all men and communities and sanctioned by constitutional law.

14. In order to be faithful to the divine command, "teach all nations" (Matt. 28:19-20), the Catholic Church must work with all urgency and concern "that the word of God be spread abroad and glorified" (2 Thess. 3:1). Hence the Church earnestly begs of its children that, "first of all, supplications, prayers, petitions, acts of thanksgiving be made for all men .... For this is good and agreeable in the sight of God our Savior, who wills that all men be saved and come to the knowledge of the truth" (1 Tim. 2:1-4). In the formation of their consciences, the Christian faithful ought carefully to attend to the sacred and certain doctrine of the Church.[35] For the Church is, by the will of Christ, the teacher of the truth. It is her duty to give utterance to, and authoritatively to teach, that truth which is Christ Himself, and also to declare and confirm by her authority those principles of the moral order which have their origins in human nature itself. Furthermore, let Christians walk in wisdom in the face of those outside, "in the Holy Spirit, in unaffected love, in the word of truth" (2 Cor. 6:6-7), and let them be about their task of spreading the light of life with all confidence [36] and apostolic courage, even to the shedding of their blood.

The disciple is bound by a grave obligation toward Christ, his Master, ever more fully to understand the truth received from Him, faithfully to proclaim it, and vigorously to defend it, never — be it understood — having recourse to means that are incompatible with the spirit of the Gospel. At the same time, the charity of Christ urges him to love and have prudence and patience in his dealings with those who are in error or in ignorance with regard to the faith.[37] All is to be taken into account — the Christian duty to Christ, the life-giving word which must be proclaimed, the rights of the human person, and the measure of grace granted by God through Christ to men who are invited freely to accept and profess the faith.

15. The fact is that men of the present day want to be able freely to profess their religion in private and in public. Indeed, religious freedom has already been declared to be a civil right in most constitutions, and it is solemnly recognized in international documents.[38] The further fact is that forms of government still exist under which, even though freedom of religious worship receives constitutional recognition, the powers of government are engaged in the effort to deter citizens from the profession of religion and to make life very difficult and dangerous for religious communities.

This council greets with joy the first of these two facts as among the signs of the times. With sorrow, however, it denounces the other fact, as only to be deplored. The council exhorts Catholics, and it directs a plea to all men, most carefully to consider how greatly necessary religious freedom is, especially in the present condition of the human family. All nations are coming into even closer unity. Men of different cultures and religions are being brought together in closer relationships. There is a growing consciousness of the personal responsibility that every man has. All this is evident. Consequently, in order that relationships of peace and harmony be established and maintained within the whole of mankind, it is necessary that religious freedom be everywhere provided with an effective constitutional guarantee and that respect be shown for the high duty and right of man freely to lead his religious life in society.

May the God and Father of all grant that the human family, through careful observance of the principle of religious freedom in society, may be brought by the grace of Christ and the power of the Holy Spirit to the sublime and unending and "glorious freedom of the sons of God" (Rom. 8:21).

Notes

1. Cf. John XXIII, encycl. "Pacem in Terris", April 11, 1963: AAS 55 (1963) p. 279; ibid., p. 265; Pius XII, radio message, Dec. 24, 1944: AAS 37 (1945), p. 14.

2. Cf. John XXIII, encycl. "Pacem in Terris", April 11, 1963: AAS 55 (1963), pp. 260-261; Pius XII, radio message, Dec. 24, 1942: AAS 35 (1943) p. 19; Pius XI, encycl. "Mit Brennender Sorge", March 14, 1937: AAS 29 (1937), p. 160; Leo XIII, encycl. "Libertas Praestantissimum", June 20, 1888: Acts of Leo XIII 8 (1888), pp. 237-238.

3. Cf. John XXIII, encycl. "Pacem in Terris", April 11, 1963: AAS 55 (1963), p. 270; Paul VI, radio message, Dec. 22, 1964: AAS 57 (1965), pp. 181-182.

4. Cf. John XXIII, encycl. "Mater et Magistra", May 15, 1961: AAS 53 (1961), p. 417; idem, encycl. "Pacem in Terris", April 11, 1963: AAS 55 (1963), p. 273.

5. Cf. John XXIII, encycl. "Pacem in Terris", April 11, 1963: AAS 55 (1963) pp. 273-274; Pius XII, radio message, June 1, 1941: AAS 33 (1941), p. 200.

6. Cf. Leo XIII, encycl. "Immortale Dei", Nov. 1, 1885: AAS 18 (1885) p. 161.

7. Cf. Lactantius "Divinarum Institutionum", Book V, 19: CSEL 19, pp. 463-464, 465: PL 6, 614 and 616 (ch. 20); St. Ambrose, "Epistola ad Valentianum Imp.", Letter 21: PL 16, 1005; St. Augustine, "Contra Litteras Petiliani", Book II, ch. 83: CSEL 52 p. 112: PL 43, 315; cf. C. 23, q. 5, c. 33, (ed. Friedberg, col. 939); idem, Letter 23: PL 33, 98; idem, Letter 34: PL 33, 132; idem, Letter 35: PL 33, 135; St. Gregory the Great, "Epistola ad Virgilium et Theodorum Episcopos Massiliae Galliarum", Register of Letters I, 45: MGH Ep. 1, p. 72: PL 77, 510-511 (Book I, ep. 47); idem, "Epistola ad Johannem Episcopum Constantinopolitanum", Register of Letters, III, 52: MGH Letter 1, p. 210: PL 77, 649 (Book III, Letter 53), cf. D. 45, c. 1 (ed. Friedberg, col. 160); Council of Toledo IV, c. 57: Mansi 10, 633; cf. D. 45, c. 5 (ed. Friedberg, col. 161-162); Clement III: X., V, 6, 9: ed. Friedberg, col. 774; Innocent III, "Epistola ad Arelatensem Archiepiscopum", X., III, 42, 3: Friedberg, col. 646.

8. Cf. CIC, c. 1351; Pius XII, allocution to prelate auditors and other officials and administrators of the tribune of the Holy Roman Rota, Oct. 6, 1946: AAS 38 (1946), p. 394; idem. Encycl. "Mystici Corporis", June 29, 1943: AAS (1943) p. 243.

9. Cf. Eph. 1:5.

10. Cf. John 6:44.

11. Cf. John 13:13.

12. Cf. Matt. 11:29.

13. Cf. Matt. 11:28-30; John 6:67-68.

14. Cf. Matt. 9:28-29; Mark 9:23-24; 6:5-6; Paul VI, encycl. "Ecclesiam Suam", Aug. 6, 1964: AAS 56 (1964), pp. 642-643.

15. Cf. Matt. 11:20-24; Rom. 12:19-20; 2 Thess. 1:8.

16. Cf. Matt. 13:30 and 40-42.

17. Cf. Matt. 4:8-10; John 6:15.

18. Cf. Is. 42:1-4.
19. Cf. John 18:37.
20. Cf. Matt. 26:51-53; John 18:36.
21. Cf. John 12:32.
22. Cf. 1 Cor. 2:3-5; 1 Thess. 2:3-5.
23. Cf. Rom. 14:1-23; 1 Cor. 8:9-13; 10:23-33.
24. Cf. Eph. 6:19-20.
25. Cf. Rom. 1:16.
26. Cf. 2 Cor. 10:4; 1 Thess. 5:8-9.
27. Cf. Eph. 6:11-17.
28. Cf. 2 Cor. 10:3-5.
29. Cf. 1 Pet. 2:13-17.
30. Cf. Acts 4 :19-20.
31. Cf. Leo XIII, letter "Officio Sanctissimo", Dec. 22, 1887: AAS 20 (1887), p. 269; idem, letter "Ex Litteris", April 7, 1887: AAS 19 (1886), p.465.
32. Cf. Mark 16:15; Matt. 28:18-20; Pius XII, encycl. "Summi Pontificatus", Oct. 20, 1939: AAS 31 (1939). pp. 445-446.
33. Cf. Pius XI, letter "Firmissiman Constantiam", March 28, 1937: AAS 29 (1937), p. 196.
34. Cf. Pius XII, allocution, "Ci Riesce", Dec. 6, 1953: AAS 45 (1953), p. 802.
35. Cf. Pius XII, radio message, March 23, 1952: AAS 44 (1952) pp. 270-278.
36. Cf. Acts 4:29.
37. Cf. John XXIII, encycl. "Pacem in Terris (1963), April 11, 1963: AAS 55 pp. 299-300.
38. Cf. John XXIII, encycl. "Pacem in Terris", April 11, 1963: AAS 55 (1963) pp. 295-296.

PART V

**SELECTED DOCUMENTS ON
THE
RELATIONSHIP BETWEEN THE
STATE AND RELIGIOUS INSTITUTIONS**

THE RELATIONSHIP BETWEEN THE STATE AND RELIGIOUS INSTITUTIONS

The myriad aspects of the relationship between the state and religious communities and institutions are governed by an extremely diverse set of state practices. In some states different laws apply to different religious communities, and some allow communities to apply their own laws in certain fields. Other states treat religious groups only as organizational entities. Some states regulate religious organizations as such (sometimes having a specific executive or administrative governmental body devoted solely to religious affairs), while others treat them in the context of non-profit charitable and educational organizations. Some states have general laws and regulations that cover all religious organizations, while others have separate laws or agreements covering the institutions of individual or classes of recognized denominations.

The subjects covered under these various laws and agreements include (1) the rights and powers of religious entities, (2) privileges granted by the state to all religious entities, or to religious entities that meet certain criteria and (3) limitations on the activities of religious entities. Examples of important rights and powers include the acquisition of legal personality, the ability to own and transfer property, the freedom to order the internal affairs of the entity according to appropriate doctrinal principles and the ability to raise funds through charitable solicitation. Typical privileges include state financial support (sometimes through a direct tax); the recognition of the jurisdiction of religious courts; access of clerics to public facilities such as prisons, hospitals and installations of the armed forces; the ability to conduct religious instruction and worship in the state-sponsored schools; and access to public broadcasting. Examples of limitations include limitations on commercial activity, political activity and occasionally on the ability to proselytize and accept converts.

INTERNATIONAL RELATIONS: THE HOLY SEE

The Holy See is the supreme organ of government of the Catholic Church and is composed of the Pope and the Roman Curia (the central administration of the church). Prior to 1870 the Pope was also the sovereign of the Papal States. In 1870 what remained of the Papal States was seized by the Kingdom of Italy, and the relationship between Italy and the Holy See was not reconciled until the two parties signed the Lateran Treaty and the Italian Concordat in 1929. These documents are reprinted in Peaslee, Constitutions of Nations, Volume III, (Rev. 3rd ed. 1968) at 1187, 1194. Under the terms of the Lateran Treaty, Italy recognized the sovereign jurisdiction of the Holy See over a new state entity: the "City of the Vatican", which consists essentially of the 101-acre Vatican complex and its residents. It is generally agreed that the Vatican City does not possess the requisite characteristics to be considered a state in international law.

There is not complete agreement in the international community as to the precise status of the Holy See. To the extent that the claim of the Holy See for international legal status is based on its religious authority and mission, it is hard to imagine governments granting similar status to other religious entities. On the other hand, it has long been the practice of states to accord the Holy See some state-like status.

The Holy See has concluded a number of bilateral agreements, and states have generally treated these as they would international treaties. The Holy See has also signed numerous multilateral agreements open only to states. Representatives of the Holy See in foreign states — called papal nuncios — are regularly treated as ambassadors. Neither the Holy See nor the Vatican City are members of the United Nations, although the Holy See has been granted the status of "non-member state permanent observer", a status similar to Switzerland. The Holy See therefore can participate in a variety of United Nations activities. It played an important and somewhat controversial role in two recent United Nations conferences: the International Conference on Population and Development held in Cairo in 1994 and the Fourth World Conference on Women held in Beijing in 1995.

The Holy See has concluded a number of bilateral agreements — usually called "Concordats" — with states regarding the position of the Catholic Church in that state. The Concordats cover a wide range of issues including state support for the church, the recognition of the ecclesiastical authority of the church and the church's role in education. Following the strengthening of international standards of non-discrimination on the basis of religion or belief and the recognition by the Catholic Church at the Second Vatican Council of the right of all to freedom of religion, a number of states have changed the constitutional position of the Catholic Church or religion and have found it necessary to negotiate new Concordats with the Holy See. Concordats concluded with Colombia (1974), Spain (1976), and Italy (1984) are the most prominent examples of this trend. The fall of communist governments in Eastern Europe and the former Soviet Union has also given rise to the negotiation of new Concordats.

The unique and unusual status accorded to the Holy See is perhaps best understood as a combination of (1) a consistent history of state practice of recognition of the international character of the Holy See and (2) the presence of a territorial entity — the Vatican City — under its jurisdiction.

PREAMBLE

The Holy See and the State of Israel,

Mindful of the singular character and universal significance of the Holy Land;

Aware of the unique nature of the relationship between the Catholic Church and the Jewish people, and of the historic process of reconciliation and growth in mutual understanding and friendship between Catholics and Jews;

Having decided on 29 July 1992 to establish a 'Bilateral Permanent Working Commission,' in order to study and define together issues of common interest, and in view of normalizing their relations;

Recognizing that the work of the aforementioned Commission has produced sufficient material for a first and Fundamental Agreement;

Realizing that such Agreement will provide a sound and lasting basis for the continued development of their present and future relations and for the furtherance of the Commission's task,

Agree upon the following Articles:

Article 1
1.   The State of Israel, recalling its Declaration of Independence, affirms its continuing commitment to uphold and observe the human right to freedom of religion and conscience, as set forth in the Universal Declaration of Human Rights and in other international instruments to which it is a party.

2.   The Holy See, recalling the Declaration on Religious Freedom of the Second Vatican Ecumenical Council, 'Dignitatis humanae', affirms the Catholic Church's commitment to uphold the human right to freedom of religion and conscience, as set forth in the Universal Declaration of Human Rights and in other international instruments to which it is a party. The Holy See wishes to affirm as well the Catholic Church's respect for other religions and their followers as solemnly stated by the Second Vatican Ecumenical Council in its Declaration on the Relation of the Church to Non-Christian Religions, 'Nostra aetate'.

Article 2
1.   The Holy See and the State of Israel are committed to appropriate co-operation in combating all forms of antisemitism and all kinds of racism and of religious intolerance, and in promoting mutual understanding among nations, tolerance among communities and respect for human life and dignity.

2.   The Holy See takes this occasion to reiterate its condemnation of hatred, persecution and all other manifestations of antisemitism directed against the Jewish people and individual Jews anywhere, at any time and by anyone. In particular, the Holy See deplores attacks on Jews and desecration of

Jewish synagogues and cemeteries, acts which offend the memory of the victims of the Holocaust, especially when they occur in the same places which witnessed it.

Article 3

1.   The Holy See and the State of Israel recognize that both are free in the exercise of their respective rights and powers, and commit themselves to respect this principle in their mutual relations and in their co-operation for the good of the people.

2.   The State of Israel recognizes the right of the Catholic Church to carry out its religious, moral, educational and charitable functions, and to have its own institutions, and to train, appoint and deploy its own personnel in the said institutions or for the said functions to these ends. The Church recognizes the right of the State to carry out its functions, such as promoting and protecting the welfare and the safety of the people. Both the State and the Church recognize the need for dialogue and co-operation in such matters as by their nature call for it.

3.   Concerning Catholic legal personality at canon law the Holy See and the State of Israel will negotiate on giving it full effect in Israeli law, following a report from a joint subcommission of experts.

Article 4

1.   The State of Israel affirms its continuing commitment to maintain and respect the 'Status quo' in the Christian Holy Places to which it applies and the respective rights of the Christian communities thereunder. The Holy See affirms the Catholic Church's continuing commitment to respect the aforementioned 'Status quo' and the said rights.

2.   The above shall apply notwithstanding an interpretation to the contrary of any Article in this Fundamental Agreement.

3.   The State of Israel agrees with the Holy See on the obligation of continuing respect for and protection of the character proper to Catholic sacred places, such as churches, monasteries, convents, cemeteries and their like.

4.   The State of Israel agrees with the Holy See on the continuing guarantee of the freedom of Catholic worship.

Article 5

1.   The Holy See and the State of Israel recognize that both have an interest in favouring Christian pilgrimages to the Holy Land. Whenever the need for coordination arises, the proper agencies of the Church and of the State will consult and cooperate as required.

2.   The State of Israel and the Holy See express the hope that such pilgrimages will provide an occasion for better understanding between the pilgrims and the people and religions in Israel.

Article 6

The Holy See and the State of Israel jointly reaffirm the right of the Catholic Church to establish, maintain and direct schools and institutes of study at all levels; this right being exercised in harmony with the rights of the State in the field of education.

Article 7

The Holy See and the State of Israel recognize a common interest in promoting and encouraging cultural exchanges between Catholic institutions worldwide, and educational, cultural and research institutions in Israel, and in facilitating access to manuscripts, historical documents and similar source materials, in conformity with applicable laws and regulations.

Article 8

The State of Israel recognizes that the right of the Catholic Church to freedom of expression in the carrying out of its functions is exercised also through the Church's own communications media; this right being exercised in harmony with the rights of the State in the field of communications media.

Article 9

The Holy See and the State of Israel jointly reaffirm the right of the Catholic Church to carry out its charitable functions through its health care and social welfare institutions, this right being exercised in harmony with the rights of the State in this field.

Article 10

1. The Holy See and the State of Israel jointly reaffirm the right of the Catholic Church to property.

2. Without prejudice to rights relied upon by the Parties:

(a) The Holy See and the State of Israel will negotiate in good faith a comprehensive agreement, containing solutions acceptable to both Parties, on unclear, unsettled and disputed issues, concerning property, economic and fiscal matters relating to the Catholic Church generally, or to specific Catholic Communities or institutions.

(b) For the purpose of the said negotiations, the Permanent Bilateral Working Commission will appoint one or more bilateral subcommissions of experts to study the issues and make proposals.

(c) The Parties intend to commence the aforementioned negotiations within three months of entry into force of the present Agreement, and aim to reach agreement within two years from the beginning of the negotiations.

(d) During the period of these negotiations, actions incompatible with these commitments shall be avoided.

Article 11

1. The Holy See and the State of Israel declare their respective commitment

to the promotion of the peaceful resolution of conflicts among States and nations, excluding violence and terror from international life.

2. The Holy See, while maintaining in every case the right to exercise its moral and spiritual teaching-office, deems it opportune to recall that, owing to its own character, it is solemnly committed to remaining a stranger to all merely temporal conflicts, which principle applies specifically to disputed territories and unsettled borders.

Article 12

The Holy See and the State of Israel will continue to negotiate in good faith in pursuance of the Agenda agreed upon in Jerusalem, on 15 July 1992, and confirmed at the Vatican, on 29 July 1992; likewise on issues arising from Articles of the present Agreement, as well as on other issues bilaterally agreed upon as objects of negotiation.

Article 13

1. In this Agreement the Parties use these terms in the following sense:

(a) The Catholic Church and the Church — including, inter alia, its Communities and institutions.

(b) Communities of the Catholic Church — meaning the Catholic religious entities considered by the Holy See as Churches sui juris and by the State of Israel as Recognized Religious Communities;

(c) The State of Israel and the State — including, inter alia, its authorities established by law.

2. Notwithstanding the validity of this Agreement as between the Parties, and without detracting from the generality of any applicable rule of law with reference to treaties, the Parties agree that this Agreement does not prejudice rights and obligations arising from existing treaties between either Party and a State or States,

which are known and in fact available to both Parties at the time of the signature of this Agreement.

Article 14

1.   Upon signature of the present Fundamental Agreement and in preparation for the establishment of full diplomatic relations, the Holy See and the State of Israel exchange Special Representatives, whose rank and privileges are specified in an Additional Protocol.

2.   Following the entry into force and immediately upon the beginning of the implementation of the present Fundamental Agreement, the Holy See and the State of Israel will establish full diplomatic relations at the level of Apostolic Nunciature, on the part of the Holy See, and Embassy, on the part of the State of Israel.

Article 15

This Agreement shall enter into force on the date of the latter notification of ratification by a Party.

Done in two original copies in the English and Hebrew languages, both texts being equally authentic. In case of divergency, the English text shall prevail.

Signed in Jerusalem, this thirtieth day of the month of December, in the year 1993, which corresponds to the sixteenth day of the month of Tevet, in the year 5754.

ADDITIONAL PROTOCOL

1.   In relation to Art. 14 (1) of the Fundamental Agreement, signed by the Holy See and the State of Israel, the 'Special Representatives' shall have, respectively, the personal rank of Apostolic Nuncio and Ambassador.

2.   These Special Representatives shall enjoy all the rights, privileges and immunities granted to Heads of Diplomatic Missions under international law and common usage, on the basis of reciprocity.

3.   The Special Representative of the State of Israel to the Holy See, while residing in Italy, shall enjoy all the rights, privileges and immunities defined by Art. 12 of the Treaty of 1929 between the Holy See and Italy, regarding Envoys of Foreign Governments to the Holy See residing in Italy. The rights, privileges and immunities extended to the personnel of a Diplomatic Mission shall likewise be granted to the personnel of the Israeli Special Representative's Mission. According to an established custom, neither the Special Representative, nor the official members of his Mission, can at the same time be members of Israel's Diplomatic Mission to Italy.

4.   The Special Representative of the Holy See to the State of Israel may at the same time exercise other representative functions of the Holy See and be accredited to other States. He and the personnel of his Mission shall enjoy all the rights, privileges and immunities granted by Israel to Diplomatic Agents and Missions.

5.   The names, rank and functions of the Special Representatives will appear, in an appropriate way, in the official lists of Foreign Missions accredited to each Party.

Signed in Jerusalem, this thirtieth day of the month of December, in the year 1993, which corresponds to the sixteenth day of the month of Tevet, in the year 5754.

Taking into account the process of political and social change that has occurred in Italy over the last decades and the developments which have taken place in the Church since the Second Vatican Council;

Bearing in mind, on the part of the Italian Republic, the principles proclaimed in its Constitution and, on the part of the Holy See, the Second Vatican Ecumenical Council's declarations on religious freedom and on the relations between the Church and the polity, as well as the new codification of canon law;

Considering further that, in accordance with Article 7, paragraph (2) of the Constitution of the Italian Republic, the relations between the State and the Catholic Church are governed by the Lateran Pacts, which, however, can be modified by common agreement of the two Parties without requiring any procedure of Constitutional revision;

Have recognized the opportunity of entering into the following mutually agreed amendments to the Lateran Concordat:

Article 1

The Italian Republic and the Holy See reaffirm that the State and the Catholic Church are, each in its own order, independent and sovereign and commit themselves to the full respect of this principle in their mutual relations and to reciprocal collabora-tion for the promotion of man and the common good of the Country.

Article 2

1.   The Italian Republic shall recognize the full freedom of the Church to develop its pastoral, educational, and charitable mission, of evangelization and sanctification. In particular, the Church shall be assured the freedom of organization, of public exercise of worship, of exercise of its magisterium and spiritual ministry as well as of exercise of jurisdiction in ecclesiastical matters.

2.   It shall be equally assured the reciprocal freedom of communication and correspondence between the Holy See, the Italian Bishops Conference, the Regional Bishops Conferences, the bishops, the clergy and the faithful, as well as the freedom of printing and circulating acts and documents concerning the mission of the Church.

3.   Catholics and their associations and organizations shall be granted the full freedom of assembly and of expression of their thoughts by oral, written, or any other means of publication.

4.   The Italian Republic acknowledges the particular significance that Rome, the Episcopal See of the Supreme Pontiff, has to Catholicism.

Article 3

1.   The boundaries of the dioceses and of the parishes shall be freely determined by the ecclesiastical authority. The

Holy See commits itself not to include any part of the Italian territory into a diocese whose Episcopal See is in the territory of another State.

2. Appointments to ecclesiastical offices shall be freely made by the ecclesiastical authority. The ecclesiastical authority shall communicate to the competent civil authorities the appointments of the Archbishops and diocesan bishops, of the coadjutors, the abbots and prelates with territorial jurisdiction as well as of the parish priests and the appointments to the other ecclesiastical offices relevant for the State legal order.

3. Except for the diocese of Rome and for the suburban ones, ecclesiastics who are not Italian citizens shall not be appointed to the offices hereof.

Article 4

1. The priests, the deacons, and the members of the religious orders who have taken vows shall have the right to obtain, at their own request, an exemption from the military service or to be assigned to the substitutive Civil Service.

2. In the event of general mobilization, the ecclesiastics who have not been assigned to the care of souls shall be called to exercise their religious office among the troops or, subordinately, they shall be assigned to the medical service.

3. Students of theology, those in the last two years of their theological preparation for ordination and novices of religious institutes and societies for apostolic life may take advantage of the same postponements of military service which are granted to the students of Italian Universities.

4. Ecclesiastics shall not be required to provide to magistrates or other authorities any information regarding persons or matters known to them by reason of their ministry.

Article 5

1. Buildings open to worship shall not be requisitioned, occupied, expropriated or demolished except for grave reasons and pursuant to a previous agreement with the competent ecclesiastical authority.

2. Except in cases of urgent necessity, the police force shall not enter buildings open to worship for the purpose of carrying out its duties without first advising the ecclesiastical authority thereof.

3. The civil authority shall take into account the religious needs of the people, as presented to it by the competent ecclesiastical authority, in connection with the construction of new buildings for Catholic worship and of the pertinent parish structures.

Article 6

The Italian Republic shall recognize as public holidays every Sunday and all the other religious feasts determined by agreement between the Parties.

Article 7

1. The Italian Republic, in accordance with the principle enunciated in Article 20 of its Constitution, reaffirms that the ecclesiastical character and the religious or worship purpose of an association or institution shall not be the motive of special legislative limitations or of special tax exemptions with regard to its constitution, legal capacity, or any other form of activity.

2. The legal personality previously granted to ecclesiastical bodies shall be retained and the Italian Republic, upon request of the ecclesiastical authority or with its consent, shall continue to recognize the legal personality of the ecclesiastical bodies whose See is in Italy, who are constituted or approved according to the norms of canon law and have a religious or worship purpose. A similar procedure shall be followed in order to recognize civil effects to any substantial change of the same bodies.

3. With respect to taxation, ecclesiastical bodies having a religious or devotional purpose, as well as activities directed to that same scope shall be treated in the same manner as those having a beneficent or educational purpose.

The activities carried out by ecclesiastical bodies that are not for religious or devotional purposes shall be subject, in accordance with the structure and purpose of such bodies, to the laws of the State concerning such activities and to the tax burden provided for the same.

4. The buildings open to worship, the publications of acts, the posting of notices in the interior or at the outside doors of the worship or ecclesiastical buildings, and the collections made in the aforesaid buildings shall continue to be subject to the regulations presently in force.

5. The administration of the property owned by ecclesiastical bodies shall be subject to the controls provided by canon law. The acquisitions made by these bodies shall also be subject, however, to the controls provided for in the Italian laws on acquisition by legal persons.

6. On the occasion of the signing of the present agreement, the Parties shall appoint a joint Commission to formulate norms, that will be subsequently submitted for their approval, for the regulation of the whole matter of ecclesiastical bodies and properties and for the revision of the financial obligations of the Italian State and of its intervention into the patrimonial management of ecclesiastical bodies.

Upon a temporary basis and until the entry into force of the new regulation, Articles 17, paragraph (3), 18, 27, 29 and 30 of the previous text of the Concordat shall remain applicable.

Article 8

1. Civil effects shall be recognized for marriages contracted according to the norms of canon law, provided that the act of marriage be entered in the registers of the vital statistics, and the notices of marriage have been previously published at the communal offices. Immediately after the ceremony, the parish priest or his delegate shall explain the civil effects of the marriage to the parties, by reading the Articles of the Civil Code concerning the rights and duties of married people and he shall thereafter draw up, in original duplicate, the certificate of marriage, in which the spouses' declarations permitted by civil law may be inserted.

The Holy See acknowledges that the registration shall not take place:

(A) When the spouses do not meet the requirements of age determined by civil law for celebration;

(B) When an impediment from which, according to civil law, no derogation is permitted, exists between the spouses.

However, registration is permitted when, according to civil law, an action for nullity or annulment can no longer be maintained.

The request for registration shall be made, in writing and within five days from the celebration, by the parish priest of the place where the marriage has been celebrated. If the conditions for registration are satisfied, the vital statistics officer shall record it within 24 hours from the receipt of the act and shall give notice thereof to the parish priest.

The marriage shall have civil effects from the moment of the celebration, even if the vital statistics officer has, for any reason, made the registration after the prescribed term.

The registration can also be made subsequently upon request of the two spouses, or of one of them with the knowledge and without the opposition of the other, provided that both have retained single status without interruption from the moment of the celebration to the request for registration and the rights legally acquired by third parties are not prejudiced.

2.   The judgments of nullity of marriage pronounced by ecclesiastical tribunals, together with the decree of execution issued by the superior controlling ecclesiastical authority, shall be declared, at the request of the parties or of one of them, effective within the Italian Republic by judgment of the competent Court of Appeal, upon verifying:

(A)   that the ecclesiastical judge was the competent judge to adjudicate the action, the marriage having been celebrated in accordance with the present Article;

(B)   that in the proceedings before the ecclesiastical tribunals the right to sue and to defend in Court has been assured to the parties in a way not dissimilar from what is required by the fundamental principles of the Italian legal system;

(C)   that the other conditions required by the Italian legislation for the declaration of efficacy of foreign judgments are present.

The Court of Appeal may, with the judgment that recognizes a canonical judgment, take temporary economical measures in favor of one of the two spouses whose marriage has been declared null, referring the parties to the competent judge for a final decision on the matter.

3.   In entering into the present regulation of matrimonial matters the Holy See herein reaffirms the unchangeable validity of the Catholic teaching on marriage and the concern of the Church for the dignity and values of the family, foundation of the society.

Article 9

1.   The Italian Republic, in conformity with the principle of freedom of schools and teaching and according to the terms provided for in its Constitution, shall guarantee to the Catholic Church the right to freely establish schools of every order and grade and educational institutes.

Full freedom shall be assured to private schools officially recognized by the State and it shall also be assured to their pupils school treatment equivalent to that applied to the pupils of schools run by the State or by the other territorial entities, also with regards to the State exam.

2.   The Italian Republic, recognizing the value of the religious culture and considering that the principles of the Catholic Church are part of the historical heritage of the Italian people, shall continue to assure, within the framework of the scope of the schools, the teaching of Catholic religion in the public schools of every order and grade except for Universities.

With respect for the freedom of conscience and educational responsibility of the parents, everyone shall be granted the right to choose whether or not to receive religious instruction. When they enroll, the students or their parents shall exercise this right at the request of the school authority and their choice shall not give rise to any form of discrimination.

Article 10

1.   The Universities, seminaries, academies, colleges, and other institutions for ecclesiastics and members of religious orders or for the training in the ecclesiastical disciplines, established according to canon law, shall continue to be subordinate to the ecclesiastical authority alone.

2.   The academic degrees in theology and in the other ecclesiastical disciplines, determined by the agreement of the contracting Parties and granted by the faculties approved by the Holy See, shall be recognized by the State. The diplomas of Paleography, Diplomacy, Custody of Historical Documents, and Library Sciences obtained at Vatican schools shall likewise be recognized.

3.   The appointment of professors to the Catholic University of the Sacred Heart and the subordinate institutes shall be sub-

ject to the approval of the candidates' religious profile by the competent ecclesiastical authority.

Article 11

1.   The Italian Republic assures that service in the army, in the police or in any other similar service, time spent in hospitals, in sanatoria or in houses of public assistance and confinment to the institutes for prevention and punishment shall not impede the exercise of religious freedom and the fulfillment of the practices of Catholic worship.

2.   The spiritual assistance to the same shall be assured by ecclesiastics appointed by the competent Italian authorities upon designation by the ecclesiastical authority and in accordance with the legal status, the personnel and the formalities determined by common agreement of these authorities.

Article 12

1.   The Holy See and the Italian Republic, each in its proper order, shall collaborate for the protection of the historical and artistic heritage.

In order to harmonize the application of Italian law with the religious needs, the competent authorities of the two Parties shall agree upon appropriate provisions for the protection, appraisal, and enjoyment of cultural property of religious interest that belongs to ecclesiastical bodies or institutions.

The preservation and consultation of archives of historical interest and of the libraries of the same bodies and institutions shall be favoured and facilitated on the basis of understandings between the competent authorities of the two Parties.

2.   The Holy See shall retain the power to dispose of the Christian catacombs that exist underground at Rome and other parts of the Italian territory, bearing the consequent responsibility for their custody, maintenance and preservation, but it shall waive the power to dispose of the other catacombs.

Subject to the laws of the State and to any rights of third parties, the Holy See shall be at liberty to proceed with any necessary excavation and removal of sacred relics.

Article 13

1.   The preceding provisions shall be amendments to the Lateran Concordat accepted by the two Parties and shall enter into force on the exchange of the instruments of ratification. Except for what is provided in Article 7, paragraph (6), the provisions of the Concordat not reproduced in the present text are herein repealed.

2.   Additional matters for which a need of collaboration between the Catholic Church and the State might arise, shall be governed by further agreements between the two Parties or by understandings between the competent authorities of the State and of the Italian Bishops Conference.

Article 14

If, in the future, any difficulties should arise with regard to the interpretation or application of the preceding provisions, the Holy See and the Italian Republic shall entrust the search for an amicable settlement to a joint Commission appointed by them.

Rome, February 18, 1984
Signed on February 18, 1984

On the occasion of the signing of the Agreement that modifies the Lateran Concordat, the Holy See and the Italian Republic, desiring to assure, by means of appropriate specifications, the best application of the Lateran Pacts and the agreed upon amendments, and willing to avoid any difficulties of interpretation thereof, herein jointly declare:

1. *In relation to Article 1*

The principle of the Catholic religion as the sole religion of the Italian State, originally referred to by the Lateran Pacts, shall be considered to be no longer in force.

2. *In relation to Article 4*

(a) With reference to Paragraph (2), the ordinaries, parish priests, parish vicars, rectors of churches open to worship and priests permanently assigned to the services of spiritual assistance referred to in Article 11 shall be considered to be in cure of souls.

(b) The Italian Republic assures that the judicial authority shall inform the ecclesiastical authority with territorial competence of any criminal proceedings against ecclesiastics.

(c) The Holy See takes advantage of the amendments to the Lateran Concordat to declare its agreement, without prejudice to the canon legal system, with the interpretation given by the Italian State to Article 23, paragraph (2) of the Lateran Treaty, according to which the civil effects of the judgments and final orders pronounced by ecclesiastical authorities and provided by this Article shall be understood in accordance with the rights of Italian citizens which are constitutionally recognized.

3. *In relation to Article 7*

(a) The Italian Republic assures that no obligation to proceed with the conversion of real property shall exist upon ecclesiastical bodies, unless contrary agreements are concluded from time to time between the competent governmental and ecclesiastical authorities when special reasons are present.

(b) The joint Commission referred to in Paragraph (6) shall terminate its work within and no later than six months from the signing of the present agreement.

4. *In relation to Article 8*

(a) In view of the application of Paragraph (1) (B), the following shall be understood to be impediments from which, according to civil law, no derogation is permitted:

(1) the fact that one of the contracting parties is interdicted for mental infirmity;

(2) the existence, between the spouses, of a previous marriage which is valid for civil purposes;

(3) the impediments which derive from crime of affinity in a direct line.

(b) With reference to Paragraph (2), in view of the application of Articles 796 and 797 of the Italian Code of Civil Procedure, the specificity of the canon legal system, that governs the bond of matrimony which had its origin therein, shall be taken into account. In particular:

(1) it shall be taken into consideration that the references made by Italian law to the law of the place where the judicial proceedings have taken place shall be understood as relating to canon law;

(2) final judgment shall be considered to be a judgment that is enforceable according to canon law;

(3) it is understood that, in any case, the merits shall not be re-examined.

(c) The provisions of Paragraph (2) shall also be applied to marriages celebrated, before the entry into force of the present agreement, in conformity with the norms of Article 34 of the Lateran Concordat and of the law No. 847 of May 27, 1929 and for which a proceeding before the civil judicial authority, as provided by the same norms, has not been initiated.

5. *In relation to Article 9*

(a) The teaching of Catholic religion in the schools indicated at Paragraph (2) shall be given — in conformity with the doctrine of the Church and with respect for the freedom of conscience of the pupils — by the teachers who are recognized by the ecclesiastical authority as being qualified thereto and who are appointed, in agreement therewith, by the school authority.

In infant and elementary schools, this teaching may be given by the class teacher, if recognized by the ecclesiastical authority as being qualified thereto and if willing to do it.

(b)   By means of a subsequent understanding between the competent school authorities and the Italian Bishops Conference, it shall be determined:

(1)   the teaching prospectus of Catholic religion in public schools of every order and grade;

(2)   the organization of this teaching, also with respect to its position in the school time table;

(3)   the criteria for selecting the textbooks;

(4)   the requirements of professional qualification for the teachers.

(c)   The provisions of this Article shall not prejudice the regulations presently in force in the regions on the borders of the Country, in which the matter is governed by special norms.

6.   *In relation to Article 10*

The Italian Republic, in interpreting Paragraph (3) — that does not change Article 38 of the Concordat signed on February 11, 1929 — shall follow the jument of the Constitutional Court, No. 195/1972, concerning the same Article.

7.   *In relation to Article 13, Paragraph (1)*

The Parties shall initiate appropriate consultations with a view of the implement, each within its proper order, the provisions of the present agreement.

The present Additional Protocol is an integral part of the Agreement that modifies the Lateran Concordat and that was contextually signed by the Holy See and the Italian Republic.

Rome, February 18, 1984

THE EXAMPLE OF SPAIN

Since the reconquest of the Iberian Peninsula by Christians in the fifteenth century, Spain has had a long history of close co-existence between the Spanish State and the Catholic Church and varying degrees of intolerance and persecution of non-Catholics (punctuated by periods of anti-clericalism). Following the end of the Franco regime, a new constitution was adopted in 1978. This Constitution rendered an historic change, as it was the first Spanish constitution that did not provide for Catholicism as the only religion recognized and accepted by the State. Article 16 addresses the issues of religious freedom and the relationship of the State to the Catholic Church and to other religious denominations:

Article 16
1.   Individual and community ideological freedom, religious freedom and freedom of worship are guaranteed, without any limitations in their expression other than those necessary for the maintaining of public order protected by law.
2.   No one shall be obliged to state their ideology, religion or beliefs.
3.   No faith shall have a State character. The public authorities shall take into account the religious beliefs of Spanish society, and shall maintain the resulting relationships of co-operation with the Catholic Church and other faiths.*

In 1976 and 1979, four new agreements were concluded between the Spanish State and the Holy See, replacing the Concordat of 1953. These new agreements — portions of which are reprinted below — covered numerous issues, including the financial support of the Catholic Church by the State, tax exemptions and benefits granted to the Church, the teaching and practice of the Catholic religion in the public schools, and the civil law effects of church marriages and decisions of the Catholic Church's ecclesiastical courts.

In 1980, a comprehensive law on religious liberty (the "1980 Religious Liberty Law") was passed by the Spanish legislature. This law sets out in some detail not only the rights of individuals, but the rights of "churches, faiths and religious communities" as well. These rights are subject to limitation to protect public safety, health, and morality and the fundamental rights and public freedoms of others (Article 3(1)). Also, the protections of the 1980 Religious Liberty Law do not apply to any activity related to "psychic or parapsychological phenomenon" and the spread of "humanistic or spiritualistic values or other similar non-religious aims" (Article 3(2)). Article 5 of the 1980 Religious Liberty Law provides for the registration of religious groups — those that meet the qualifications set out in the law — in a Religious Entities Registry maintained by the Ministry of Justice. Groups that do not meet the criteria of the 1980 Religious Liberty Law may be qualified to organize under the 1964 Associations Law.

Article 7(1) of the 1980 Religious Liberty Law provides that certain religious groups, that is, those that have achieved "notorious influence in Spanish society due to their domain or number of followers," can negotiate agreements of co-operation with the Spanish government. These agreements regulate some of the same matters as the agreements with the Holy See, although the rights, privileges and limitations provided in the co-operation agreements are not identical to those provided to the Catholic Church. As of 1997, co-operation agreements have been signed with the Federation of Evangelical Religious Entities of Spain, the Islamic Commission of Spain (reprinted below) and the Federation of Israelite Communities of Spain. It should be noted that these three groups have refused to accept any financial aid collected by the State from the income tax of their believers (thereby rejecting an arrangement similar to that of the Catholic Church).

In light of the above legal arrangements, there are basically four classes of formally organized and arguably religious entities in Spain, with each class (1) having different rights, powers, privileges and immunities and (2) being primarily regulated by different laws and/or agreements:

(1) The Catholic Church;
(2) Those groups covered under co-operation agreements with the State;
(3) Those groups not covered under co-operation agreements but are registered pursuant to and fall under the protection of the 1980 Religious Liberty Law; and
(4) Those groups not registered but organized under the 1964 Associations Law.

This arrangement, similar in many respects to the systems in some other European countries, reflects an attempt to balance the evolving principles of religious freedom, equality of religious groups, and the social and cultural primacy of a traditional, dominant religious faith.

AGREEMENTS BETWEEN THE SPANISH STATE AND THE HOLY SEE [SELECTIONS]

Translation prepared by the Spanish Ministry of Justice.

**AGREEMENT OF 28 JULY 1976
(RATIFIED 19 AUGUST 1976; B.O.E. NO.
230, 24 SEPTEMBER 1976)**

The Holy See and the Spanish Government: in view of the profound process of transformation experienced by Spanish society in recent years concerning relations between the political community and religious faiths, and between the Catholic Church and the State; taking into account that on its part Vatican Council II established as fundamental principles, to which the relations between the political community and the Church should adapt, both the mutual independence of both parties in their respective areas, as well as positive collaboration between them; asserted religious freedom as a right that should be recognized in society's legal code; and taught that the freedom of the Church is an essential principle of the relationship between the Church and Public Authority and the civil system, given that the Spanish State included in its laws the right to religious freedom, based on the dignity of persons (Law of 1 July 1967) and recognized in this same code that there shall be norms appropriate to the fact that the majority of the Spanish people profess the Catholic religion, deem it necessary to regulate by means of specific Agreements, those subjects of common interest that, under the new circumstances arising after the signing of the Concordat of 27 August 1953, require new regulation; therefore, they agree to undertake, by common consent, the study of these different subjects for the purpose of concluding, as soon as possible, the Agreements that will gradually substitute the corresponding provisions of the Concordat currently in force.

On the other hand, taking into account that the free naming of Bishops and the equality of all citizens in the administration of justice has priority and special urgency in the revision of the provisions of the present Concordat, both contracting Parties conclude, as a first step in said revision, the following:

AGREEMENT
I

1.   The appointment of Archbishops and Bishops shall be the exclusive responsibility of the Holy See.

2.   Before proceeding with the appointment of resident Archbishops and Bishops and of Coadjutors with the right to succession, the Holy See shall communicate the name of the person designated to the Spanish Government, in case there may be, with respect to this person, possible specific objections of a general political nature, the appraisal of which shall correspond to the judicious consideration of the Holy See. It shall be understood that there are no objections if the Government has not expressed these within fifteen days. Both Parties shall maintain the corresponding formalities secret.

3.   The appointment of the Military Vicar General shall be made by means of the proposal of three names, drawn up by common consent between the Apostolic Nunciature and the Ministry of Foreign Affairs and submitted for approval to the Holy See. The King shall present, within

fifteen days, one of these to be appointed by the Supreme Pontiff.

4. Article VII and Paragraph 2 of Article VIII of the current Concordat are hereby abolished, as is the Agreement stipulated between the Holy See and the Spanish Government of 7 June 1941.

II

1. Article XVI of the current Concordat is hereby abolished.

2. If a clergyman is criminally charged, the competent Authority shall notify his respective Ordinary. If the person charged is a Bishop, or a person of similar rank under Canon law, the Holy See shall be notified.

3. In no case may a clergyman or member of a religious order be enjoined by Judges or other Authorities to give information concerning persons or subjects that they may have obtained in the course of their ministry.

4. The Spanish State recognizes and respects the exclusive legal authority of the church Courts over those offenses which exclusively violate an ecclesiastic law in accordance with Canon Law. Civil Authorities shall have no right to appeal sentences served by Church Courts.

* * *

AGREEMENT OF 3 JANUARY 1979 CONCERNING LEGAL AFFAIRS (RATIFIED 4 DECEMBER 1979; B.O.E. NO. 300, 15 DECEMBER 1979)

* * *

AGREEMENT
I

1. The Spanish State recognizes the right of the Catholic Church to carry out its apostolic mission and guarantees the Church free and public exercise of those activities inherent of it, especially worship, jurisdiction and teaching.

2. The Church is free to establish its own organization. In particular, it may create, modify or suppress Dioceses, Parishes and other territorial circumscriptions, which shall be considered legal under civil law at the time they acquire legality under canon law and this is notified to the State's competent agencies. The Church may also establish, confirm and suppress Orders, Religious Congregations, other religious institutions, other Ecclesiastical Institutions and Organizations. No part of Spanish Territory shall be dependent upon the Bishop whose seat is in an a area subject to the sovereignty of another State, and no Diocese or Spanish territorial district shall include territorial areas subject to a foreign sovereignty. The principality of Andorra will continue to pertain to the Diocese of Urgel.

3. The State recognizes the civil legal nature of the Spanish Episcopal Assembly, in accordance with the Statutes approved by the Holy See.

4. The State recognizes the civil legal nature and full capacity to act of the Orders, religious congregations and other religious institutions and their Provincials, Monasteries and Convents, and that of other religious Organizations and Foundations that have this status at the time at which this Agreement goes into effect. The Orders, Religious Congregations and other religious institutions and their Provincials, Monasteries and Convents that, having been established under canon law at that date, are not considered legal under civil law, and those established in accordance with canon law in the future, shall acquire civil legality upon registration at the corresponding State Registry Office, by virtue of an authentic document stating the establishment, purpose, identification, representative bodies, rules of operation and faculties of said agencies. For the purpose of determining the

extent of and limitations to their capacity to act and, therefore, to dispose of their goods, they shall be governed by canon law, which will act in this case as statutory law. The Associations and other religious Organizations and Foundations that, having been established under canon law at the date on which this Agreement goes into effect, but that are considered legal under civil law, and those established by the competent Ecclesiastical Authority in accordance with canon law in the future, may acquire civil legality, and subject to stipulations in the State's regulations, upon registration at the corresponding Registry, by virtue of an authentic document stating the establishment, purpose, rules of operation and faculties of said agencies.

5.   Churches are guaranteed inviolability according to the Law. They may not be demolished unless they are no longer consecrated. In the case of necessary expropriation, the competent Church Authority shall first be heard.

6.   The State shall respect and protect the inviolability of archives, registers and other documents belonging to the Spanish Episcopal Conference, to the Episcopal Curiae, the Curiae of the Superiors of religious Orders and Congregations, Parishes an other Church Institutions and Organizations.

II

The Holy See may freely promulgate and publish any resolutions referring to the governing of the Church and may freely communicate with prelates, the clergy and the faithful, as they may with the Holy See. Ordinaries and other Church Authorities shall have the same rights with respect to the clergy and the faithful.

III

The State recognizes Sunday as a holiday. Other religious activities to be recog-

nized as holidays shall be decided by common consent.

IV

1.   The State recognizes and guarantees the exercise of the right of religious attendance of those citizens in prisons, hospitals, sanatoriums, orphanages and similar centers, both private and public.

2.   Catholic religious attendance and pastoral activities of priests and members of religious orders in the above-mentioned centers that are public shall be regulated by common consent of the competent authorities of the Church and the State. In any case, the right to religious freedom and due respect for religious and ethical principles shall be safeguarded.

V

1.   The Church may carry out its own charitable or welfare activities. Those Institutions or Organizations of a charitable or welfare nature that are part of the Church or dependent upon it shall be run according to the Church's statutory regulations and shall have the same rights and benefits as those organizations classified as private charities.

2.   The Church and the State may, by common consent, establish the bases for appropriate co-operation between charitable or welfare activities carried out by their respective institutions.

VI

1.   The State recognizes the civil effects of marriages celebrated according to Canon Law. Canon marriage is considered legal under civil law from the moment of the celebration. For full recognition of these effects, the marriage must be registered in the Civil Registry; this may be done with the presentation of the church certificate of the existence of the marriage.

2.   The marriage partners, in accor-

dance with the provisions of Canon Law, may go to the Ecclesiastical Courts to request a declaration of annulment or to request a pontifical decision concerning a valid but unconsummated marriage. By request of either of the parties, said ecclesiastical resolutions shall be considered valid under civil law if declared in compliance with State Law by sentence of the competent Civil Court.

3. The Holy See reaffirms the permanent value of its doctrine concerning marriage and reminds those who celebrate marriage in accordance with Canon Law of the serious obligation they assume to abide by the canon rules regulating marriage and, especially, to respect their essential meaning.

VII

The Holy See and the Spanish Government shall proceed by common consent in the resolution of any doubts or difficulties that may arise in the interpretation or application of any clause of this Agreement, guided by the principles informing it.

* * *

AGREEMENT OF 3 JANUARY 1979 CONCERNING EDUCATION AND CULTURAL AFFAIRS (RATIFIED 4 DECEMBER 1979; B.O.E. NO. 300, 15 DECEMBER 1979)

The Spanish Government and the Holy See, continuing with revision of the concordat texts in the spirit of the Agreement of 28 July 1976, confer essential importance to matters related to education. On one hand, the State recognizes the fundamental right to religious education and has ratified international agreements that guarantee the exercise of this right.

On the other hand, the Church must coordinate its educational mission with the principles of civil liberty in religious affairs

and with the rights of families and all students and teachers, to avoid any discrimination or privilege.

The so-called social media have become an efficient school of knowledge, criteria and customs. Therefore, the same principles of religious freedom and equality without special privilege that the Church and State profess in educational affairs shall be applied in the legal regulation of the media. Finally, the Church's Historical, Artistic and Documental Patrimony continue to be an extremely important part of the cultural estate of the Nation. Therefore, placing this Patrimony in the service and for the enjoyment of society, its conservation and its increase justify collaboration of the Church and State. For this reason, both Parties conclude the following:

AGREEMENT
I

In view of the principle of religious freedom, educational activity shall respect the fundamental right of parents concerning the moral and religious education of their children in schools. In any case, education imparted in public teaching centers shall respect the values of Christian ethics.

II

Educational plans at the levels of preschool, Elementary School (EGB) and High School (BUP) and technical colleges for students of the corresponding ages, shall include the teaching of the Catholic Religion in all Educational Centers, in conditions equal to those of the basic subjects.

Out of respect for freedom of conscience, this religious education shall not be obligatory for all students. However, the right to receive it is guaranteed.

Academic authorities shall adopt the necessary means so that receiving or not receiving religious instruction shall not suppose any discrimination at the school.

At the teaching levels previously named, the corresponding academic authorities shall allow the Ecclesiastical Hierarchy to establish, under the specific conditions agreed upon, other complementary activities of training and religious attendance.

III

At the educational levels referred to in the previous article, religious instruction shall be imparted by those persons who, each school year, shall be appointed by the academic authority from among those proposed by the diocesan Ordinary. With sufficient advance notice, the diocesan Ordinary shall make known the names of those teachers and persons considered competent for said education.

In public preschool, elementary schools and technical colleges, the designation, as previously described, shall preferably fall to those elementary school teachers who have requested it. No one shall be compelled to teach religion.

Teachers of religion shall be part, for all purposes, of the faculty of their respective schools.

IV

The teaching of Catholic doctrine and its teaching at the University Schools for Teacher Training, under the same conditions as the other basic disciplines, shall be voluntary for all students. Teachers of Catholic doctrine shall be named by the academic authorities in the same manner as that established in Article III and they too shall be considered part of the their respective faculties.

V

The State guarantees that the Catholic Church may organize voluntary teaching courses and other religious activities in Public Universities, using the premises and resources of these centers. The Church Hierarchy shall come to an agreement with the Centers' Authorities for the suitable exercise of these activities in all aspects.

VI

It shall be the responsibility of the Church Hierarchy to decide the contents of Catholic teaching and training courses, as well as to propose textbooks and educational material relative to said teaching and training.

The Church Hierarchy and the State's agencies, within the scope of their respective competence, shall ensure that the teaching and training are suitably imparted, with the religious teaching subject to the general control of the Centers.

VII

The economic situation of teachers of the Catholic religion at the different educational levels, who are not part of the State's teaching staff, shall be arranged by the central government and the Spanish Episcopal Conference, in order that it be applied when this Agreement takes effect.

VIII

The Catholic Church may establish diocesan and religious Minor Seminaries, the specific nature of which shall be respected by the State.

In order to be considered elementary schools, high schools or universities, the general legislation shall be applied, although neither a minimum number of registered students nor the acceptance of students in accordance with their geographical origin or family residence shall be required.

IX

Teaching centers that are not universities, independent of their grade or specialty, established by the Church now or in the future, shall conform to the legislation in force, concerning the exercise of their activities.

X

1. Universities, University Colleges, University Schools and other University Centers established by the Catholic Church, shall conform to the legislation in force, concerning the exercise of their activities.

In order for studies carried out in these Centers to be recognized under civil law, they shall be governed according to current legislation concerning those subjects at all times.

2. The State recognizes the legal existence of those Universities established by the Church in Spain as of the date in which this Agreement comes into effect. The legal regulations of these Universities must adapt to the legislation in force, except for that stipulated in Article XVII.2.

3. Students at these Universities shall have the same benefits in matters of health care, student security, student aid and research and other forms of student protection as those established for students at State universities.

XI

The Catholic Church, in accordance with its own law, maintains its autonomy in the establishment of Universities, Departments, Institutes of higher learning and other Centers of Ecclesiastic Science for training priests, religious and laymen.

Confirmation of studies and recognition by the State of the civil effects of degrees conferred by these centers of higher learning, shall be the subject of specific regulation between the competent authorities of the Church and the State. As long as this regulation is not in effect, possible confirmations of those studies and the granting of civil value to the degrees conferred shall be made in accordance with the general norms on this subject.

The confirmation and recognition of studies carried out and degrees obtained by clergymen or laymen in Departments approved by the Holy See abroad shall also be regulated by common consent.

XII

State Universities, upon prior agreement with the competent Church authority, may establish Centers of higher learning for the study of Catholic theology.

XIII

The Church's teaching centers, regardless of their grade and specialization, and their students shall have the right to receive those subsidies, scholarships, fiscal benefits and other aid that the State grants to private centers and to the students at these centers, in accordance with the system of equal opportunity.

XIV

Safeguarding the principles of religious freedom and freedom of expression, the State shall ensure that its social media shall respect the feelings of Catholics and shall establish the corresponding agreements concerning these matters with the Spanish Episcopal Conference.

XV

The Church reiterates its disposition to continue to place its historic, artistic and documental patrimony at the service of society in general and shall come to an agreement with the State concerning the basis for effecting the common interests and collaboration of both parties, for the purpose of preserving, making known and cataloging the Church's cultural patrimony, facilitating its viewing and study, assuring its best possible conservation and preventing all losses, within the framework of Article 46 of the Constitution.

For these purposes and any others related with said patrimony, a Mixed Commission shall be formed within a year's time at the latest, from the date on which this Agreement becomes effective in Spain.

XVI

The Holy See and the Spanish Government shall proceed by common consent in the resolution of any doubts or difficulties that may arise in the interpretation or application of any clause of this Agreement, guided by the principles informing it.

XVII

* * *

[T]he rights acquired by those Universities that the Church has established in Spain at the time of the signing of this Agreement are assured. These, however, may choose to adapt to the general legislation concerning private universities.

AGREEMENT OF 3 JANUARY 1979 CONCERNING ECONOMIC AFFAIRS (RATIFIED 4 DECEMBER 1979; B.O.E. NO. 300, 15 DECEMBER 1979)

The review of the system of economic contributions made by the Spanish State to the Catholic Church is of special importance when substituting the Concordat of 1953 with new Agreements.

On the one hand, the State cannot indefinitely ignore or prolong legal obligations undertaken in the past. On the other hand, given the spirit shaping the relations between Church and State, in Spain it is necessary to give new meaning to both the sections concerning economic contributions as well as to the common system according to which said contributions shall be made. Consequently, the Holy See and the Spanish

government conclude the following:

AGREEMENT

I

The Catholic Church may freely obtain payment from the faithful, organize public collections and receive alms and offerings.

II

1. The State promises to collaborate with the Catholic Church in the obtention of adequate economic support, absolutely respecting the principle of religious freedom.

2. Three complete fiscal years after this Agreement is signed, the State may assign to the Catholic Church a percentage of the yield from income taxes or net patrimony or other taxes of a personal nature following the most suitable technical method. To do this, each taxpayer must, on the respective tax form, expressly declare his decision concerning the use he wishes to make of the money concerned. In the absence of such a declaration, the corresponding amount shall be assigned to other purposes.

3. This system shall substitute the bequest referred to in the next section, in such a way that the Catholic Church shall receive funds of a similar amount.

4. As long as the new system is not applied, the State, in the General Budget, shall consign a suitable bequest to the Catholic Church, in the form of one lump sum, that shall be updated yearly.

During the substitution process, which shall take place over a period of three years, the budgetary bequest shall be decreased in proportion to the tax assignation received by the Catholic Church.

5. The Catholic Church declares its intention of obtaining sufficient resources for its needs of its own accord. Once this has been achieved, both parties shall agree

to substitute the systems of financial collaboration described in the preceding paragraphs of this article, in other areas and by other means of economic collaboration between the Catholic Church and the State.

III

The following shall not be subject to income tax or value-added tax, as appropriate:

a) Apart from the concepts mentioned in Article I of this Agreement, the publication of instructions, statutes, pastoral letters, diocesan bulletins and any other document written by the competent church authorities, nor their placement in the usual places.

b) Teaching activities in diocesan and religious Seminaries, as well as ecclesiastical disciplines at Church Universities.

c) The purchase of objects intended for worship.

IV

1. The Holy See, the Episcopal Conference, the Diocese, Parishes and other territorial Districts, religious Orders and Congregations and religious Institutions and their Provincials and their convents and monasteries are entitled to the following exemption:

A) Total and permanent exemption from property taxes on the following real estate:

1. Churches and chapels designated as places of worship, and their branches and annexed local buildings designated for pastoral purposes.

2. Bishops' residences, canons' residences and residences of parish priests.

3. Premises designated as offices for the diocesan Curia and parish offices.

4. Seminaries designated for training diocesan and religious clergy, and Church Universities, as long as they impart teaching related to church disciplines.

5. Those buildings designated fundamentally as Houses or Convents of the Orders, religious Congregations and religious Institutions.

B) Total and permanent exemption from excise duties, income tax and capital gains taxes. This exemption does not include those products obtained through financial operations, nor those derived from its patrimony, when it has been transferred, nor to capital gains, nor to earnings subject of withholding at the source on income tax.

C) Total exemption from taxes on succession, donations and transfer taxes, as long as the acquired goods or rights are intended for worship, maintenance of the Clergy, the sacred apostolate and charitable purposes.

D) Exemption from special contributions and rates, when these taxes fall on the goods listed in section A) of this article.

2. The amounts donated to the church organs listed in this article and assigned for the purposes stated in section C), have the right to the same deductions on income tax as those amounts given to organizations classified or declared as charitable or of public utility.

V

The religious Associations and Organs not included among those listed in article IV of this Agreement and that are dedicated to religious, charitable, teaching, medical or hospitable or social care, shall have the right to the fiscal benefits that the Spanish State's legal and tax regulations provide for non-profit organizations, and in any case, those granted to private charitable organizations.

VI

The Holy See and the Spanish Government shall proceed by common consent in the resolution of any doubts or difficulties that may arise in the interpretation or application of any clause of this Agreement, guided by the principles that inform it.

RELIGIOUS LIBERTY LAW OF SPAIN
General Act 7 of 5 July 1980. B.O.E. no. 177, 24 July 1980.
Translation prepared by the Spanish Ministry of Justice.

H.M. Juan Carlos I, King of Spain

May all men know by these presents:

That Parliament has enacted and I ratify the following General Act:

Article 1
1.   The State guarantees the fundamental right to freedom of worship and religion recognized by the Constitution, in accordance with the provisions of the present Act.

2.   Religious beliefs shall not occasion unequal or discriminatory treatment under the Law. No one may be deprived of any occupation or activity or public positions or employment for reasons of religion.

3.   No faith shall be the official State religion.

Article 2
1.   The freedom of worship and religion guaranteed by the Constitution secures the right, which may therefore be exercised by all without duress, to:

a)   Profess whatever religious beliefs they freely choose or profess none at all; change or relinquish their faith; freely express their own religious beliefs or lack thereof or refrain from making any statement in such regard.

b)   Take part in the liturgy and receive spiritual support in their own faith; celebrate their festivities; hold their marriage ceremonies; receive decent burial, with no discrimination for reasons of religion; be free from any obligation to receive spiritual support or participate in religious services that are contrary to their personal convictions.

c)   Receive and deliver religious teaching and information of any kind, orally, in writing or any other means; choose religious and moral education in keeping with their own convictions for themselves and any non-emancipated minors or legally incompetent persons, in and outside the academic domain.

d)   Meet or assemble publicly for religious purposes and form associations to undertake their religious activities in community in accordance with ordinary legislation and the provisions of this General Act.

2.   It also comprises the right of Churches, Faiths and Religious Communities to establish places of worship or assembly for religious purposes, appoint and train their ministers, promulgate and propagate their own beliefs and maintain relations with their own organisations or other religious faiths, within the national boundaries or abroad.

3.   To ensure true and effective application of these rights, public authorities shall adopt the necessary measures to facilitate assistance at religious services in public, military, hospital, community and penitentiary establishments and any other under its aegis, as well as religious training in public schools.

Article 3
1.   The rights deriving from the freedom of worship and religion may not be exercised to the detriment of the rights of others to practise their public freedoms and fundamental rights or of public safety, health and morality, elements which constitute the order ensured under the rule of Law in democratic societies.

2.   Activities, purposes and Entities relating to or engaging in the study of and experimentation with psychic or parapsychological phenomena or the dissemination of humanistic or spiritualistic values or other similar non-religious aims do not qualify for the protection provided in this Act.

Article 4

The rights recognised in this Act, practised within the limits indicated herein, shall guarantee effective legal protection before ordinary Courts and constitutional protection before the Constitutional Court under the terms stipulated in the General Act related thereto.

Article 5

1. Churches, Faiths and Religious Communities and their Federations shall acquire legal personality once registered in the corresponding public Registry created for this purpose and kept in the Ministry of Justice.

2. Registration shall be granted by virtue of an application together with an authentic document containing notice of the foundation or establishment of the organisation in Spain, declaration of religious purpose, denomination and other particulars of identity, rules of procedure and representative bodies, including such body's powers and requisites for valid designation thereof.

3. Entities relating to a given religious Entity may only be cancelled at the request of its representative bodies or in compliance with a final court sentence.

Article 6

1. Registered Churches, Faiths, and Religious Communities shall be fully independent and may lay down their own organisational rules, internal and staff by-laws. Such rules, as well as those governing the institutions they create to accomplish their purposes, may include clauses on the safeguard of their religious identity and own personality, as well as the due respect for their beliefs, without prejudice to the rights and freedoms recognised by the Constitution and in particular those of freedom, equality and non-discrimination.

2. Churches, Faiths and Religious Communities may create and promote, for the accomplishment of their purposes, Associations, Foundations and Institutions pursuant to the provision of ordinary legislation.

Article 7

1. The State, taking account of the religious beliefs existing in Spanish society, shall establish, as appropriate, Co-operation Agreements or Conventions with the Churches, Faiths or Religious Communities enrolled in the Registry where warranted by their notorious influence in Spanish society, due to their domain or number of followers. Such Agreements shall, in any case, be subject to approval by an Act of Parliament.

2. Subject to the principle of equality, such Agreements or Conventions may confer upon Churches, Faiths or Religious Communities the tax benefits applied by ordinary legislation to non-profit Entities and other charitable organisations.

Article 8

1. An advisory Committee on Freedom of Worship is hereby created in the Ministry of Justice whose membership, which shall be stable, shall be divided equally between the representatives of the Central Government and of the corresponding Churches, Faiths and Religious Communities or their Federations including, in any case, those that have a notorious influence in Spain, with the participation as well of persons of renowned competence whose counsel is considered to be of interest in matters related to this Act. Such Committee may have, in turn, a standing commission whose membership shall be likewise equally apportioned.

2. The functions of such Committee shall consist of reviewing, reporting on and setting forth proposals with respect to issues relating to the enforcement of this Act and such intervention shall be mandatory in the preparation and recommendations for the Co-operation Agreements or Conventions referred in the preceding article.

3. The State acknowledges the legal personality and full legal capacity of the religious Entities in possession thereof on the date the present Act enters into force. Beginning three years thereafter, they may substantiate their legal personality only via certificate of enrollment in the Registry referred to herein.

SECOND TRANSITIONAL PROVISION

When applying for legal recognition, Religious Associations which, pursuant to the provisions of Act forty-four/nineteen hundred sixty-seven of the twenty-eight day of June, had expressly claimed to own real or other kinds of property whose full and effective conveyance is subject to public registration, where ownership thereof has been registered in the name of third parties and those which, having lodged this statement of property with the Government apply for legal registration thereof pursuant to the provisions of the present Act may, within one year's time, normalise the legal status of such property, by delivering the documents attesting to their ownership of property appearing under the names of intermediaries or by using any other legal procedure to substantiate their rights, until the corresponding deeds are registered in the Registry of Deeds, and such registration shall be exempt from all taxes, fees and rates that may be levied on conveyance or the documents or action generated on the occasion thereof.

REVOCATORY PROVISION

Act forty-four/nineteen hundred and sixty-seven of the twenty-eighth day of June as well as any other legal provisions that contradict the terms of the present Act are hereby repealed.

FINAL PROVISION

The Government, at the proposal of the Ministry of Justice, shall establish any such regulatory provisions as may be necessary for the organisation and operation of the Registry and the Advisory Committee on Freedom of Worship.

COOPERATION AGREEMENT BETWEEN THE SPANISH STATE AND THE ISLAMIC COMMISSION OF SPAIN

Law 26 of 10 November 1992.
B.O.E. no 272, 12 November 1992.
Translation prepared by the Spanish Ministry of Justice.

STATED PURPOSE

The Spanish Constitution of 1978, in providing for a democratic and pluralistic State, entailed a profound change in the State's traditional attitude towards religious matters, whereby the rights to equality and freedom of religion are confirmed and the practise thereof guaranteed under the broadest possible terms, subject only to the imperatives of public order under the Law and to due respect for the fundamental rights of others.

Such freedom of worship, conceived originally to pertain individually to each citizen is, likewise and by extension, applicable to the faiths or communities that groups of individuals may establish to comply collectively with their religious aims, subject to no prior authorisation or enrollment in any public Registry.

From the standpoint of the deepest respect for such principles, the State is obliged by constitutional mandate, to the extent that religious beliefs prevailing in Spanish society demand, to maintain cooperative relations with the various religious faiths, which may involve different avenues for each of the faiths enrolled in the Registry of Religious Entities.

The General Act of the Freedom of Worship provides that the State may cooperate with religious faiths under more specific terms through Co-operation Agreements or Conventions when such faiths, duly enrolled in the Registry of Religious Entities, have gained obvious or notorious influence in Spanish society due to the number of their followers and the impact of their beliefs. This is the case of the Muslim religion, which has a centuries-old tradition in our country and primary relevance in the make-up of Spanish identity, consisting of various communities of that faith registered in the Registry of Religious Entities and members of one of the two Federations, likewise registered, known respectively as the Spanish Federation of Islamic Religious Entities and the Union of Islamic Communities of Spain which have, in turn, constituted a religious entity enrolled in said Registry under the name Islamic Commission of Spain, which is their representative to the State for negotiating, adopting and subsequently implementing the Agreements adopted.

The present Co-operation Agreement was concluded in response to the request formulated by the two Federations, as an expression of the will of Spanish Muslims, and after the corresponding negotiation; it addresses matters of great importance to citizens professing the Muslim faith: the status of Islamic Religious Leaders and Imams, determining the specific rights deriving from the practise of their religious office, their personal status in areas of such importance as Social Security and ways of complying with their military duties, legal protection for their mosques, civil validity of marriage ceremonies held pursuant to Muslim rites, religious services in public centres or establishments, Muslim religious education in schools, the tax benefits applicable to certain property pertaining to the Federations that constitute the Islamic Commission of

Spain, commemoration of Muslim religious holidays and finally, co-operation between the State and such Commission for the conservation and furthering of Islamic Historic and Artistic Heritage.

The religious delegates' negotiating positions have always been scrupulously respected, such as in the clear expression of particularly Muslim doctrinary content and the specific matters of conscience deriving therefrom, to make real and effective practise of the right of freedom of worship possible for members of the Muslim faith.

Article 1

1. The rights and obligations deriving from the Act adopting the present Agreement shall be applicable to the Islamic Communities which, having enrolled in the Registry of Religious Entities, are or subsequently become members of the Islamic Commission of Spain or of one of the Islamic Federations registered as belonging to such Commission, for as long as their membership therein is on record in such Registry.

2. Islamic Community and Federation membership in the Islamic Commission of Spain, for the intents and purposes of entry thereof in said Registry, shall be substantiated by a certificate issued by the corresponding legal representatives under the endorsement of the Commission. Caveats on their withdrawal or exclusion shall be entered at the request of the community in question or the Islamic Commission of Spain.

3. The certification of religious purpose required pursuant to R.D. 142/1981 of 9 January for enrollment of associative religious entities constituted as such in accordance with the regulations governing Islamic Communities, may be issued by the Federation to which they belong, as endorsed by the Islamic Commission of Spain or issued by the latter if they are not members of either Federation.

Article 2

1. The buildings or premises permanently and exclusively dedicated to Islamic prayer, training or spiritual support shall, for all legal intents and purposes, be considered to be mosques and places of worship of the Islamic Communities members of the Islamic Commission of Spain, when such use is certified by the community in question and endorsed by such Commission.

2. The places of worship of Islamic Commission of Spain member Communities shall enjoy immunity under the terms laid down by Law. In the event of expropriation, the Islamic Commission of Spain must first be heard and they may not be demolished unless first divested of their sacred nature, except where otherwise provided by law in the event of emergency or hazard. They shall also be excepted from temporary occupation and the imposition of easements in the terms provided in article 119 of the Act on Expropriation.

3. The State respects and protects the inviolability of the files and other documents pertaining to the Islamic Commission of Spain as well as of its member communities.

4. Places of worship may be included in the Registry of Religious Entities.

5. Muslim cemeteries shall be entitled to the legal benefits laid down in paragraph 2 of this article for places of worship. Islamic Communities that are members of the Islamic Commission of Spain are entitled to assign the plots reserved for Muslim burials in municipal cemeteries, as well as to own private Muslim cemeteries. All due measures shall be adopted to observe traditional Islamic rules regarding internments, graves and funeral rites, which shall be conducted by the local Islamic Community. The right to transfer the remains of the Muslim deceased to cemeteries belonging to the Islamic Communities, both from tombs in municipal cemeteries and from towns in which there is no Muslim cemetery is hereby

acknowledged, subject to the provisions of legislation on local government and health ordinances.

Article 3

1. Natural persons devoted on a regular basis to guiding the communities referred in article 1 of the present Agreement, leading prayer, training and Islamic spiritual support, who substantiate compliance with such requirements under a certificate issued by the respective community to which they pertain, endorsed by the Islamic Commission of Spain, shall, for all legal intents and purposes, be considered to be Islamic religious leaders and Imams of the Islamic Communities.

2. The persons mentioned in the preceding paragraph shall not under any circumstances whatsoever be compelled to declare about events revealed to them in their liturgical practice or when officiating at religious services or tendering spiritual support, under the legally established provisions on professional secrecy.

Article 4

1. The imams and Islamic religious leaders shall be subject to the general provisions on Military Service. Should they so request, they shall be assigned to missions compatible with their religious functions.

2. Enrollment in courses on religious training for the persons referred in article 3 in Islamic institutions recognised by the Ministry of Education and Science shall entitle students to second class deferral of their enlistment under the terms provided in the legislation on Military Service in force.

Application for such deferral must include substantiation of enrollment in the form of a certificate issued by the corresponding Islamic institution.

Article 5

In accordance with the provisions of article 1 of R.D. 2398/77 of 27 August, the persons meeting the requirements set forth in article 3 of the present Agreement shall be included in the Ordinary Social Security Scheme, under employee status. The respective Islamic Communities shall assume the employer rights and obligations laid down under such Ordinary Social Security Scheme.

Article 6

For all legal intents and purposes, practices conducted in accordance with Islamic law and tradition, issuing from the Qu'ran or the Sunna and protected under the General Act on Freedom of Worship, shall be considered to be Islamic religious services or training or spiritual support.

Article 7

1. Civil validity of marriage administered in accordance with the religious ceremony established under Islamic Law is acknowledged from the time the wedding is held if the parties thereto meet the legal capacity requirements established by the Civil Code.

The bride and groom shall lend their consent in the presence of one of the persons mentioned in article 3, paragraph 1 above and at least two witnesses, who must be of age.

Full recognition of such validity shall call for registration of such marriages in the Civil Registry.

2. Persons who wish to register their marriage held in the manner provided in the preceding paragraph must furnish prior witness of their ability to marry, consisting of a certificate issued by the corresponding Civil Registry. The marriage may not be registered if more than six months elapse after the issue date of such certificate.

3. After marrying the couple, the representative of the Islamic Community in which they were married shall send a certificate attesting thereto to the Civil Registry for registration, which certificate must include the particulars required by legislation relating to the Civil Registry.

4. Without prejudice to the responsibilities that may be incurred and rights acquired in good faith by third parties, registration may be undertaken at any time by presenting the certificate, duly processed, referred in the preceding paragraph.

5. The rules of this article relating to the procedures for effective exercise of the rights stipulated herein shall be adopted to accommodate any future amendments which may be made to the legislation regarding the Civil Registry, after hearing the recommendations made by the Islamic Commission of Spain.

Article 8

1. The right of all Muslim military personnel, be they career staff or otherwise, and all other persons of such faith rendering services in the Armed Forces, to receive Islamic spiritual support and participate in Islamic religious services and rites is hereby acknowledged, subject to authorisation from their superiors, who shall endeavour to make such assistance compatible with duty, facilitating the premises and means required to make this possible.

2. Muslim servicemen unable to comply with their religious obligations, in particular collective prayer on Friday because there is no mosque or, as appropriate, oratory in the place they are stationed, may be authorised to comply therewith in the closest mosque in the vicinity, service permitting.

3. Islamic religious services shall be rendered by ministers designated by the imams or persons designated on a regular basis by the Islamic Communities belonging to the Islamic Commission of Spain and authorised by Army commanders, who shall lend such aid as needed so they can perform their duties on the same footing as the clergy of other Churches, faiths or communities that have signed Co-operation Agreements with the State.

4. The corresponding authorities shall notify the families of the decease of Muslim servicemen occurring while they are in the service of the military.

Article 9

1. The right to spiritual support is hereby guaranteed for all persons committed to penitentiaries, hospitals, social service or other analogous public institutions, provided by imams or persons designated by the communities, subject to authorisation by the corresponding administrative bodies. Public centre and establishment management shall be bound to forward the request for spiritual support received from interns or their families to the corresponding Islamic Community if the parties concerned are unable to do so personally.

The spiritual support provided for in this article shall include that administered to the dying, as well as Islamic funeral rites.

2. In any case, the spiritual support referred to in the preceding paragraph shall be provided with due respect for the principle of freedom of religion and observing the organisational regulations and rules of procedure of the centres in question, freely and with no restrictions with respect to timetable. As far as penitentiaries are concerned, religious services shall be conducted in accordance with the provisions of the corresponding legislation.

3. The expenses incurred to provide the above religious services shall be defrayed in the manner covenanted by the representatives of the Islamic Commission of Spain and the public centre and establishment management authorities referred to in

paragraph 1 of this article, without prejudice to the use of the premises set aside for such purposes in the corresponding centres.

Article 10

1.   In order to make the provisions of article 27.3 of the Constitution, and of General Act 8/75 of 3 July on Regulation of the Right to Education and Act 1/90 of 3 October on the General Regulation of the Education System effective, Muslim pupils, their parents and any school governing bodies who so request, are guaranteed the right of the first mentioned to receive Islamic religious teaching in public and private subsidised schools at the infant, primary and secondary education levels, providing, in the case of private institutions, that the exercise of such right does not conflict with the nature of the school itself.

2.   Islamic religious teaching shall be delivered by teachers designated by the communities belonging to the Islamic Commission of Spain, with the endorsement of the respective Federation.

3.   The content of Islamic religious teaching as well as the textbooks relating thereto shall be provided by the respective communities, as endorsed by the Islamic Commission of Spain.

4.   The public and publicly subsidised schools referred to in paragraph 1 of this article must provide suitable premises for the exercise of the right whose exercise is regulated in this article, but this may not be to the detriment of other academic activities.

5.   The Islamic Commission of Spain and its member communities may organise courses on religious teaching in public universities, making use of these institutions' premises and resources for such purposes under agreements reached in this regard with academic authorities.

6.   The Islamic Commission of Spain and its member communities may establish and run schools on the educational levels mentioned in paragraph 1 of this article, as well as Islamic Universities and Training Centres, subject to the ordinary legislation in force on the matter.

Article 11

1.   The Islamic Commission of Spain and its member communities may freely request services of their followers, organise public donation campaigns and receive offerings and other contributions.

2.   The following operations shall be subject to no taxation whatsoever:

a)   The provision, free of charge, of publications, instructions and internal Islamic religious bulletins directly to the faithful by communities belonging to the Islamic Commission of Spain.

b)   Islamic religious teaching in centres belonging to the Islamic Commission of Spain or its member communities, devoted to training imams and Islamic religious leaders.

3.   The Islamic Commission of Spain, as well as its member communities, shall be exempt:

A)   From real estate tax and any excise taxes, as appropriate, on the following real property owned thereby:

a)   Mosques or places of worship and outbuildings or ancillary premises devoted to religious services or spiritual support or used as abode by imams and Islamic religious leaders.

b)   Premises used for Islamic Commission of Spain member community offices.

c)   Institutions devoted solely to training imams and Islamic religious leaders.

B)   From the Corporation Tax under the terms of Act 61/78 of 27 December, article 5, paragraphs 2 and 3, regulating such tax.

From the Corporation Tax levied on increases in wealth obtained gratuitously, providing such property and rights so acquired are devoted to worship or social services.

C) From the Transfer Tax and Stamp Duty, providing the respective property or rights acquired are devoted to religious services or spiritual support under the terms provided in the Consolidated Text of such Tax, enacted by Royal Legislative Decree 3050/1980 of 30 December and the Regulations, enacted by Royal Decree 3494/1981 of 29 December, with regard to the requirements and procedures to be met to qualify for such exemption.

4. Without prejudice to the provisions of the preceding paragraphs, the Islamic Commission of Spain and its member communities as well as the associations and entities created and managed thereby devoted to religious, charitable-educational, medical and hospital or social service activities, shall be entitled to all other tax benefits that Spanish State ordinary legislation on taxes applies at any given time to non-profit organisations and in any case, those granted to private charitable organisations.

5. The Personal Income Tax regulations shall govern the treatment given to donations to the Islamic Commission of Spain member communities, including any applicable deductions.

Article 12

1. The members of the Islamic Communities belonging to the Islamic Commission of Spain who wish to do so may request that their work cease every Friday, the Muslim day of compulsory collective prayer, from one thirty p.m. to four thirty p.m., and, during the month of fasting (Ramadan), one hour before sundown.

In both cases, prior agreement must be reached between the parties concerned. The hours not worked must be made up, with no compensation therefor whatsoever.

2. The holy days listed below which, according to Islamic law, are religious holidays, may, subject to agreement between the parties concerned, replace those established in article 37.2 of the Workers' By-laws as a general rule, under the same terms of paid, holidays with no time payback, at the request of persons of the Muslim faith belonging to the Islamic Communities that are members of the Islamic Commission of Spain.

- AL HIYRA, corresponding to the 1st day of Muharram, first day of the Islamic New Year.
- ACHURA, tenth day of Muharram.
- IDU AL-MAULID, corresponding to 12 Rabiu Al Awwal, nativity of the prophet.
- AL ISRA WA AL-MI'RAY, corresponding to 27 Rayab, date of the Night of Determining and the prophet's Ascension.
- IDU AL-FITR, corresponding to the 1st, 2nd and 3rd days of Shawwal, which celebrates the culmination of the Ramadan fast.
- IDU AL-ADHA, corresponding to the 10, 11 and 12 Du Al-Hyyah to celebrate the sacrifice made by the prophet Abraham.

3. Muslim pupils enrolled in public or publicly subsidised schools shall be excused from attending class on Friday during the time referred to in paragraph 1 of this article and on the religious holidays and commemorations listed above, at their own request or at the request of their parents or guardians.

4. Exams, State competitive examinations or selective tests convened for enrollment in the Public Administration which are to be held on the days referred in the preceding paragraph shall be indicated for an alternative date for the Muslims so requesting, unless otherwise warranted by just cause.

Article 13

The State and the Islamic Commission of Spain shall co-operate to conserve and further Islamic historic, artistic and cultural heritage in Spain, which shall remain at the service of society, for contemplation and study.

Such co-operation shall include drawing up a catalogue and inventory of such heritage and embrace the creation of Trusts, Foundations or other institutions of a cultural nature, whose membership shall include representatives of the Islamic Commission of Spain.

Article 14

1.   In accordance with the spiritual dimension and specific peculiarities of Islamic Law, the denomination "HALAL" serves to distinguish food products prepared in accordance therewith.

2.   In order to protect the proper use of such denominations, the Islamic Commission of Spain must apply for and obtain registration of the corresponding trademarks from the Patent and Trade Mark Office, pursuant to the legal standards in force.

Once the above requirements are met, products bearing the Islamic Commission of Spain mark on the package shall be guaranteed, for the intents and purposes of marketing, import and export, to have been prepared in accordance with Islamic Law.

3.   The slaughtering of animals in accordance with Islamic laws must abide by health standards in force.

4.   Where requested, attempts shall be made to adapt the food provided interns in public centres or establishments and military premises, as well as to Muslim pupils in public and publicly subsidised private educational institutions to Islamic religious precepts and to mealtimes during the Ramadan fast.

FIRST ADDITIONAL PROVISION

The Government shall notify the Islamic Commission of Spain of all legislative initiatives that affect the contents of these presents, in order for it to express its opinion thereon.

SECOND ADDITIONAL PROVISION

The present Agreement may be denounced by either of the parties hereto, who must notify the other six months in advance. It may also be subject to full or partial revision at the initiative of either party, without prejudice to subsequent parliamentary procedure.

THIRD ADDITIONAL PROVISION

A Mixed Committee shall be constituted, on which the Central Government and the Islamic Commission of Spain shall be equally represented, for the implementation and follow-through of the present Agreement.